Secondary English

Sadler
Hayllar

Book Two

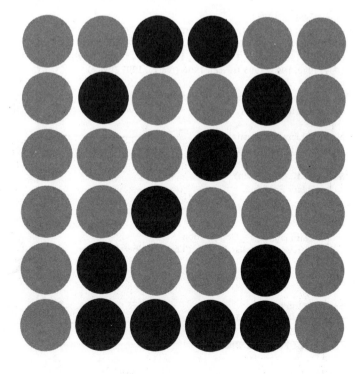

MACMILLAN

First published 1984 by
MACMILLAN EDUCATION AUSTRALIA PTY LTD
627 Chapel Street, South Yarra 3141
Reprinted 1985 (twice), 1986, 1987, 1988, 1989, 1990 (twice),
1991, 1992, 1993, 1995 (twice), 1996 (twice), 1997 (twice).

Associated companies and representatives
throughout the world.

National Library of Australia
cataloguing in publication data.

Sadler, R. K. (Rex Kevin)
    Secondary English 2.

    For secondary students.
    ISBN 0 333 38034 7.

    1. English language – Composition
    and exercises. I. Hayllar, T. A. S. (Thomas Albert S.)
    II. Title.

428

Set in Plantin by
Graphicraft Typesetters, Hong Kong
Printed in Malaysia by
Chee Leong Press Sdn. Bhd, Ipoh

Contents

Preface

Secondary English 2 is a comprehensive, integrated language and literature text for students in their second year of secondary schooling. Teachers and students will find here a solid coverage of the areas of importance in any junior English course. The language work includes usage, vocabulary, comprehension, punctuation, and practical language concepts. The clear-thinking strands also examine aspects of language use. The writing workshops, with their emphasis on the development of writing skills, meet a major need that most texts ignore or treat superficially. The poetry strands, and the many that contain passages of prose, offer a rich and stimulating body of writing from the pens of some of the most skilled practitioners of our language. A special short dictionary at the back of the book provides a valuable vocabulary and spelling reservoir, while acting as a handy reference/refresher list of some of the words encountered in the comprehension strand of each Unit.

The book is divided into 16 Units, each of which contains seven strands:

- **Comprehension.** A passage chosen for its high interest level, and for aspects of its style and language. Questions accompanying the passage probe the student's understanding, response and sensitivity.

- **Language.** This strand focuses on important aspects of language with which all junior students should be familiar. It provides opportunities for students to work with words in as many interesting and varied ways as possible, so that their competence and creativity in the use of language can be enhanced.

- **Punctuation.** The punctuation strand aims to provide an opportunity for the mastery of punctuation skills through practice.

- **Creative Writing.** This is a practical writing course. Models of writing by famous authors are analysed to bring students into touch with the ways in which skilful writing is achieved. Striking pictures of exceptional interest and relevance are then presented to students as stimuli for their own creative writing efforts.

- **Poetry.** The poems chosen have a high level of interest for students, while not neglecting the needs of quality. Accompanying discussion points, questions or exercises are designed to elicit a finer response from students. Furthermore, special topics — such as simile, metaphor, rhythm, etc. — are treated and provide an introduction to poetry technique.

- **Spelling.** This practical spelling, vocabulary and word-skills strand contains a broad range of exercises and activities designed to foster the student's knowledge, control and mastery of words.

- **Try Thinking.** A variety of intriguing puzzles and quizzes present the student with practice in reasoning and problem-solving. This strand promotes clear thinking as students develop confidence in their ability to reason effectively.

We have built this series on the conviction that the study of English should be enjoyable, and believe that teachers and students alike will find *Secondary English 2* an engaging and highly practical text and resource book.

Unit One

Comprehension 1

INVENTORS AND INVENTIONS

The Man Who Almost Invented the Vacuum Cleaner

The man officially credited with inventing the vacuum cleaner is Hubert Cecil Booth. However, he got the idea from a man who almost invented it.

In 1901 Booth visited a London music-hall. On the bill was an American inventor with his wonder machine for removing dust from carpets.

The machine comprised a box about one foot square with a bag on top. After watching the act — which made everyone in the front six rows sneeze — Booth went round to the inventor's dressing room.

'It should suck not blow,' said Booth, coming straight to the point. 'Suck?' exclaimed the enraged inventor. 'Your machine just moves the dust around the room,' Booth informed him. 'Suck? Suck? Sucking is not possible,' was the inventor's reply and he stormed out. Booth proved that it was by the simple expedient of kneeling down, pursing his lips and sucking the back of an armchair. 'I almost choked,' he said afterwards.

The Most Unsuccessful Inventor

Between 1962 and 1977 Mr Arthur Paul Pedrick patented 162 inventions, none of which were taken up commercially.

Among his greatest inventions were 'A bicycle with amphibious capacity', spectacles which improved vision in poor visibility and an arrangement whereby a car may be driven from the back seat.

The grandest scheme of Mr Pedrick, who described himself as the 'One-Man-Think-Tank Basic Physics Research Laboratories of 77 Hillfield Road, Selsey, Sussex', was to irrigate deserts of the world by sending a constant supply of snowballs from the Polar regions through a network of giant peashooters.

He patented several golf inventions — including a golf ball which could be steered in flight — that contravened the rules of the game.

from *The Book of Heroic Failures*
by STEPHEN PILE

The Man Who Invented the Ball-point Pen

Ladislo Biro lived in Hungary and worked as proofreader, reading manuscripts when they were first printed and correcting any mistakes before the final printing.

He had an old-fashioned pen that he had to dip in a jar of ink before making a correction.

Ladislo didn't like that process. It was a bother, and there was always the danger of getting ink splotches on the page.

So he decided he would invent a pen that would not have to be dipped in ink.

He called it an inspiration. His friends called the idea plain foolishness.

Ladislo didn't worry about them. With his brother he tried many ways to make the new pen. Finally they hit upon putting a tiny metal ball at the tip, then filling the pen with paste-like ink.

That is the basic idea of today's ball-points. But it took many years to perfect the process.

When first manufactured, the new pens were very expensive, and few saw a good reason for buying them. Interestingly, it was the fighter pilots of World War II who popularized ball-point pens. Ordinary fountain-pens leaked at high altitudes, and so the Air Force bought for the airmen the 'high-altitude writing sticks' that Biro made.

After that, ball-points became increasingly popular, and today many more are sold than fountain-pens.

The Woman Who Caused the Invention of the Band-Aid

Josephine Dickson married a man who worked for a company that manufactured gauze and adhesive tape called Johnson & Johnson.

We will never know the reason, but it is a fact that Josephine Dickson was accident prone. During the first week that she was married to Mr Dickson, she cut herself twice with the kitchen knife.

After that, it just went from bad to worse. It seemed that Josephine was always cutting herself.

One day her husband had an idea. He sat down with some tape and gauze and a pair of scissors. Then he cut the tape into strips. In the middle of each strip he stuck a little square of gauze.

From then on, whenever Josephine had an accident, ready-made bandages were on hand for her to use quickly and without a lot of fuss.

At Johnson & Johnson they heard about these new bandages that could be put on in thirty seconds. Soon the company was making them to sell on a small scale.

Four years later, in 1924, the company installed machines for mass-producing the new product, and the trade name Band-Aid was adopted.

from *Why Didn't I Think of That?*
by WEBB GARRISON

How Well Did You Understand?

The Man Who Almost Invented the Vacuum Cleaner

(1) What is the meaning of 'officially credited'?

(2) What was wrong with the American inventor's scheme for removing dust from carpets?

(3) How did Booth provide proof that his method was the right one?

(4) What comments would you make about the character of the American inventor?

The Most Unsuccessful Inventor

(5) What evidence can you find to show that Mr Arthur Paul Pedrick was a very hard-working inventor?

(6) What do you think a bicycle 'with amphibious capacity' could do?

(7) Why was Mr Pedrick a failure as an inventor?

(8) What comments would you make about Mr Pedrick's character?

The Man Who Invented the Ball-point Pen

(9) Why did Ladislo Biro decide to invent a new kind of pen?

(10) What clues tell you that Ladislo was a determined man?

(11) What hindered the sales of the ball-point pen?

(12) Why did the ball-point pen eventually become accepted by the public?

The Woman Who Caused the Invention of the Band-Aid

(13) What does 'accident prone' mean?

(14) What was the main advantage of Mr Dickson's new bandages?

Dictionary Words

Give the meaning of each of these words from the passages you have just read. You may like to consult the dictionary at the back of the book.

(a) inspiration   (b) adhesive   (c) expedient   (d) contravene.

Language 1

The Sentence

Without sentences, we would have a great deal of difficulty in communicating with each other. A sentence is a group of words that makes complete sense by itself. In its simplest form, a sentence may consist of just a noun and a verb; or even of a single word.

Fish swim.   Yes.   Inventors create.

A sentence has two main parts, called the **subject** and the **predicate**. The subject is the part of the sentence which tells us *who* or *what* performs the action. The main word in the subject is usually a noun or a pronoun. Whatever is said about the subject is called the predicate. The predicate always contains a verb.

When you look at the examples below, you will notice that the subject of a sentence can be a single word or a group of words; and that the same is true for the predicate.

Subject	Predicate
He	lived.
Ladislo Biro	lived in Hungary.
Josephine Dickson and her husband	were responsible for the invention of the Band-Aid.
The grandest scheme of Mr Pedrick	was to irrigate the deserts of the world.
The enraged American inventor	stormed out of the room.

Finding the subject and predicate

Write down the subject and predicate of each of the following sentences. One good way of identifying the subject is to put the question 'Who?' or 'What?' in front of the verb.

(1) Levi Strauss made the first pair of jeans out of canvas.

(2) Prehistoric man created rope by twisting vines together.

(3) The invention of water-pipes took place about five thousand years ago.

(4) The Chinese and Mongols had used rockets from about AD 1200 onwards.

(5) The first traffic-light was installed in Cleveland, USA, in 1914.

(6) The development of plastic led to the invention of the long-playing record.

(7) By the time of Christ, taps were in use by the Romans.

(8) Originally, windows were designed as openings to let light in.

Adding predicates

Using the information contained in the comprehension passages, add predicates to these subjects to form complete sentences.

(1) Ladislo Biro's friends ....

(2) Ordinary fountain-pens ....

(3) The basic idea of today's ball-points ....

(4) Josephine Dickson ....

(5) Johnson & Johnson ....

(6) Hubert Cecil Booth ....

(7) The American inventor's machine ....

(8) A network of giant peashooters ....

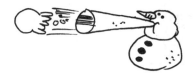

Matching up subjects and predicates

Correctly match up the subjects and predicates of these proverbs.

SUBJECT	PREDICATE
The early bird	flock together.
Absence	sweep clean.
Many hands	has a silver lining.
A drowning man	makes the heart grow fonder.
Familiarity	is the mother of invention.
Necessity	catches the worm.
Too many cooks	make light work.
Birds of a feather	breeds contempt.
New brooms	will clutch at a straw.
Every cloud	spoil the broth.

Missing subjects

Write out the following sentences, inserting the appropriate subjects from the box below.

seismograph	barometer	stethoscope	periscope	microscope
telegraph	megaphone	compass	telescope	thermometer

(1) The .... is an instrument used for listening to the heart.

(2) The .... is an instrument for determining direction.

(3) The .... is an instrument for observing the movements of the stars.

(4) The .... is an instrument for examining tiny objects.

(5) The .... is an instrument for measuring temperature.

(6) The .... is an instrument for amplifying and directing the voice.

(7) The .... is an instrument for measuring atmospheric pressure.

(8) The .... is an instrument for recording and measuring earthquakes.

(9) The .... is an instrument for viewing the surface from underwater.

(10) The .... is an instrument for sending messages between places far apart.

Punctuation 1

When we are speaking, we *stop* naturally at the end of a sentence. We also use *pauses* to help our listeners follow our meaning. We can even indicate a *question* or *exclamation* by changing the pitch of our voice.

In our writing, we use punctuation marks to indicate these pauses and changes of expression. Can you imagine how confusing it would be to read and write without punctuation? Punctuation marks were invented to clarify written language. It is possible for one punctuation mark to alter the whole meaning of a sentence. Look at the difference a mere comma (,) makes in these two sentences:

- Has the bear eaten, Fred?
- Has the bear eaten Fred?

Using punctuation to change the meaning

Change the punctuation in each of the following to produce a different meaning. Hints are given in the brackets.

(1) King Charles walked and talked half an hour after his head was cut off.
   [*Insert a full stop, a capital letter and a comma.*]

(2) The reindeer, having eaten the Eskimos, moved on.
    [*Remove the two existing commas and add a new comma.*]

(3) Have you eaten Father?
    [*Add a comma.*]

(4) Have you seen Carol Smith?
    [*Add a comma.*]

(5) Caesar entered on his head
    A helmet on each foot
    A sandal in his hand he had
    His trusty sword to boot.
    [*Add full stops, commas and capital letters.*]

Creative Writing 1

The Approach

When the moment comes to take up your pen and put down your own ideas in a clear and interesting way, you will find it easier if you have an *approach* in mind. A simple approach that will work for most pieces of writing consists of:

(a) An **introduction**, made up of a sentence or a short paragraph in which you bring to the attention of your reader the topic or subject you are going to write about.

(b) The **main part** or **body** of your piece of writing — two to five paragraphs in length.

(c) The **conclusion**. This may take the form of a sentence or short paragraph that sums up, or neatly finishes off, your piece of writing.

Here's your approach at a glance:

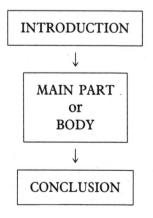

Collecting and Organizing Your Ideas

Keeping in mind the approach just described (page 7), you are now ready to collect and organize your ideas on the topic or subject you have been given to write about.

Just suppose your topic is 'The Gun'. According to the approach, you first need an INTRODUCTION. Various ideas range through your mind; possibilities occur to you.... For instance, you come upon the gun by chance: you enter a ranch bunkhouse and spot a saddle-roll, which you casually touch. There's a gun inside! A beautiful but deadly-looking weapon is revealed when you unroll the blankets.

Now for the MAIN PART or BODY of your piece of writing. You describe the gun in detail: the design, the model and the features that make this weapon very special. You handle the gun. You even admire it.

With what kind of CONCLUSION will you now round off your description of the gun? Well, you might suddenly *feel* the deadly, dark nature of the weapon. You might then return it to its hiding-place, and hurry out of the bunkhouse and away from it.

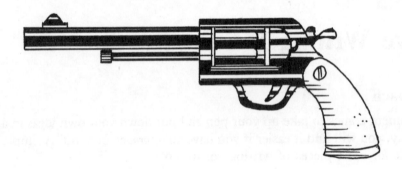

Now let's turn to a piece of writing that *is* about a gun, and is famous for the clear and interesting way in which it describes the weapon.

There is an introductory paragraph, and this is followed by six paragraphs of description making up the main part or body of the writing. A single paragraph then provides a satisfying conclusion. Note that the above section on the collection and organization of ideas is based on this skilful description of a revolver.

THE GUN

Shane never carried a gun. And that was a peculiar thing because he had a gun.

I saw it once. I saw it when I was alone in the barn one day and I spotted his saddle-roll lying on his bunk. Usually he kept it carefully put away underneath. He must have forgotten it this time, for it was there in the open by the pillow. I reached to sort of feel it — and I felt the gun inside. No one was near, so I unfastened the straps and unrolled the blankets. There it was, the most beautiful-looking weapon I ever saw. Beautiful and deadly-looking.

The holster and filled cartridge belt were of the same soft black leather as the boots tucked under the bunk, tooled in the same intricate design. I knew enough to know that the gun was a single-action Colt, the same model as the Regular Army issue that was the favourite of all men in those days, and that oldtimers used to say was the finest pistol ever made.

This was the same model. But this was no Army gun. It was black, almost blue black, with the darkness not in any enamel but in the metal itself. The grip was clear on the outer curve, shaped to the fingers on the inner curve, and two ivory plates were set into it with exquisite skill, one on each side.

The smooth invitation of it tempted your grasp. I took hold and pulled the gun out of the holster. It came so easily that I could hardly believe it was there in my hand. Heavy like father's, it was somehow much easier to handle. You held it up to aiming level and it seemed to balance itself into your hand.

It was clean and polished and oiled. The empty cylinder, when I released the catch and flicked it, spun swiftly and noiselessly. I was surprised to see that the front sight was gone, the barrel smooth right down to the end, and that the hammer had been filed to a sharp point.

Why should a man do that to a gun? Why should a man with a gun like that refuse to wear it and show it off? And then, staring at that dark and deadly efficiency, I was again suddenly chilled, and I quickly put everything back exactly as before and hurried out into the sun.

from *Shane* by JACK SCHAEFER

Your Turn to Write

Try your hand at writing about *one* of these:

(1) Describe in detail an important invention that affects your life. Pretend your description is being written for someone who has never seen this invention before.

(2) The best/worst thing ever invented was . . .
(Be sure to give reasons for your viewpoint.)

(3) 'Something I think should be invented now!'

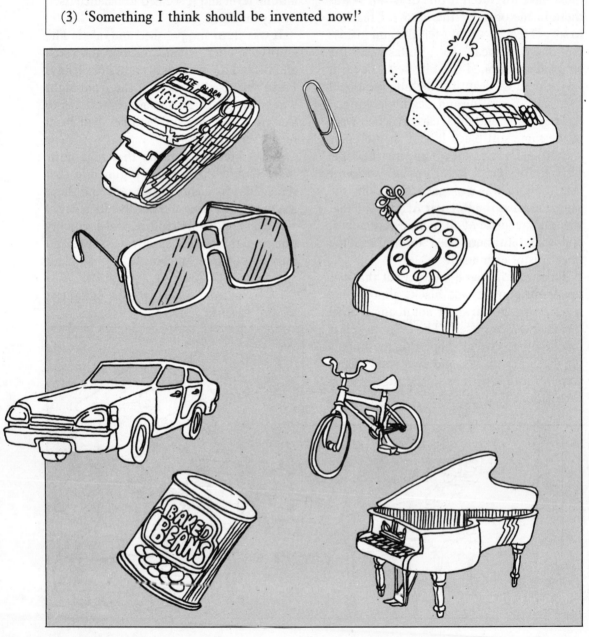

Poetry 1

'The Microscope' is a serious poem focusing on the life of Anton Leeuwenhoek, who was at first ridiculed because nobody really understood his passion and his purpose in constructing his lenses.

THE MICROSCOPE

Anton Leeuwenhoek was Dutch.
He sold pincushions, cloth, and such.
The waiting townsfolk fumed and fussed
As Anton's dry goods gathered dust.

He worked, instead of tending store,
At grinding special lenses for
A microscope. Some of the things
He looked at were:

        mosquitoes' wings,
the hairs of sheep, the legs of lice,
the skin of people, dogs, and mice;
ox eyes, spiders' spinning gear,
fishes' scales, a little smear
of his own blood,

        and best of all,
the unknown, busy, very small
bugs that swim and bump and hop
inside a simple water drop.

Impossible! Most Dutchmen said.
This Anton's crazy in the head.
We ought to ship him off to Spain.
He says he's seen a housefly's brain.
He says the water that we drink
Is full of bugs. He's mad, we think!

They called him dumkopf, which means dope.
That's how we got the microscope.

MAXINE KUMIN

Thinking about Microscopes

(1) What was Leeuwenhoek's attitude to his dry-goods shop?

(2) How did his customers react?

(3) What evidence can you find to show that Leeuwenhoek's lenses were successful?

(4) Why did people think that Leeuwenhoek was crazy?

(5) What impression of Leeuwenhoek did you get from reading this poem?

(6) Why do you think the poet wrote 'The Microscope'?

Sometimes car-owners can become very attached to their cars. The poet Pam Ayres is one such car-owner. But despite her Morris 1000's faithful and enduring service, she hardens her heart and leaves it in the scrapyard to its fate.

GOODBYE WORN-OUT MORRIS 1000

Oh love, you got no poke left
I didn't want to say
It seems we are outmoded,
Much too slow, and in the way.
You know how much I love you
I'd repair you in a flash
But I haven't got the knowledge
And I haven't got the cash.

There is rust all round your headlamps
I could push through if I tried
My pot of paint can't cure it
'Cause it's from the other side.
All along your sides and middle
You are turning rusty brown
Though you took me ninety thousand miles
And never let me down.

Not the snapping of a fan belt
Nor the blowing of a tyre
Nor the rattling of a tappet
And nor did you misfire.
All your wheels stayed on the corners
And your wipers on the screen
Though I didn't do much for you
And I never kept you clean.

All your seats are unupholstered
And foam rubber specks the floor.
You were hit by something else once
And I cannot shut the door.
But it's not those things that grieve me
Or the money that I spent,
For you were my First-driven,
Ninety thousand miles we went.

I could buy a bright and new car
And go tearing round the town
A BGT! A Morgan!
(With the hood all battened down).
But as I leave you in the scrapyard,
Bangers piled up to the skies,
Why do your rusty headlamps
Look like sad, reproachful eyes?

PAM AYRES

Thinking about Old Morrises

(1) In the first stanza, what criticism does the poet make of the car?

(2) Why doesn't the poet go ahead and repair her Morris 1000?

(3) In the second stanza, what reason does Pam Ayres give for getting rid of her car?

(4) What evidence can you find to show that the car has performed well for its owner?

(5) How has the poet treated her Morris 1000?

(6) Explain how the poet has personified (given human qualities to) her Morris 1000?

(7) What onomatopoeic (sound) words does the poet use to suggest car noises?

(8) Do you feel sympathetic towards the poet's Morris 1000? Why or why not?

(9) In the final line, why does the car seem to be reproaching its owner?

(10) How would you summarize the poet's feelings towards her car?

Spelling 1

INVENTIONS

electricity	progress	designer	skilful	telephone
invention	television	efficient	development	advancement
generate	energy	necessity	discovery	equipment
produce	beginning	useful	bicycle	manufacture

Words on the Go

Read through *The Invention*, below, and then write down in your workbook the words from the spelling box which will correctly fill the blanks. Note the helpful letters.

The Invention

A recent advertisement on t.......... showed a famous d.......... of scientific .... pedalling a .... and, at the same time, talking into a t.......... . You could see he was able to g.......... enough .... from all the pedalling to make a phone call. What a marvellous i..........! U.......... too. But surely this is just a b.......... . A s.......... inventor ought to be able to p.......... an even more e.......... machine — one that combines pedalling and telephoning with making milkshakes and whipping up ice-cream. That would be *real* p.......... .

Work Out the Word

Go to words in the spelling box for answers to the following:

(1) The opposite of an **ending** is a ....

(2) Form two new words from **energy**: .... and ....

(3) Form two adjectives from **electricity**: ....ic and ....al.

(4) A two-wheeled form of transport propelled by the feet: ....

(5) If something is **essential**, it is a ....

(6) The person who creates an **invention** is called its ....

(7) Give the word for a device that communicates using a screen: ....

(8) The noun that comes from **skilful** is ....

(9) A verb that relates to the production of power is ....

(10) Something with an earpiece, a mouthpiece and a dial is called a ....

(11) Give the adjective that comes from **progress**: ....

(12) Find a word that will change to its opposite when its ending is changed to -*less*: ....

Jumbled Words

Unjumble the spelling-box words in the brackets.

(1) He can .... [cdreopu] any electronic gadget in that workshop of his.

(2) This .... [meqtenpui] needs a charge of .... [celcetyirit] before it can operate.

(3) .... [sivniletoe] has become a .... [yensectis] for many people.

(4) People can talk over long distances thanks to the .... [nentnovii] of the .... [penhoteel].

(5) The leg-driven .... [yiblecc] is .... [nignigneb] to be much used by those who like exercise.

(6) A great .... [veodcisyr] usually means .... [sopegrsr].

(7) The .... [rutfamcenau] of any machine calls for much .... [flisklu] planning.

(8) The .... [lomvedtenep] of nuclear .... [greyne] is an important aim of some countries.

Try Thinking 1

Who goes with What?

Complete each of the following pairs by selecting the correct words from the box. The first pair has been done to help you.

typewriter	money	camera	food	compass
violence	bat	aqualung	speech	rifle
robbery	language	microscope	glass	oven
tricks	blackboard	intelligence	telescope	stethoscope

(1) A .....*telescope*..... is to an astronomer as a .....*stethoscope*..... is to a doctor.

(2) A .... is to a photographer as .... is to a glazier.

(3) .... is to a glutton as an .... is to a cook.

(4) A .... is to a soldier as a .... is to a sailor.

(5) .... are to a conjurer as a .... is to an orator.

(6) An .... is to a diver as a .... is to a cricketer.

(7) .... is to a terrorist as ..,............ is to a burglar.

(8) A .... is to a teacher as a .... is to a secretary.

(9) .... is to an interpreter as .... is to a genius.

(10) A .... is to a biologist as .... is to a cashier.

Car Words

Given the clues, complete the following words that begin with CAR. Note your example.

(1) A soft floor-covering: CAR <u>P</u> <u>E</u> <u>T</u>

(2) A shelter for a car: CAR_ _ _ _

(3) A large box: CAR_ _ _

(4) A kind of jumper that can be unbuttoned: CAR_ _ _ _ _

(5) A funny drawing: CAR_ _ _ _

(6) A flesh-eating animal: CAR_ _ _ _ _ _

(7) A fun place to go; a festival: CAR_ _ _ _ _

(8) One who works with wood: CAR_ _ _ _ _ _

(9) To shape or cut up with a sharp knife: CAR_ _

(10) Goods carried by a ship or plane: CAR_ _

(11) A small piece of stiffened paper, often used in games: CAR_

(12) The powder-container for a bullet: CAR_ _ _ _ _ _

A Puzzling Poem

The poet has presented the reader with a poem full of puzzles. See how well you can unravel them.

MISSIONARY BILL

A missionary 1ce and a good 1 2
Though he spoke with a bit of a lisp
Said 'Whatever'th that terrible 3k
From that track on that thide of that hill?'
So he packed some lunch and a thermos of tea
4 he never did things by ½s
And his toothbrush, pyjamas, then he set 4th
And he found a horrible find
4 there on the hill were cannibals 5
Munching on 1 of their kind.
'Of that,' said he, 'I cannot approve;
Fellow man wath meant to love.
You mutht never indulge in odiouth thlaughterth
Or carving of men into therving ¼th —
I've told you b4 it ith wrong.'
But the cannibals 5 in their cannibal tongue
Said 'Walgett. Pockataroo.

We karved him in ⅕s not ¼s U C —
B kwiat oar weeleat U 2.'
Then Missionary Bill at 6es and 7s
Berated them very severely
So they knocked him down and tied him up
And finished their meal quite cheerly;
But as they were eating he loosened an arm
And wrote with his paper and quill
'Dear Mum, if I'm late it'th becauthe I've been 8'
And he signed it 'Miththionary Bill'.
Then he added 'P. Th. Have no dithtrethth,
A miththionary'th life ith fine
And a cannibal'th life ith a dithmal methth
Though I fear I wath athi9
2 chide thethe men again and again
Till I did it 1th 2 of-10.'

ERIC C. ROLLS

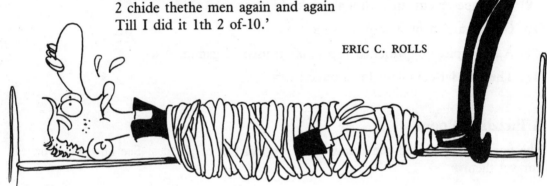

Unit Two

Comprehension 2

When he experienced this horrifying encounter with an octopus, the writer, Arthur Grimble, was a cadet officer working in the Gilbert and Ellice Islands for the British Colonial Office.

OCTOPUS!

But that very quality of the octopus that most horrifies the imagination, its relentless tenacity, becomes its undoing when hungry man steps into the picture. The Gilbertese happen to value certain parts of it as food, and their method of fighting it is coolly based upon the one fact that its arms never change their grip. They hunt for it in pairs. One man acts as the bait, his partner as the killer. First, they swim eyes-under at low tide just off the reef, and search the crannies of the submarine cliff for sight of any tentacle that may flicker out for a catch. When they have placed their quarry, they land on the reef for the next stage. The human bait starts the real game. He dives and tempts the lurking brute by swimming a few strokes in front of its cranny, at first a little beyond striking range. Then he turns and makes straight for the cranny, to give himself into the embrace of those waiting arms. Sometimes nothing happens. The beast will not always respond to the lure. But usually it strikes.

The partner on the reef above stares down through the pellucid water, waiting for his moment. His teeth are his only weapon. His killing efficiency depends on his avoiding every one of those strangling arms. He must wait until his partner's body has been drawn right up to the entrance of the cleft. The monster inside is groping then with its horny mouth against the victim's flesh, and sees nothing beyond it. That point is reached in a matter of no more than thirty seconds after the decoy has plunged. The killer dives, lays hold of his pinioned friend at arms' length, and jerks him away from the cleft; the octopus is torn adrift from the anchorage of its proximal suckers, and clamps itself the more fiercely to its prey. In the same second, the human bait gives a kick which brings him, with quarry annexed, to the surface. He turns on his back, still holding his breath for better buoyancy, and this exposes the body of the beast for the kill. The killer closes in, grasps the evil head from behind, and wrenches it away from its meal. Turning the face up towards himself, he plunges his teeth between the bulging eyes, and bites down and in with all his strength. That is the end of it. It dies on the instant; the suckers release their hold; the arms fall away; the two fishers paddle with whoops of delighted laughter to the reef, where they string the catch to a pole before going to rout out the next one.

Any two boys of seventeen, any day of the week, will go out and get you half a dozen octopus like that for the mere fun of it. Here lies the whole point of this story. The hunt is, in the most literal sense, nothing but child's play to the Gilbertese.

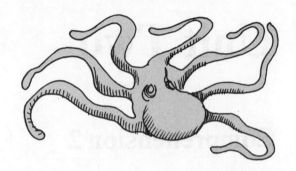

When two Gilbertese boys unexpectedly ask the author to participate in the hunt for an octopus, he reluctantly agrees.

I was dressed in khaki slacks, canvas shoes and a short-sleeved singlet. I took off the shoes and made up my mind to shed the singlet if told to do so; but I wildly determined to stick to my trousers throughout. Dead or alive, said a voice within me, an official minus his pants is a preposterous object, and I felt I could not face that extra horror. However, nobody asked me to remove anything.

I hope I did not look as yellow as I felt when I stood to take the plunge; I have never been so sick with funk before or since. 'Remember, one hand for your eyes,' said someone from a thousand miles off, and I dived.

I do not suppose it is really true that the eyes of an octopus shine in the dark; besides, it was clear daylight only six feet down in the limpid water; but I could have sworn the brute's eyes burned at me as I turned in towards his cranny. That dark glow — whatever may have been its origin — was the last thing I saw as I blacked out with my left hand and rose into his clutches. Then, I remember chiefly a dreadful sliminess with a herculean power behind it. Something whipped round my left forearm and the back of my neck, binding the two together. In the same flash, another

something slapped itself high on my forehead, and I felt it crawling down inside the back of my singlet. My impulse was to tear at it with my right hand, but I felt the whole of that arm pinioned to my ribs. In most emergencies the mind works with crystal-clear impersonality. This was not even an emergency, for I knew myself perfectly safe. But my boyhood's nightmare was upon me. When I felt the swift constriction of those disgusting arms jerk my head and shoulders in towards the reef, my mind went blank of every thought save the beastliness of contact with that squat head. A mouth began to nuzzle below my throat, at the junction of the collar-bones. I forgot there was anyone to save me. Yet something still directed me to hold my breath.

I was awakened from my cowardly trance by a quick, strong pull on my shoulders, back from the cranny. The cables around me tightened painfully, but I knew I was adrift from the reef. I gave a kick, rose to the surface and turned on my back with the brute sticking out of my chest like a tumour. My mouth was smothered by some flabby moving horror. The suckers felt like hot rings pulling at my skin. It was only two seconds, I suppose, from then to the attack of my deliverer, but it seemed like a century of nausea.

My friend came up between me and the reef. He pounced, pulled, bit down, and the thing was over — for everyone but me. At the sudden relaxation of the tentacles, I let out a great breath, sank, and drew in the next under water. It took the united help of both boys to get me, coughing, heaving and pretending to join in their delighted laughter, back to the reef. I had to submit there to a kind of war-dance round me, in which the dead beast was slung whizzing past my head from one to the other. I had a chance to observe then that it was not by any stretch of fancy a giant, but just plain average. That took the bulge out of my budding self-esteem. I left hurriedly for the cover of the jetty, and was sick.

from *A Pattern of Islands*
by ARTHUR GRIMBLE

How Well Did You Understand?

(1) What quality of the octopus enables the Gilbertese to catch and kill it?

(2) Why do the Gilbertese hunt the octopus?

(3) 'The beast will not always respond to the lure.' In your own words explain the meaning of this sentence.

(4) What 'moment' is the partner, on the reef above, waiting for?

(5) What does the octopus do when it is torn away from its cranny?

(6) What are some of the things the decoy does to help his friend?

(7) What evidence can you find to show that the Gilbertese enjoy catching the octopus?

(8) How did Arthur Grimble feel before he plunged into the water?

(9) What evidence can you find to show that the octopus was very powerful?

(10) In his description of the octopus, the author shows his horror and repulsion. Jot down two or three of his words or phrases that indicate this.

(11) How is it that Grimble, in his horrifying predicament, knew himself to be 'perfectly safe'?

(12) When the incident was over, Arthur Grimble's feelings were very different from those of the Gilbertese boys. Explain why this was so.

Dictionary Words

Give the meaning of each of the following words. Use the back-of-the-book dictionary to help you.

(a) relentless   (b) tenacity   (c) cranny   (d) lure   (e) limpid   (f) nuzzle.

Language 2

Phrases and Sentences

A group of words that does not make complete sense by itself is called a **phrase**. Look at these phrases, taken from 'Octopus!'

in pairs	of the submarine cliff	to its prey
at low tide	between the bulging eyes	

Each group of these words needs other words added to it to make complete sense. When this takes place you have a sentence. Look what happens when these five phrases are made into sentences.

- The Gilbertese hunt **in pairs**.
- **At low tide** they swim eyes-under.
- They search the crannies **of the submarine cliff**.
- The octopus clamps itself the more fiercely **to its prey**.
- **Between the bulging eyes** the killer plunges his teeth.

Identifying phrases and sentences

Arrange the following into two columns, headed PHRASES and SENTENCES.

(1) Into the picture

(2) I was the bait

(3) His teeth are his only weapon

(4) By some flabby moving horror

(5) Sometimes nothing happens

(6) It was only two seconds

(7) Of my budding self-esteem

(8) From my cowardly trance

(9) This was not even an emergency

(10) Sticking out of my chest

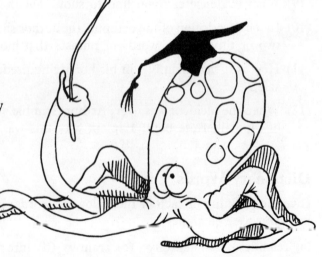

Turning phrases into sentences

Use the information contained in 'Octopus!' to change the following phrases into sentences.

(1) In the cranny ....

(2) With its tentacles ....

(3) .... in khaki slacks.

(4) .... to the surface.

(5) .... for the mere fun of it.

Missing phrases

Correctly insert the phrases from the box into the passage below it.

of the room	in all the glow	of plain boards
from the rafters overhead	of spotless plates	on the wide hearth
of eggs	of onions	of logs

Badger's Kitchen

Badger flung open the door, and Ratty and Mole found themselves .... and warmth of a large fire-lit kitchen. The floor was well-worn red brick, and .... burnt a fire .... between two attractive chimney-corners. In the middle .... stood a long table .... placed on trestles, with benches down each side. At one end of it, where an arm-chair stood pushed back, were spread the remains of the Badger's plain but ample supper. Rows .... winked from the shelves of the dresser at the far end of the room, and .... hung hams, bundles of dried herbs, nets ...., and baskets ....

A word for a phrase

Here is a list of eighteen phrases. Write down one word for each phrase. The first letters are given to help you. Note the example.

(1) to give oneself up to the enemy: <u>s u r r e n d e r</u>

(2) to drink in small amounts: <u>s</u> _ _

(3) a person under the care of a doctor: <u>p</u> _ _ _ _ _

(4) the poison of snakes and spiders: <u>v</u> _ _ _ _

(5) a paid driver of a motorcar: <u>c</u> _ _ _ _ _ _ _

(6) a hoarder of money: <u>m</u> _ _ _ _

(7) a bunch of flowers: <u>b</u> _ _ _ _ _

(8) the greater number or part: m _ _ _ _ _ _ _

(9) troops mounted on horseback: c _ _ _ _ _ _

(10) to stare open-mouthed: g _ _ _

(11) lasting only for a time: t _ _ _ _ _ _ _

(12) to put off or defer: p _ _ _ _ _ _

(13) to walk with long steps: s _ _ _ _ _

(14) not true or genuine: f _ _ _ _

(15) to bite a little at a time: n _ _ _ _

(16) feeling sleepy: d _ _ _ _

(17) far away: d _ _ _ _ _

(18) a person entertained at another's house: g _ _ _ _

Punctuation 2

Capital Letters and Full Stops

A capital letter begins a sentence. A full stop is used to end a sentence.

> The eyes of an octopus shine in the dark.

Separating the sentences

Write the following paragraphs into your workbook, using capital letters to begin sentences and full stops to end them wherever necessary. The number of sentences in each paragraph is given in brackets. The first sentence of the first paragraph is given as your example.

(1) The ragged boy came and went at his own free will. He slept on doorsteps in fine weather in the wet weather he slept in empty hogsheads he could go fishing and swimming whenever he chose [*4 sentences*]

from *Huckleberry Finn* by MARK TWAIN

(2) the great witch hunt is planned for to-night many will be smelled out as witches and wizards they will be slain no one's life will be safe Gagool will dance and point the bone of death at the guilty ones [*5 sentences*]

from *King Solomon's Mines* by RIDER HAGGARD

(3) that night was bitterly cold snow lay heavily on the ground a hard, thick crust had formed in doorways and on fences the wind that howled abroad was savage it caught the snow and scattered it into the air [*5 sentences*]

from Oliver Twist by CHARLES DICKENS

(4) i looked at the wretch the monster I had created glared back at me his jaws opened vague sounds came forth he lifted a withered hand horrified I rushed away now I am trembling downstairs [*7 sentences*]

from Frankenstein by MARY SHELLEY

Creative Writing 2

The Opening Sentence

Coming up with just the right way to begin your piece of creative writing is possibly the hardest task of all. This is because your opening sentence is so important — as everybody realizes. The opening sentence must *appeal* to the reader's interest and imagination, so that he or she will want to read on to find out what follows.

When you are ready to write, try to think up the kind of opening sentence that will appeal to or even *tantalize* your reader. How is this possible? Here's one way.

Read through the twenty opening sentences that follow. Each one is famous for the way it appeals or tantalizes. As you look through them, dwell on each one as a possible *model* for your own creative-writing effort. This does not mean that you should just copy the sentence, but you could certainly try to imitate some special touch it exhibits which you think might work for you too.

The special touch might be a hint of mystery or humour; it may be a touch of the uncanny, or the suspenseful, or the strange; a scene may be vividly set, or an emotion strongly introduced. Find out for yourself by taking a thoughtful look at what follows.

Effective Opening Sentences

(1) It was a bright cold day in April, and the clocks were striking thirteen.
[Nineteen Eighty-Four by George Orwell]

(2) The eyes behind the wide black rubber goggles were as cold as flint.
[For Your Eyes Only by Ian Fleming]

(3) I was tired and very cold; a little scared, too.
[The Wreck of the Mary Deare by Hammond Innes]

(4) 'Tom!'
[Tom Sawyer by Mark Twain]

(5) During the greater part of the day the guillotine had been kept busy at its horrible work: many noble heads had fallen.　[*The Scarlet Pimpernel* by Baroness Orczy]

(6) The great fish moved silently through the night water, propelled by short sweeps of its crescent tail.   [*Jaws* by Peter Benchley]

(7) The telephone rang.   [*My Turn to Make the Tea* by Monica Dickens]

(8) The boy with the fair hair lowered himself down the last few feet of rock and began to pick his way towards the lagoon.   [*Lord of the Flies* by William Golding]

(9) The Espresso machine behind my shoulder hissed like an angry snake.
                                                                [*The Pale Horse* by Agatha Christie]

(10) When a day that you happen to know is Wednesday starts off by sounding like Sunday, there is something seriously wrong somewhere.
                                                          [*The Day of the Triffids* by John Wyndham]

(11) I am fourteen years old, five foot four and still growing (I hope).
                                                            [*A Billion for Boris* by Mary Rodgers]

(12) No one would have believed, in the last years of the nineteenth century, that human affairs were being watched keenly and closely by intelligences greater than man's and yet as mortal as his own; that as men busied themselves about their affairs they were scrutinized and studied, perhaps almost as narrowly as a man with a microscope might scrutinize the transient creatures that swarm and multiply in a drop of water.
                                                        [*The War of the Worlds* by H.G. Wells]

(13) 'Off there to the right — somewhere — is a large island,' said Whitney.
                                              ['The Most Dangerous Game' by Richard Connell]

(14) The trouble with Harrowby Hall was that it was haunted, and, what was worse, the ghost did not merely appear at the bedside of a person, but remained there for one mortal hour before it disappeared.
                                    ['The Water Ghost of Harrowby Hall' by John Kendrick Bangs]

(15) This is a story of revenge.   ['Out of the Past' by Jack Schaefer]

(16) Choking, dense, impenetrable, the black smoke lay pall-like over the dying city.
                                                      [*South by Java Head* by Alistair Maclean]

(17) Whoever has made a voyage up the Hudson, must remember the Kaatskill mountains.   ['Rip Van Winkle' by Washington Irving]

(18) Just occasionally you find yourself in an odd situation.
                                                    [*The Kon-Tiki Expedition* by Thor Heyerdahl]

(19) How many of us have ever got to know a wild animal?
                                                      ['Silverspot' by Ernest Thompson Seton]

(20) In a hole in the ground there lived a hobbit.   [*The Hobbit* by J.R.R. Tolkien]

Your Turn to Write

See how interestingly you can write about *one* of these topics:

(1) Write a composition beginning, 'I was all alone in the middle of the ocean.'

(2) My Favourite Pastime.

(3) Write a newspaper or radio advertisement for a brand of one of these products:
(a) suntan lotion   (b) sunglasses   (c) swimming costume   (d) surfboard
(e) beach umbrella.

(4) The Creature from the Black Lagoon.

Poetry 2

Lifesavers at our beaches save thousands of lives each year. Because they are such strong swimmers, it is most unusual for them to meet their death in the sea. 'Lifesaver' is a very sad poem. It describes the moving scene of a drowned lifesaver being carried up the beach.

LIFESAVER

He was brought up out of the sea,
His tall body dead.
He was carried shoulder high
Between the sea and the sky.

The sun and the water trembled down
From his fingers and from the brown
Valley between his shoulders; and the spray
Fell before him as he passed on his way.

His eyes were dead, and his lips
Closed on death, and his feet
Chained with death, and his hands
Cold with death. He is one now with ships
And the bones of pirate bands
Steeped in salt and knavery.
One with fish and weed and pearl
And the long lonely beat
Of the waves that curl
On shell and rock and sand
Of a deep drowned land.

He was carried shoulder high
Up the alleys of the sun;
And the heat
Washed him over from his head to his feet,
But you cannot give the body back breath
With a flagon full of sun.
He is drowned, the tall one.
Thin brother Death
Has him by the throat
On the sand, in the sun.

ELIZABETH RIDDELL

Thinking about the Poem

(1) What words tell you that the lifesaver had a fine physique?

(2) What evidence can you find to show that the dead lifesaver had been brought up out of the sea only recently?

(3) What words of the poet emphasize that the lifesaver cannot be given back his life?

(4) What does the poet mean by: 'He is one now with ships / And the bones of pirate bands'?

(5) At the end of the poem, the poet gives human qualities to death. Explain how.

(6) Do you think the poet actually witnessed the scene described in the poem? Why?

(7) What were your feelings towards the lifesaver after reading the poem?

(8) Did you like 'Lifesaver'? Why or why not?

Spelling 2

OCTOPUS

horrifying	ordeal	quality	extraordinary	procedure
imagination	ability	spectacle	determined	usually
octopus	assist	especially	anxiety	system
tentacles	enveloped	essential	relaxation	astonishment

Missing Words

Rewrite *The Decoy* in your notebook, filling the blank spaces with words from the spelling box above.

The Decoy

In his book *A Pattern of Islands*, Arthur Grimble described the e.......... s.......... used by the Gilbertese to kill the .... When Grimble made his decision to become the decoy, he experienced great ...., but nevertheless he was .... to go ahead. He knew it was .... to keep his eyes covered with one hand, before the .... of the octopus .... him. The p.......... was e.......... successful, with Grimble even being able to a.......... the Gilbertese boy in getting to the surface with the octopus. Nevertheless, after the h.......... o.......... was over, Grimble was sick under cover of the jetty.

Single Words

Give a single word from the spelling box for each of the following:

(1) a remarkable sight: ....

(2) a difficult, painful experience: ....

(3) a worry about what may happen: ....

(4) unusual: ....

(5) absolutely necessary: ....

(6) surrounded completely: ....

(7) with one's mind firmly made up: ....

(8) on most occasions: ....

(9) amazement: ....

(10) to help: ....

Word Forms

Insert the correct form of each of the words in brackets into the space provided.

(1) The killing of the octopus was .... [**spectacle**].

(2) .... [**determined**] was one of the .... [**quality**] displayed by Arthur Grimble.

(3) At no stage was Grimble .... [**ability**] to .... [**relaxation**].

(4) Arthur Grimble .... [**procedure**] to take off his shoes, even though he ....
[**imagination**] the plan could fail.

(5) It was .... [**usually**] for the Gilbertese to hunt and kill the octopus ....
[**system**].

(6) The success of the system depended on the octopus's .... [**enveloped**] of the
decoy.

Try Thinking 2

Homes for Creatures

Put the creature on the left in touch with its usual home on the right.

(1)	spider	hive
(2)	rabbit	cave
(3)	ant	stable
(4)	lion	burrow
(5)	snail	pen
(6)	dog	shell
(7)	bat	den
(8)	bee	nest
(9)	horse	kennel
(10)	sheep	web

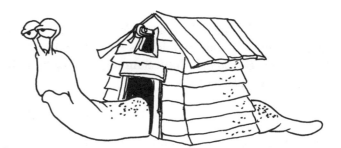

Detective Work

Try yourself out for the job of detective by looking closely at the following receptacles or containers and then deciding what thing or substance would most likely be found inside. (For example, the answer to the first one is *flowers*.)

(1) vase	(5) compact	(9) scabbard	(13) silo	(17) urn
(2) envelope	(6) flagon	(10) cellar	(14) holster	(18) goblet
(3) keg	(7) wallet	(11) bath	(15) percolator	(19) glove
(4) scuttle	(8) wardrobe	(12) punnet	(16) attaché case	(20) tureen

Name Game

Given that Jean, a brunette like Mary, isn't reading and that she has the same sunshade as Connie and a bathing costume like Clara's but different from Mabel's, can you determine the respective names of these five beach beauties? (Answer on p. 258.)

Unit Three

Comprehension 3

What is it *really* like to be spastic? What's it like to be young and bursting with physical and mental energy — but unable to get your limbs and muscles to obey you? In this extract from *Let the Balloon Go* John Sumner thinks about all the things the adults in his life have told him he must not do.

DISABLED

'You must remember that you are different from other children. You can never be sure that your limbs will obey you. It's no one's fault that you're "spastic"; no one can be blamed; least of all yourself; but we've all got to learn to live with it. If we ignore some things they go away, but if we ignore this or if you ignore it we may have serious accidents on our hands. Other children, particularly, sometimes expect too much of you. They may put you into dangerous situations even though they don't mean to. Perhaps even dangerous for them and doubly dangerous for you.

'You mustn't chop wood or use a saw or hammer nails or swing on the monkey bars or ride a bike or get into fights or play football or cricket or softball or rough games with boys or girls in case you injure yourself. You mustn't run fast in case you fall. You mustn't go near the edge of cliffs or climb trees or ladders in case you overbalance. You mustn't play with matches or boiling water or this or that or the next thing.

'Of course there are lots of things you can do and we must be thankful for that, mustn't we? You don't, after all, have to go to a special school. You can swim in shallow water if someone is with you. You can go fishing with your friends as long as one of them will bait your hook. You can go for nice walks with other people. You can be time-keeper for the football team and scorer for the cricket team and they're both very important jobs. You can see all the beauty of the world around you. You can read books and watch TV and listen to music and collect things. And you do have a marvellous imagination. With that there is almost nothing you cannot do. In your imagination you can swim the broadest river, run the fastest race, climb the highest mountain — and believe you me, lad, the adventures of the mind in the long run are far more exciting than the adventures of the body.'

How stupid it was, all those grown-up words, all those grown-up meanings. How could they expect him to like it? Even when they were telling him about the things he could do they were saying it in such a way that the fun was about as joyful as a stab of toothache. And when he did use his imagination, as they said he should, someone would end up shouting, 'John

Clement Sumner, your imagination will be the death of me.'

It made him sick and they thought he didn't mind; patted him on the head and called him a good boy (perhaps he should purr), squeezed his shoulders and smiled at him, told him he was wonderful, he was clever, he was brave. But all the time they were only telling him that he was different, was as good as useless, was a dreadful worry to everybody, was half a boy, not a whole boy, was a peculiar little object known as John Clement Sumner who had to be handled carefully like a broken egg.

Sometimes he thought he would ex-plode. Bang. And someone would have to rush round with a broom to sweep up a billion bits.

Surely by now they should have guessed that he was a whole boy bound hand and foot, that they had made his body into a prison, that he was a young lion in chains, that he was an eagle with clipped wings, that he was really a Herb Elliott, an Edmund Hillary, a *Hercules*? Didn't they know that a balloon was not a balloon until someone cut the string?

from *Let the Balloon Go*
by IVAN SOUTHALL

How Well Did You Understand?

(1) What three words in the opening sentence sum up John Sumner's problem?

(2) Why have the adults told him that he must not ignore the fact that he is spastic?

(3) The list of things John must not do is a terrible one for a young boy. Why is this?

(4) Why are nearly all the things he *can* do somehow bitterly disappointing?

(5) John is assured that 'the adventures of the mind in the long run are far more exciting than the adventures of the body'. Why do you think such an argument is unlikely to appeal to a disabled person?

(6) What is wrong with the kind of fun proposed by the adults for the disabled boy?

(7) What does John think about the praise he continually receives?

(8) Why do the adults think John has to be handled carefully?

(9) In what way is John 'a whole boy bound hand and foot'?

(10) What have the adults made of John's body?

(11) What does John believe himself to be?

(12) 'Didn't they know that a balloon was not a balloon until someone cut the string?' Can you explain what John *really* means by these words?

Dictionary Words

Use the back-of-the-book dictionary to work out the meanings of these medical words:

(a) pneumonia (b) psychiatrist (b) haemorrhage (d) epilepsy.

Language 3

Nouns

A noun is the name of a person, animal, place, thing or quality. Here are some nouns from *Let the Balloon Go* to give you the idea of what a noun is: *boy* (person), *lion* (animal), *world* (place), *bike* (thing), *beauty* (quality).

Identifying the nouns

Write down the following sentences and underline the nouns. (*Note:* 'You' is a **pronoun**.)

(1) You can see all the beauty of the world around you.

(2) You can go for nice walks with other people.

(3) You can read books and watch TV and listen to music and collect things.

(4) In your imagination you can swim the broadest river, run the fastest race, climb the highest mountain.

(5) You mustn't ride a bike or get into fights or play football or cricket or softball or rough games.

(6) You mustn't go near the edge of cliffs or climb trees or ladders in case you over-balance.

(7) And you do have a marvellous imagination.

(8) He was a young lion in chains.

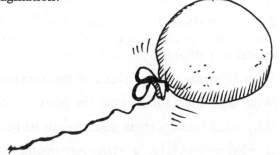

Singular and Plural Nouns

A noun is **singular** when it names *one* person, animal, place, thing or quality; and **plural** when it names *more than one*.

SINGULAR	PLURAL
balloon	balloons
boy	boys
eagle	eagles

Most nouns form the plural simply by adding 's' to the singular form. However, you will soon learn that this is not always so. Here are some valuable rules and examples:

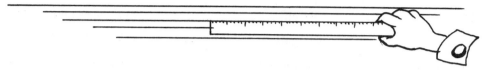

For nouns whose singular ends with 's', 'sh', 'ch', 'x' or 'z', the ending 'es' has to be added to form the plural.

> fox — foxes   church — churches   lass — lasses

Nouns that end with 'y', with a *consonant* coming before the 'y', form their plural by changing the 'y' into 'i' and adding 'es'.

> city — cities   fairy — fairies   mystery — mysteries

But nouns that end with 'y', with a *vowel* coming before the 'y', just add 's'.

> monkey — monkeys   kidney — kidneys   jockey — jockeys

Nouns that end with 'f' form their plural either by simply adding 's' or by changing the 'f' to 'v' and then adding 'es'.

> reef — reefs   wolf — wolves

Most nouns that end with 'o' form their plural by adding 'es'.

> potato — potatoes   echo — echoes   cargo — cargoes

However, there are a few nouns ending with 'o' which form the plural simply by adding 's'.

> studio — studios   piano — pianos   solo — solos

Finally, some words have peculiar plurals that you'll just have to learn as you meet up with them.

> child — children   phenomenon — phenomena   tooth — teeth

Forming the plurals

Form the plurals of these nouns:

(1) baby ....

(2) basis ....

(3) chief ....

(4) chimney ....

(5) cry ....

(6) datum ....

(7) diary ....

(8) echo ....

(9) elf ....

(10) gallery ....

(11) journey ....

(12) mosquito ....

(13) oasis ....

(14) piano ....

(15) salary ....

(16) salmon ....

(17) secretary ....

(18) self ....

(19) silo ....

(20) society ....

(21) story ....

(22) tomato ....

(23) torch ....

(24) turkey ....

Forming the singulars

Change these nouns into their singular forms:

(1) appendices ....

(2) batteries ....

(3) brothers-in-law ....

(4) buffaloes ....

(5) bureaux ....

(6) charities ....

(7) colonies ....

(8) commandos ....

(9) curricula ....

(10) economies ....

(11) heroes ....

(12) infernos ....

(13) journeys ....

(14) leaves ....

(15) lice ....

(16) memories ....

(17) photos ....

(18) potatoes ....

(19) radii ....

(20) remedies ....

(21) summaries ....

(22) tornadoes ....

(23) trolleys ....

(24) worries ....

Gender

A **masculine** noun names a male, a **feminine** noun names a female, and a **neuter** noun names a thing. ('Neuter' means that the word is neither masculine nor feminine.)

Masculine and feminine

Write down the masculine and feminine term for each of the persons in the list following. The first one has been done to help you.

(1) A person who practises magic: ....*wizard*.....   ....*witch*.....

(2) A person who rules an empire: ....

(3) A person who entertains guests: ....

(4) A person who acts: ....

(5) A person who is a parent: ....

(6) A person whose spouse has died: ....

(7) A person who reigns supreme: ....

(8) A person whose parent is a monarch: ....

(9) A person about to be married: ....

(10) A person who serves food: ....

Missing males and females

Insert the missing males and females into the two tables below.

MASCULINE	FEMININE
duke	....
....	niece
gentleman	....
priest	....
....	mistress
....	hostess
....	daughter
lad	....
hero	....
....	madam

MASCULINE	FEMININE
....	mare
....	duck
boar	....
....	goose
ram	....
bull	....
buck	....
....	vixen
dog	....
....	peahen

Punctuation 3

Using the Full Stop for Abbreviations

The full stop is used to show that a word has been abbreviated. For example, **Co.** = Company, **Sept.** = September. However, when the last letter of the abbreviation is also the last letter of the complete word, the full stop is omitted. Thus, **Rd** = Road. No full stop is needed here because 'd' (the last letter of the abbreviation) is the same as the last letter of the complete word.

Abbreviations and their meanings

See if you can match the useful abbreviations on the left with their meanings on the right.

(1) R.S.V.P. (*répondez s'il vous plaît*)   namely

(2) v. (*versus*)   after noon

(3) e.g. (*exempli gratia*)   something written afterwards

(4) N.B. (*nota bene*)   note well

(5) p.a. (*per annum*)   that is to say

(6) etc. (*et cetera*)   against

(7) i.e. (*id est*)   for example

(8) p.m. (*post meridiem*)   yearly

(9) P.S. (*postscriptum*)   and so on

(10) viz. (*videlicet*)   please reply

Abbreviations undone

Rewrite the following sentences, using the complete spelt-out form of each of the abbreviations.

(1) Next year, we hope to visit the U.S.A., G.B. and the U.S.S.R.

(2) Gen. Clark, Maj. Rogers and Capt. Jones inspected the troops.

(3) The bookshop has only one vol. of *Ulysses*.

(4) The satellite will fall to earth on Sat., the first of Aug., 1990.

(5) The Macmillan Co. of Aust. sent the parcel C.O.D.

(6) You have written approx. four pages.

Creative Writing 3

The Writer's Technique

The passage that follows is from *I Can Jump Puddles* by Alan Marshall. This writer describes how, as a boy crippled in both legs by polio, he met the fearful challenge of swimming in really deep water.

In this passage Alan has just left his wheelchair and crawled down the shore to the edge of the water. He now makes the attempt to swim in deep water by himself. Read carefully, and then answer the questions on technique (on page 40).

A FEARFUL CHALLENGE

It was the loneliness that frightened me. No trees grew around this lake. It lay open to the sky and there was always a still silence above it. Sometimes a swan called out but it was a mournful cry and only accentuated the lake's isolation.

After a while I crawled into the water and continued on, keeping erect by moving my arms in a swimming stroke on the surface, till I reached the edge of the drop into the dark blue and the cold. I stood there moving my arms and looking down into the clear water where I could see the long, pale stems of weeds swaying like snakes as they stretched out from the steep side of the submerged terrace.

I looked up at the sky and it was immense above me, an empty dome of sky with a floor of blue water. I was alone in the world and I was afraid.

I stood there a little while then drew a breath and struck out over the drop. As I moved forward a cold tendril of leaves clung for a moment to my trailing legs then slipped away and I was swimming in water that I felt went down beneath me for ever.

I wanted to turn back but I kept on, moving my arms with a slow rhythm while I kept repeating over and over in my mind, 'Don't be frightened now; don't be frightened now; don't be frightened now.'

I turned gradually and when I was facing the shore again and saw how far away it seemed to be I panicked for a moment and churned up the water with my arms, but the voice within me kept on and I recovered myself and swam slowly again.

I crawled out on to the shore as if I were an explorer returning home from a long journey of danger and privation. The lakeside was now no longer a lonely place of fear but a very lovely place of sunshine and grass and I whistled as I dressed.

I could swim!

from *I Can Jump Puddles*
by ALAN MARSHALL

Questions on the writer's technique

(1) 'It was the loneliness that frightened me.' This is an effective opening sentence because the writer introduces the words 'loneliness' and 'frightened', which intrigue the reader. However, this is just a beginning. How does the writer then proceed to provide the reader with the sights and sounds of the frightening loneliness?

(2) Next, we follow the boy's progress as he swims away from the shore of the lake and comes to the cold, dark-blue water, where he can see 'the long, pale stems of weeds swaying like snakes'. What would you say is the writer's purpose in comparing the swaying of the weeds to such deadly creatures as snakes?

(3) 'I was alone in the world and I was afraid.' In order to prepare the reader for the overwhelming nature of these emotions, the writer describes the form that the sky and water seem to take on. How are sky and water linked into one overwhelming presence from the lone young swimmer's point of view?

(4) 'I wanted to turn back . . . .' It is important for the reader to know about the crisis that is going on in the boy's mind when he reaches the point at which he feels tempted to turn back. In what special way does the writer show the reader what is going through the boy's mind at this crisis-point?

(5) When the boy successfully completes the swim, his happy mood changes the lake from a lonely place of fear into something very different. What does the lake now become for the boy?

(6) A good writer strives for a satisfying ending to a piece of writing, and Alan Marshall has achieved this here. Why, in your opinion, is his ending satisfying?

Your Turn to Write

Try your hand at writing about *one* of the following:

(1) You have been forced to leave your home. You have nowhere to go. How will you cope?

(2) 'My thoughts on helping and caring for handicapped people.'

(3) 'The unluckiest person I've ever met.'

(4) Life wasn't meant to be easy.

(5) There are many ways of helping the poor throughout the world. Discuss some of them.

(6) 'My most precious possession.'

Poetry 3

'Outside the General Hospital' and 'Timothy Winters' are poems about disadvantaged people. The schoolboy and the elderly woman outside the hospital are physically handicapped, while Timothy Winters is handicapped by his environment. The two poets approach their subjects in very different ways. Bruce Dawe focuses on a specific happening; Charles Causley, on the other hand, looks at Timothy's life and background.

OUTSIDE THE GENERAL HOSPITAL

The six-foot lank-faced schoolboy
with the cleft palate panted
on the bus-steps while the driver
wrenched the gear-stick in its socket
like a rheumaticky knee. Can't wait, he said,
as the blue-shirted kid, staring his desperation, groaned
over the first syllable, Sorry ...
The boy waved his arm
across the road to the general hospital where an elderly
woman with one leg taken off at the knee
jerked forward upon crutches.

Where had I seen that stricken look before?
The sun ached then for all of us, my tongue
clove to the roof of my mouth.
The bus waited.
But none of us were fooled.

BRUCE DAWE

Looking Closely at the Poem

(1) How do you know that the schoolboy had been hurrying for the bus?

(2) How did the boy react to the bus-driver's 'Can't wait'?

(3) 'The bus waited.' Why did the bus-driver wait after all?

(4) When you finished reading the poem, what was your attitude to the bus-driver?

(5) What are your feelings towards the schoolboy and the elderly lady?

(6) What clues in the poem tell you that the poet was personally involved in the incident?

(7) What do you think the poet was trying to make the reader aware of with this poem?

(8) What different title could you give the poem?

TIMOTHY WINTERS

Timothy Winters comes to school
With eyes as wide as a football-pool,
Ears like bombs and teeth like splinters;
A blitz of a boy is Timothy Winters.

His belly is white, his neck is dark,
And his hair is an exclamation mark;
His clothes are enough to scare a crow,
And through his britches the blue winds blow.

When teacher talks he won't hear a word,
And he shoots down dead the arithmetic-bird;
He licks the patterns off his plate,
And he's not even heard of the Welfare State.

Timothy Winters has bloody feet,
And he lives in a house on Suez Street;
He sleeps in a sack on the kitchen floor,
And they say there aren't boys like him any more.

Old Man Winters likes his beer,
And his missus ran off with a bombardier;
Grandma sits in the grate with a gin,
And Timothy's dosed with an aspirin.
The Welfare Worker lies awake,
But the law's as tricky as a ten-foot snake;
So Timothy Winters drinks his cup,
And slowly goes on growing up.

At Morning Prayers the Master helves,
For children less fortunate than ourselves;
And the loudest response in the room is when,
Timothy Winters roars 'Amen!'
So come one angel, come on ten:
Timothy Winters says 'Amen
Amen amen amen amen.'
Timothy Winters, Lord.

Amen.

CHARLES CAUSLEY

Looking Closely Again

(1) Why are Timothy's teeth 'like splinters'?

(2) 'Blitz' was a word used to describe wartime bombing raids. Why do you think Timothy is described as a 'blitz of a boy'?

(3) 'His belly is white, his neck is dark . . . .' What do these words tell us about Timothy?

(4) Why do you think Timothy's hair is 'an exclamation mark'?

(5) Why do you think Timothy has 'bloody feet'?

(6) 'His clothes are enough to scare a crow . . . .' What is the poet telling us about Timothy's clothes?

(7) We don't usually think of winds as being coloured. Why do you think the poet refers to the winds as 'blue'?

(8) How does Timothy react to school?

(9) What is the poet suggesting with 'He licks the patterns off his plate'?

(10) Why do you think the Welfare Worker lies awake?

(11) Why do you think Timothy is dosed with aspirin?

(12) How do you know that Timothy doesn't realize how badly off he is?

(13) Why do you think the poet wrote: '*Timothy Winters, Lord.* / Amen.'?

(14) What are your feelings towards Timothy Winters?

Spelling 3

DISABLED

accident	diagnosis	symptom	predicament	balance
specialist	assistance	invalid	genuine	accomplish
paralysed	thorough	circumstances	fulfil	situation
conscious	precaution	exhausted	different	responsibility

Find the Word

For each clue given, find the correct word in the spelling box.

(1) The antonym of 'similar'.

(2) A synonym of 'help'.

(3) The word for a sign or indicator of some (medical) condition.

(4) The word for a person who is an expert in a particular field.

(5) A word that can be changed to its opposite by addition of the prefix 'un'.

(6) A synonym of 'achieve'.

(7) The word for a medical opinion on a disease or condition.

(8) The word that can be changed to its opposite by addition of the prefix 'ir'.

(9) The word for a disabled person.

(10) The word for a difficult or unpleasant situation.

Word Forms

Complete each of the following sentences by using the correct form of the word in brackets.

(1) The risk of .... [**accident**] injury is great.

(2) After the smash, the driver of the car lost .... [**conscious**].

(3) An .... [**assistance**] helped him along the corridor.

(4) Every step that she took was a real .... [**accomplish**].

(5) The doctor has been .... [**specialist**] in infectious diseases.

(6) The .... [**different**] between the two treatments was soon apparent.

(7) The nurse was .... [**responsibility**] for the cleanliness of the ward.

(8) The teacher could see that the boy was suffering from complete .... [**exhausted**].

Given the Vowels

Given the vowels, insert the rest of the letters needed to complete the words. All the words come from the spelling box.

(1) _ _ o _ o u _ _
(2) _ a _ a _ _ e
(3) _ u _ _ i _
(4) a _ _ i _ e _ _
(5) _ o _ _ _ i o u _

(6) _ _ _ _ _ _ o _
(7) _ e _ _ o _ _ i _ i _ i _ _
(8) _ _ e _ a u _ i o _
(9) _ i _ u a _ i o _
(10) _ i a _ _ o _ i _

Try Thinking 3

Threesomes

Complete each of the following threesomes. The first one is done for you.

(1) Sun, moon and ....*stars*........

(2) Morning, noon and ....

(3) Stop, look and ....

(4) Ear, nose and ....

(5) Animal, vegetable and ....

(6) Lock, stock and ....

(7) Faith, hope and ....

(8) Ready, set, ...

(9) Knife, fork and ....

(10) Hop, skip and ....

(11) This, that and the ....

(12) Reading, writing and ....

Letter Shuffle

Shuffle the letters in each of the opening words to arrive at a new word suggested by the clue. Note the example.

(1) ART becomes a rodent: R A T

(2) SWAP becomes a stinging insect: _ _ _ _

(3) FRINGE becomes a human digit: _ _ _ _ _ _

(4) SINK becomes a body-covering: _ _ _ _

(5) MALE becomes something you eat: _ _ _ _

(6) USE becomes a girl's name: _ _ _

(7) HINGE becomes the sound made by a horse: _ _ _ _ _

(8) CAUSE becomes something to make food tasty: _ _ _ _ _

(9) EARTH becomes a beating organ of the body: _ _ _ _ _

(10) SAVE become a flower-holder: _ _ _ _

(11) STAIN becomes a very holy person: _ _ _ _ _

(12) ITEM becomes something shown by a clock: _ _ _ _

(13) TIP becomes a deep hole: _ _ _

(14) SLIP becomes what you kiss with: _ _ _ _

(15) DEAR becomes something you'd do to a book: _ _ _ _

Spare a Thought

Spare a thought for the following. But beware — each contains a special twist! (Answers on p. 258.)

1. Rungs of a ladder

A fishing boat is at anchor in the harbour. Over the side hangs a rope-ladder containing twelve rungs exactly one foot apart. The bottom rung is just touching the water at midday, which is dead low tide. The tide rises at the rate of eight inches an hour. At six p.m. how many of the rungs will be covered with water?

2. Family tally

Donald has as many sisters as brothers, but each of his sisters has only half as many sisters as brothers. How many brothers and sisters are there in Donald's family?

3. A weather forecast

On Sunday at midnight it is raining heavily. I look outside and predict that in 72 hours' time it will not be sunny. How can I make such a forecast for a time so far into the future?

Unit Four

Comprehension 4

This graphic description of a locust attack is written from the author's own experience in Rhodesia.

A PLAGUE OF LOCUSTS

By now the locusts were falling like hail on to the roof of the kitchen. It sounded like a heavy storm. Margaret looked out and saw the air dark with a criss-cross of the insects, and she set her teeth and ran out into it — what the men could do, she could. Overhead the air was thick, locusts everywhere. The locusts flopping against her, and she brushed them off, heavy red-brown creatures, looking at her with their beady old-men's eyes while they clung with hard serrated legs. She held her breath with disgust and ran through into the house. There it was even more like being in a heavy storm. The iron roof was reverberating, and the clamour of iron from the lands was like thunder. Looking out, all the trees were queer and still, clotted with insects, their boughs weighed to the ground. The earth seemed to be moving, locusts crawling everywhere, she could not see the lands at all, so thick was the swarm. Towards the mountains it was like looking into driving rain — even as she watched the sun was blotted out with a fresh onrush of them. It was a half-night, a perverted blackness. Then came a sharp crack from the bush — a branch had snapped off. Then another. A tree down the slope leaned over, and settled heavily to the ground. Through the hail of insects a man came running. More tea, more water was needed. She supplied them. She kept the fires stoked and filled tins with liquid, and then it was four in the afternoon, and the locusts had been pouring across overhead for a couple of hours. Up came old Stephen again, crunching locusts underfoot with every step, locusts clinging all over him, cursing and swearing, banging with his old hat at the air. At the doorway he stopped briefly, hastily pulling at the clinging insects and throwing them off, then he plunged into the locust-free living-room.

'All the crops finished. Nothing left,' he said.

But the gongs were still beating, the men still shouting, and Margaret asked: 'Why do you go on with it, then?'

'The main swarm isn't settling. They are heavy with eggs. They are looking for a place to settle and lay. If we can stop the main body settling on our farm, that's everything. If they get a chance to lay their eggs, we are going to have everything eaten flat with hoppers later on.' He picked a stray locust off his shirt, and split it down with his thumb-nail — it was clotted inside with eggs. 'Imagine that multiplied by

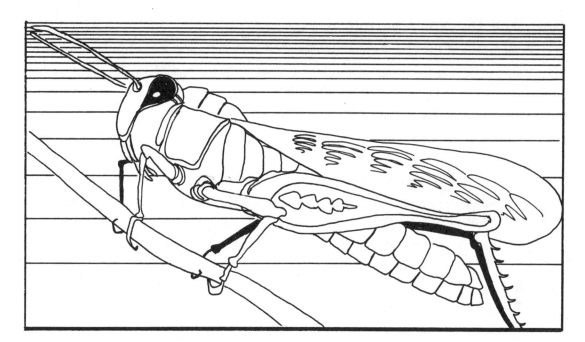

millions. You ever seen a hopper swarm on the march? Well, you're lucky.'

Margaret thought an adult swarm was bad enough. Outside now the light on the earth was a pale thin yellow, clotted with moving shadow, the clouds of moving insects thickened and lightened like driving rain. Old Stephen said: 'They've got the wind behind them, that's something.'

'Is it very bad?' asked Margaret fearfully, and the old man said emphatically: 'We're finished. This swarm may pass over, but once they've started, they'll be coming down from the north now one after another. And then there are the hoppers — it might go on for two or three years.'

Margaret sat down helplessly, and thought: 'Well, if it's the end, it's the end. What now? We'll all three have to go back to town ...' But at this, she took a quick look at Stephen, the old man who had farmed forty years in this country, been bankrupt twice, and she knew nothing would make him go and become a clerk in the city. Yet her heart ached for him, he looked so tired, the worry-lines deep from nose to mouth. Poor old man ... He had lifted up a locust that had got itself somehow into his pocket, holding it in the air by one leg. 'You've got the strength of a steel-spring in those legs of yours,' he was telling the locust, good-humouredly. Then, although he had been fighting locusts, squashing locusts, yelling at locusts, sweeping them in great mounds into the fires to burn for the last three hours, nevertheless he took this one to the door, and carefully threw it out to join its fellows as if he would rather not harm a hair of its head. This comforted Margaret, all at once she felt irrationally cheered. She remembered it was not the first time in the last three years the men had announced their final and irremediable ruin.

from *The Habit of Loving*
by DORIS LESSING

How Well Did You Understand?

(1) What words in the first three sentences show that there was a multitude of locusts?

(2) Margaret 'set her teeth and ran out into it — what the men could do, she could'. What do these words reveal about her character?

(3) What was Margaret's main task during the passing of the locusts?

(4) What were the men doing to try to prevent the main swarm of the locusts from settling on the farm?

(5) Why was old Stephen so concerned about a possible hopper swarm?

(6) 'They've got the wind behind them, that's something.' Why do you think old Stephen was glad about the wind?

(7) What evidence can you find to show that old Stephen had had previous experience of locust swarms?

(8) Can you suggest why Stephen did not kill the locust that had got into his pocket?

(9) Why did Margaret believe that old Stephen would not give up the farm?

(10) What comments would you make about Stephen's character?

Dictionary Words

Use the back-of-the-book dictionary to work out the meanings of these words:

(a) serrated   (b) reverberating   (c) clamour   (d) irrationally   (e) irremediable.

Language 4

Four Kinds of Noun

- COMMON NOUNS. A common noun is a word used for *any* person, animal, place or thing belonging to a certain category or class — e.g. girl, country, radio, athlete, cat, building.

- PROPER NOUNS. A proper noun is the name of a *particular* person, animal, place or thing, and always begins with a capital letter — e.g. Margaret, Scotland, Sony, Raylene Boyle, Sylvester, Centrepoint.

- COLLECTIVE NOUNS. A collective noun is a word used for a collection or group of similar persons, animals or things — e.g. herd, crowd, class, bunch, gang.

- ABSTRACT NOUNS. Abstract nouns are nouns that name feelings or qualities — e.g. hatred, love, pain, cowardice.

Look at the cartoon strip below.

   (1) What kind of noun is 'octopus'?

   (2) What would be *your* definition of 'octopus'?

Identifying nouns

Rule up four columns, heading them, COMMON, PROPER, COLLECTIVE and ABSTRACT. Then place each of the following nouns into the right category.

anxiety	kindness	choir	Shakespeare	Canada
woman	flock	Thursday	army	cruelty
Volvo	banana	swarm	amazement	fear
purse	loneliness	dog	congregation	Mozart

Forming nouns

Form nouns ending with 'ion' from each of these words. The first one has been done to help you.

(1) admit ....*admission*............

(2) collide ....

(3) navigate ....

(4) select ....

(5) explode ....

(6) include ....

(7) create ....

(8) supervise ....

(9) explain ....

(10) evade ....

(11) expel ....

(12) cultivate ....

(13) apply ....

(14) extend ....

(15) reduce ....

(16) isolate ....

Forming people-nouns

By adding 'er', 'or', 'ant' or 'ist', form the word for a person associated with each of the following. Sometimes you'll have to change the ending of a word before you add the suffix. The first one has been done to help you.

(1) operate ....*operator*............

(2) pension ....

(3) carry ....

(4) organ ....

(5) travel ....

(6) govern ....

(7) swim ....

(8) consult ....

(9) conquer ....

(10) depend ....

(11) science ....

(12) commission ....

(13) journal ....

(14) educate ....

(15) council ....

(16) assist ....

Missing nouns

Correctly insert the nouns from the group below into the passage that follows. Occasionally the first letter is given to help you. The passage is from *South* by Ernest Shackleton.

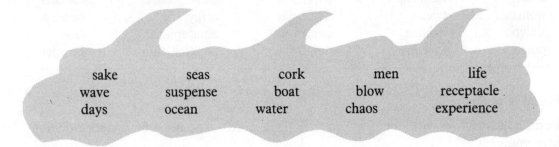

sake	seas	cork	men	life
wave	suspense	boat	blow	receptacle
days	ocean	water	chaos	experience

The Wave

During twenty-six years' .... of the ocean in all its moods I had never seen a .... so gigantic. It was a mighty upheaval of the ...., a thing quite apart from the big white-capped s........... which had been our tireless enemies for many .... I shouted, 'For God's ...., hold on! It's got us!' Then came a moment of .... which seemed to last for hours. We felt our boat lifted and flung forward like a .... in breaking surf. We were in a seething c........... of tortured water; but somehow the .... lived through it, half-full of w..........., sagging to the dead weight and shuddering under the b........... . We bailed with the energy of .... fighting for life, flinging the water over the sides with every .... which came into our hands; and after ten minutes of uncertainty we felt the boat renew her .... beneath us.

Punctuation 4

Capital Letters for Proper Nouns

Use capital letters to begin the names of people, places, commercial products, films, books and TV shows.

EXAMPLES: (a) people — Princess Diana, Elvis Presley

(b) places — Disneyland, Eiffel Tower, Ayers Rock

(c) products — Rolls Royce, National, Vegemite, Cadbury

(d) films — *Mad Max, Return of the Jedi*

(e) books — *The Silver Sword, Animal Farm*

(f) TV shows — 'Happy Days', 'Doctor Who'

Note: In titles, watch the little words such as 'the', 'from', 'in'. These are not capitalized when they are used *within* a title; they are normally given capital letters only when they begin a title — e.g. *The Man from Snowy River*.

Using capital letters

Capital letters are used for proper nouns but not for common nouns. In each of the following sentences the same word is used as a common noun and as a proper noun. Write out the sentences, putting in the necessary capitals.

(1) The captain of your jet aircraft is captain hunt.

(2) The doctor on duty tonight is doctor mary jones.

(3) The name of his school is forest agricultural high school.

(4) The closest park is dawson park.

(5) The river thames is a world-famous river.

(6) The new road is called telegraph road.

(7) The church closest to our house is st andrew's church.

(8) The moscow state circus is an outstanding circus.

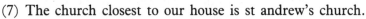
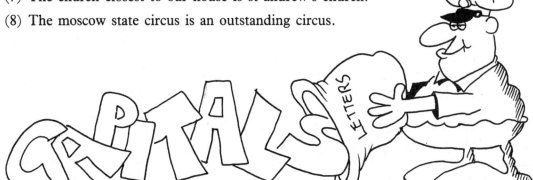

Creative Writing 4

This passage is from the short story 'Leiningen versus the Ants', in which Leiningen defends his plantation against the march of the ferocious Brazilian army ants. Immediately you begin reading, you'll find yourself involved in a gripping description of the sighting and approach of the Army of the Ants.

THE ARMY OF THE ANTS

It was a sight one could never forget. Over the range of hills, as far as eye could see, crept a darkening hem, ever longer and broader, until the shadow spread across the slope from east to west, then downwards, downwards, uncannily swift, and all the green herbage of that wide vista was being mown as if by a giant sickle, leaving only the vast moving shadow, extending, deepening, and moving rapidly nearer.

When Leiningen's men, behind their barrier of water, perceived the approach of the long-expected foe, they gave vent to their suspense in screams and imprecations. But as the distance began to lessen between the 'sons of hell' and the water ditch, they relapsed into silence. Before the advance of that awe-inspiring throng, their belief in the powers of the boss began to steadily dwindle. Even Leiningen himself, who had ridden up just in time to restore their loss of heart by a display of unshakable calm, even he could not free himself from a qualm of malaise. Yonder were thousands of millions of voracious jaws bearing down upon him and only a suddenly insignificant narrow ditch lay between him and his men and being gnawed to the bones 'before you can spit three times'.

Hadn't his brain for once taken on more than it could manage? If the blighters decided to rush the ditch, fill it to the brim with their corpses, there'd still be more than enough to destroy every trace of that cranium of his. The planter's chin jutted; they hadn't got him yet, and he'd see to it they never would. While he could think at all, he'd flout both death and the devil.

The hostile army was approaching in perfect formation; no human battalions, however well-drilled, could ever hope to rival the precision of that advance. Along a front that moved forward as uniformly as a straight line, the ants drew nearer and nearer to the water ditch. Then, when they learned through their scouts the nature of the obstacle, the two outlying wings of the army detached themselves from the main body and marched down the western and eastern sides of the ditch.

This surrounding manoeuvre took rather more than an hour to accomplish; no doubt the ants expected that at some point they would find a crossing.

During this outflanking movement by the wings, the army on the center and southern front remained still. The besieged were therefore able to contemplate at their leisure the thumb-long, reddish black, long-legged insects; some of the Indians believed they could see, too, intent on them, the brilliant, cold eyes, and the razor-edged mandibles, of this host of infinity.

from 'Leiningen versus the Ants'
by CARL STEPHENSON

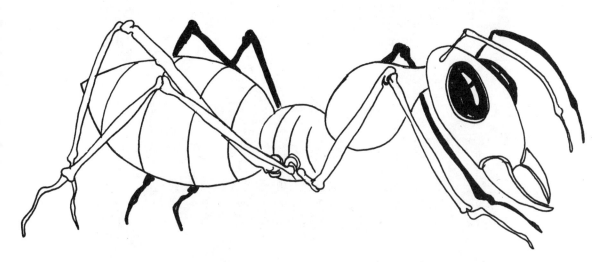

The Writer's Technique — Questions

(1) A good opening sentence is one that grips the reader and urges him or her to read on so as to find out what follows. Look at the opening sentence of the passage you have just read. In your own words, say why this is a good opening sentence.

(2) The second sentence in the passage, beginning 'Over the range . . .', flows on to the end of the paragraph. Why do you think the writer chose to create such a long, flowing sentence?

(3) The second paragraph reveals the feelings of the humans as they watch the approach of the ant army. Does the writer use the technique of:
  (a) having the characters themselves tell us what they are feeling? *or*
  (b) simply informing us of their feelings as if he and the reader were able to enter into the characters' minds?

(4) What thoughts are present in Leiningen's mind in the third paragraph?

(5) In the fourth and fifth paragraphs, the emphasis shifts from Leiningen to the ants. A manoeuvre of the ant army is described and, as you would expect, army-type words and phrases such as 'perfect formation' keep the reader aware of the military nature of the ants. Find at least six other words or phrases that emphasize the military nature of the ant army.

(6) The last paragraph focuses in like a zoom lens on the features of individual ants. The writer uses the following *adjectives* (descriptive words) to present the appearance, the coldness and the efficiency of the ants to the reader:
  • the *thumb-long, reddish black, long-legged* insects
  • the *brilliant, cold* eyes
  • the *razor-edged* mandibles

Notice how apt (fitting) the adjectives are. Now see if you can replace each of the italicized adjectives with an adjective of your own which is just as apt.

Your Turn to Write

Here's a chance to let your imagination go as you write about *one* of these:

(1) Write a composition beginning: 'It was a sight one could never forget. Millions of flesh-eating ants were rapidly moving towards us.'

(2) Attacked by Killer Wasps.

(3) Write a piece beginning: 'Rats! Rats! We were surrounded by rats!'

(4) The Day the Birds Went Mad.

(5) The Day the Insects Started Growing.

Poetry 4

A Pair of Poems

Here are two poems concerned with frogs. The first, 'Boy with Frogs', tends to concentrate on the boy's attitude to the frogs he has captured. The second, 'Frogs', reveals the poet's personal feelings towards these lively amphibians.

BOY WITH FROGS

Under his relentless eye,
jarred and jeered,
The small frogs hop
And pulse in their
Suddenly glass world.

He, blond and curious,
Captive and captivated,
Holds in his hands
World of water, pebbles, grass
And the power
Of topsy-turvy and crash.

But he is content
To study them a while,
With their delicate legs
Pressed against the glass,
The futile leaps to freedom
And their frantic eyes.

It's a game for a God
Of course.
Later, the vibrant frogs,
Still leaping with protest
And life, are forgotten
On a shelf. He is out
Wondering about the waterbugs.

SY KAHN

Thinking about the Boy

(1) What is the boy's attitude to the frogs in the first three stanzas?

(2) Why has the world of the frogs become 'Suddenly glass'?

(3) What is the boy's power 'Of topsy-turvy and crash'?

(4) Why is the boy 'Captive and captivated'?

(5) Why are the frogs' leaps to freedom futile?

(6) What does the poet mean by 'It's a game for a God'?

(7) How has the boy's attitude to the frogs changed by the end of the poem?

(8) What are your feelings towards the frogs?

(9) What is your attitude to the boy?

(10) What other suitable title could you suggest for this poem?

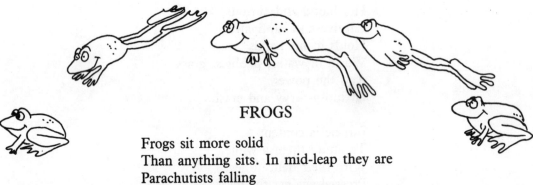

FROGS

Frogs sit more solid
Than anything sits. In mid-leap they are
Parachutists falling
In a free fall. They die on roads
With arms across their chests and
Heads high.

I love frogs that sit
Like Buddha, that fall without
Parachutes, that die
Like Italian tenors.

Above all, I love them because,
Pursued in water, they never
Panic so much that they fail
To make stylish triangles
With their ballet dancer's
Legs.

NORMAN MACCAIG

Thinking about the Frogs

(1) In what way are the frogs like Buddha?

(2) Why do you think the poet compares dying frogs to Italian tenors?

(3) Why do you think the poet likens the legs of the frogs to those of ballet dancers?

(4) Why does the poet especially like frogs?

(5) Which poem did you prefer, 'Boy with Frogs' or 'Frogs'? Give a reason for your choice.

Spelling 4

LOCUST PLAGUE

catastrophe	announced	threatening	destruction	organization
occurrence	tragic	futility	truly	bewildered
creatures	despair	courageous	arrangements	multiplied
hastily	desperate	destroy	appealed	emphasized

Missing Words

Fit the correct words from the spelling box into the spaces left blank in the passage below.

The Locusts

It was .... a d........... situation. At first the farmers were b...........
when it was a........... that the locusts had already m........... and that swarms
of them were advancing and t........... to invade the neighbouring properties.
But although most of the farmers considered that the future appearance of
these greedy c........... would be a c..........., they all adopted a c...........
attitude. H..........., a........... were made to try to limit the d........... that
the locusts would cause. The farmers' leaders a........... to the farmers not to
give in to .... They e........... the f........... of trying to save the crops
once the swarms had landed. However, they also asserted that it would be a
t........... mistake not to try to prevent the locusts from landing with whatever
means were available.

Using the Clues

Using the clues, write down the appropriate words from the spelling box.

(1) A word that means 'brave': ....

(2) A word opposite in meaning to 'creation': ....

(3) A word that means 'a happening': ....

(4) A word opposite in meaning to 'comic': ....

(5) A word that means 'hurriedly': ....

(6) A word opposite in meaning to 'falsely': ....

(7) A word that means 'to wipe out' or 'to ruin': ....

(8) A word that means 'made known': ....

(9) A word that means 'uselessness': ....

(10) A word that means 'increased in number': ....

Creating New Words

Form new words by filling the blank letter-spaces.

(1) h _ st _ n

(2) c _ t _ str _ ph _ c

(3) trag _ d _

(4) announce _ _ _ t

(5) desper _ t _ _ n

(6) tr _ _ _

(7) creat _ o _

(8) organ _ z _ r

(9) courag _ _ _ _ s _ y

(10) fut _ l _

(11) emphat _ c _ _ _ _ y

(12) destruct _ _ e

(13) multipl _ c _ t _ _ _ _

(14) occu _ _ ed

(15) appeal _ n _

(16) bewilderm _ _ _

Try Thinking 4

Food and Drink

A food or drink is described on the left and named on the right. See if you can correctly link each description of a food or drink with its name.

(1) A food made from crushed grains	JELLY
(2) A drink made from roasted beans	COFFEE
(3) A thick, sweet, liquid food produced by bees	EGG
(4) A drink from a cow	TEA
(5) A nourishing, roundish food within a shell	BEER
(6) A drink brewed from leaves	BREAD
(7) Fresh vegetables sliced, chopped or shredded	HONEY
(8) A drink made from fermented grapes	MILK
(9) A dessert made of gelatine and flavouring	SALAD
(10) A drink made with hops	WINE

Word Ladders

By altering only one letter at a time, turn the top word into the bottom word. Use the number of steps given, and make sure you use a real word at each step. (Answers p. 258.)

Example: B O Y
          B A Y
          D A Y
          D A D

(1) D O G	(2) S A W	(3) S A N D
− − −	− − −	− − − −
− − −	− − −	− − − −
R A T	F L Y	L A K E

(4) S I N K	(5) B U L L	(6) W E T
− − − −	− − − −	− − −
− − − −	− − − −	− − −
− − − −	− − − −	− − −
D A R K	D O Z E	D R Y

From A to Z

Enter the maze at A at the top of the rectangle and pass to Z at the bottom, moving through all the intermediate letters of the alphabet in the right order. Move along inside the path formed by the outlines of the letters as in a classical maze, never crossing a solid black line. You need not move through the whole of each letter. (Answer on p. 258.)

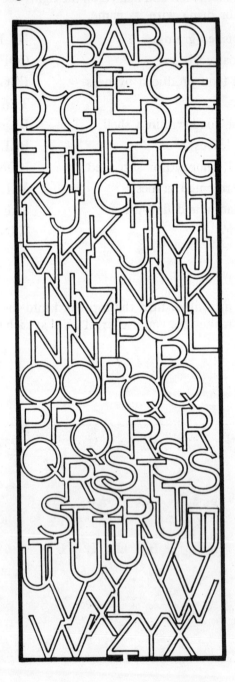

Unit Five

Comprehension 5

A rather boring Friday afternoon at school suddenly erupts into absolute chaos when a rat escapes from its owner's possession.

GOODBYE TO THE RAT

January. Friday. 3.30. The last dragging period before school ended for the week.

Mike Morgan and Louie Kam were in the school hall, with two hundred and ninety-eight other boys. They were sitting in the front, next to the door. This was to be ready for a quick get-away when the bell rang.

'My bum's gone to sleep,' Mike grumbled to Louie, in a whisper.

'Lucky bum,' Louie sighed.

'Well, boys,' the man with the dark suit and striped tie was saying, 'I hope I have given you some idea of the careers that are open to you. As I said, many of you here will be leaving school in six months' time, at the end of the summer term. And to you I would say —'

Louie yawned. Mike rubbed his numb bottom. Behind them, Tony Johnston fell off his chair and was picked up by his neighbours.

'Dropped off!' Louie whispered, and beamed at his own joke.

The school hall was hot. The windows had been steamed over by the breaths of three hundred boys. Portholes had been cleared in the steam. Through the portholes Mike could see snow, and two tall factory chimneys, and circles of grey sky.

Most Fridays at 3.30 Louie and Mike and Tony were in their classroom, listening to their form teacher complaining about the cigarette ends he had found in the biology cupboard. But they weren't in Class 5D today, banging desk lids or having a quick squint at a comic. They were in the school hall, listening to a lecture from this Careers man. They were listening to a Careers man because they were fifteen years old (coming up to sixteen) and they were leaving school in the summer.

'Boys, you must not feel that you are failures,' the Careers man was saying, 'just because you are not one of the academic boys who are good at lessons and all that sort of thing. No indeed. Your contribution to society will be just as valuable, even if you are only mixing concrete or screwing bits of steel together. Indeed, in my opinion —'

'D'you reckon he's wearing a wig?' Mike whispered to Louie. 'All that hair. T'isn't natural in a feller his age.'

Behind, Tony Johnston gave a snore.

'Ssh!' the Deputy-Head hissed from the platform.

The boys were getting restless. Feet were

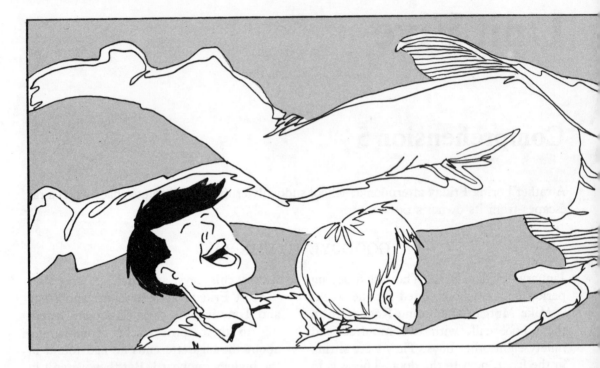

shuffling. Chairs were scraping. Thoughts were rushing towards paper rounds, and tomorrow's football match, and fish and chips, and bikes, and girl friends.

'Who cares about stupid old careers?' Louie groaned.

'Take a pride in your job, boys,' the Careers man was saying. His hair was certainly very black and glossy. Could it be a wig?

'Wish something would happen,' Mike muttered.

There was an upheaval at the back of the hall. A boy shouted something. Chairs started squeaking on the floor. Mike and Louie jumped up and peered towards the back to see what was happening.

'Don't tread on him!' a boy shouted.

'What's happening?' Louie asked, and Mike stood up on his chair to have a look.

'Boys, sit down!' the Deputy-Head cried. But no one took any notice.

Mike saw boys bending over. He saw boys staring between their legs. Boys were pushing towards the windows. A few fell over.

'Man, you were just wishing something would happen,' Louie said happily. Louie just loved things to happen.

'What's up?' Tony asked sleepily.

'It's Pete Dunn. His rat got out.'

Peter Dunn was charging forward, sending chairs tipping and crashing. 'Don't trample him!' he yelled. 'Where's he gone?'

'Here he is!'

'No, he's here. The rat's here.'

'This way, Pete. He went this way.'

The hall was in an uproar. Boys were pretending to be scared and leaping up the parallel bars. 'Save me!' Louie wailed, like a terrified lady. Mike dived under the chairs. He saw a stamping forest of legs. Out of the forest shot a brown shape. It whisked past his face, flicking him with its tail. 'He's here, Pete! Mike bellowed. He

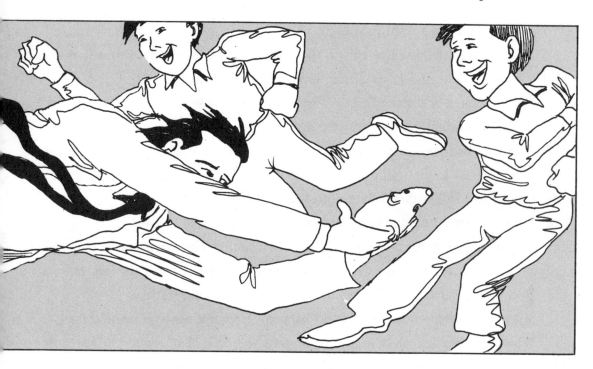

felt terrifically excited. This was better than an old careers lecture.

'Archie, come back,' Peter Dunn called.

The rat's name was Archie.

Archie skimmed over a yard of floor and ran straight up the side of the platform.

'Go away!' the Deputy-Head squeaked. He jumped up on to his chair. 'Go away!' He pulled his trouser legs up above his socks. All the boys began to laugh. The Deputy-Head looked so funny, hauling up his trousers and showing his white hairy legs.

'He won't hurt you, Sir,' Peter Dunn puffed.

Archie sped across the platform, like a little furry football. He was heading straight for the Careers man. Mike expected the Careers man to leap out of the way. But the Careers man didn't. He threw himself forward, like a goal keeper saving a goal, and clutched Archie with both hands. Archie wriggled and squealed.

But the Careers man hung on. He was full length on the platform. His head was bobbing up and down as he struggled to keep his grip on Archie.

'Man, that's no wig,' Louie said. 'It'd have fell off if it was a wig.'

Peter Dunn scrambled up on to the platform. He rescued Archie from the Careers man's clutches. He slipped Archie into the inside pocket of his jacket. The Deputy-Head got down from his chair, now the danger was over. 'Dunn,' he said sternly. 'Come and see me in my office after —'

The bell rang.

'Are there any questions?' the Deputy-Head shouted.

No one answered. Everyone was rushing to get away. Friday! No more school for two whole days!

from *Goodbye to the Rat*
by PRUDENCE ANDREW

How Well Did You Understand?

(1) What word in the first line tells us that last period on Friday was a wearisome one?

(2) Why were Mike and Louie sitting in the front of the school hall?

(3) Louie 'beamed at his own joke'. What was Louie's joke?

(4) What was uncomfortable about the inside of the school hall?

(5) 'Portholes had been cleared in the steam.' Why is the word 'portholes' used here?

(6) Where would Louie, Mike and Tony usually be in the last period on Fridays?

(7) Name three things they would normally be doing.

(8) Why were they listening to a Careers man this particular Friday?

(9) How do we know that the Careers man was not addressing the top class in the school?

(10) What was there about the Careers man which clearly fascinated the boys?

(11) How do we know that the boys in the hall were growing restless?

(12) Mike wished that 'something would happen'. How did his wish come true?

(13) What did Mike see when he peered towards the back of the hall?

(14) 'The hall was in an uproar.' What was the cause of this uproar?

(15) What did the Deputy-Head do when Archie ran up the side of the platform?

(16) What action did the Careers man take?

(17) What did the boys discover about the Career man's hair?

(18) The Deputy-Head shouted: 'Are there any questions?' Why did everyone disregard him?

Dictionary Words

Give the meaning of each of the following words from the passage. You may like to use the back-of-the-book dictionary.

(a) squint   (b) academic   (c) contribution   (d) upheaval   (e) lecture.

Language 5

Verbs

Verbs express action. They are *doing*, *being* and *having* words. Sometimes verbs consist of one word only, but at other times they consist of more than one word.

Louie **whispered**.   Louie **was whispering**.   Louie **had been whispering**.

The little words that help to complete the verbs are called *auxiliary verbs*. The main auxiliary verbs are: am, is, are, be, was, were, shall, will, should, could, would, has, have, had, may, might, do, did, can. Sometimes these words are used by themselves as full verbs.

The hall **was** in an uproar.   Here he **is**!   They **were** in the school hall.

Identifying the verbs

Write down these sentences and underline the verbs.

(1) They were sitting in front next to the door.

(2) Behind them, Tony Johnston fell off his chair and was picked up by his neighbours.

(3) Portholes had been cleared in the steam.

(4) 'As I said, many of you here will be leaving school in six months' time.'

(5) Boys were pushing towards the windows.

(6) Out of the forest shot a brown shape.

(7) Peter Dunn was charging forward.

(8) Mike and Louie jumped up and peered towards the back to see what was happening.

(9) The boys were getting restless.

(10) His hair was certainly very black and glossy.

Matching verbs with their subjects

All the sentences in the following list (which continues over the page) have been taken from the comprehension passage. Match up the verbs in heavy type (right column) with their subjects.

(1) The bell   **scrambled** up on to the platform.

(2) Louie   **yawned**.

(3) Feet   **was** hot.

(4) Chairs   **rang**.

(5) Thoughts	**had been steamed** over.
(6) The school hall	**were scraping**.
(7) The windows	**wriggled** and **squealed**.
(8) Tony Johnston	**were shuffling**.
(9) Archie	**gave** a snore.
(10) Peter Dunn	**were rushing** towards paper rounds.

Forming verbs

Write down the verbs formed from each of these words. The first one has been done to help you.

(1) false .... *falsify* ....   (11) provision ....

(2) soft ....   (12) grief ....

(3) speech ....   (13) proof ....

(4) food ....   (14) song ....

(5) horror ....   (15) dark ....

(6) colony ....   (16) resident ....

(7) tight ....   (17) moisture ....

(8) simple ....   (18) pure ....

(9) fertile ....   (19) sharp ....

(10) dictation ....   (20) large ....

Verbs and meanings

Match up the following verbs with their meanings.

(1) strive	to wait about, without purpose
(2) impede	to save from possible destruction
(3) scrutinize	to make great effort
(4) loiter	to hinder
(5) salvage	to knock down into ruins
(6) assemble	to ask earnestly
(7) abscond	to give as a sign of favour
(8) demolish	to come together
(9) entreat	to run away and hide from authority
(10) bestow	to examine closely

Punctuation 5

Using the Question Mark

The question mark is used at the end of a word or sentence that asks a question. For example:

> Why?   Me, sir?   Has the rat really escaped?

Often, a sentence that is in the form of a statement, such as:

> The last period on Friday afternoon is always boring.

can be changed into a question by the rearrangement of the words and the addition of a question mark:

> Is the last period on Friday afternoon always boring?

Forming questions

Change the following statements into questions.

(1) He is wearing a wig.

(2) The hall was in an uproar.

(3) Boys were pretending to be scared.

(4) The Deputy-Head lost his temper.

(5) This rat is called 'Archie'.

(6) The rat has run up the side of the platform.

Forming statements

Change the following questions into statements.

(1) Is it a wig?

(2) Is all that hair natural?

(3) Did one boy scramble up onto the platform?

(4) Has Archie escaped?

(5) Was the school hall very hot that afternoon?

(6) Were some chairs broken?

Creative Writing 5

The passage in this section is from *This School Is Driving Me Crazy!* by Nat Hentoff. It is a piece about the confrontation between an irascible teacher and a tardy student.

The teacher wins. However, before you go on to read it, let's put down the kind of *outline* the writer might have prepared to help him plan an interesting teacher–student confrontation that would captivate the reader.

OUTLINE FOR A CLASSROOM CONFRONTATION

1. Approaching the classroom
The tardy student, Sam, is first of all annoyed at being late for class; then he's fearful because the teacher is the terrible Mr Kozodoy! The reader will want to read on to find out what happens when the fearful student meets the terrible teacher.

2. Creeping in
Sam tries to creep into the classroom without being noticed but Kozodoy sees him and makes a caustic, sarcastic comment: Is the mayor the cause of his being late? Has he been asking Sam's advice on what to wear to a White House dinner?

3. The rest of the class sides with the teacher
Some boys in the class pretend to laugh at the teacher's humour. What the class really wants is fun, so Sam can't expect any help from them.
    Sam tries to bring things back to normal by explaining that he has lost his watch — that he's always losing them. The teacher seizes on the word 'them' to inject more sarcasm: Are Sam's parents so rich that they can afford to keep supplying him with watches while he keeps on losing them?

4. The climax — the teacher crushes the student
Dropping his sarcasm, the terrible teacher begins shouting and exerting his authority. He won't let Sam sit down, he accuses him of contempt for the class *and* he calls him a *slitherer*. Sam tries to fight back but is defeated by the teacher's firmness.

5. The conclusion
The teacher wins. Sam has to accept the term 'slitherer' if he wants to remain in the classroom. He sinks into his seat with something between a moan and a growl.

Of course, you don't have to put so much detail into an outline for your own creative writing: some headings and a few notes would be enough. However, a piece of creative writing is under better control, and often turns out to be more interesting and appealing to a reader, if some kind of outline is first prepared.

Now read and enjoy 'The Classroom Slitherer'.

THE CLASSROOM SLITHERER

Dragging his book bag behind him, Sam began moving slowly up the stairs until he saw the clock on the wall of the second-floor corridor.

Damn, Sam thought. I'm late — and for Kozodoy! Terrific.

Sam crept in the back door of the classroom. But as he feared and expected, Mr Kozodoy stopped in mid-sentence as soon as he saw Sam.

'Undoubtedly you were detained by a message from the mayor,' Mr Kozodoy said caustically. 'I read this morning in the *Times* that the mayor is a dinner guest this evening at the White House. He must have called for your advice on what to wear.'

Fat Jake snickered. Blake pantomimed uproarious laughter, his mouth opening in huge, silent guffaws as he clutched at his stomach. The rest of the class tensed in anticipation, waiting to hear Sam's response and waiting to see how soon he'd be gunned down. Before he bit the dust, Sam was always good for a few laughs.

Not today though. 'I'm sorry,' Sam said to Mr Kozodoy, 'I forgot what time it was.'

'You don't have a watch?' Mr Kozodoy asked solicitously.

'I lost it,' Sam said. 'I'm always losing them.'

'Them! Them!' Mr Kozodoy sounded like a clock that marked the hours with a thud rather than a gong. 'How fortunate you are to have parents who keep making up for your carelessness.'

'I only lost two watches. Then they said I couldn't have another one for a year.'

'*Poor* child,' Mr Kozodoy said, to the obbligato of Fat Jake's giggling. 'Why are you tardy?' Mr Kozodoy suddenly shouted.

'I told you,' Sam said, sitting down. 'I was thinking of something else and I just plain forgot.'

'I did not say you could sit down!' Mr Kozodoy boomed. 'I have not yet decided whether you are to remain in this class after showing your contempt of us by slithering in late. Get *up*, young man!'

Sam rose slowly. His head aimed at Mr Kozodoy, his lower lip thrust out, Sam half shouted, 'What do you mean *contempt*? I said I was sorry, and I didn't *slither*.'

'Boys who come in the back door after the class is already in session,' Mr Kozodoy said firmly, 'are known as slithering boys. It is a well known term in the history of pedagogy. Sit down, *slitherer*!'

For a moment Sam seemed suspended in mid-air, torn between obeying and storming out of the room. With a strange sound, something between a moan and a growl, he sank into his seat.

from *This School Is Driving Me Crazy!*
by NAT HENTOFF

Your Turn to Write

See how well you can write about *one* of these:

(1) Write a description beginning, 'I was sitting on the park bench and when I turned around I saw ...'

(2) 'Myself in Ten Years' Time.'

(3) 'What I'd Like to Do When I Leave School.'

(4) 'People I Admire.'

(5) 'People I Dislike.'

(6) 'What I hate/like most about school.'

Poetry 5

'Tom's Bomb' is a light-hearted, humorous poem about the effect that Tom's harmless home-made bomb has on all the people that come near it.

TOM'S BOMB

There was a boy whose name was Tom,
Who made a high explosive bomb,
By mixing up some iodine
With sugar, flour and plasticine.
Then, to make it smell more queer,
He added Daddy's home-made beer.
He took it off to school one day,
And when they all went out to play,
He left it by the radiator.
As the heat was getting greater,
The mixture in the bomb grew thick
And very soon it seemed to tick.
Miss Knight came in and gazed with awe
To see the bomb upon the floor.
'Dear me,' she said, 'it is a bomb,
An object worth escaping from.'
She went to Mr Holliday
And said in tones that were not gay,
'Headmaster, this is not much fun;
There is a bomb in Classroom One.'
'Great snakes,' said he, and gave a cough
And said, 'I hope it won't go off.
But on the off-chance that it does,
I think we'd better call the fuzz.'
A policeman came and said, 'Oh God,
We need the bomb disposal squad,
Some firemen and a doctor too,
A helicopter and its crew,
And, since I'm shaking in the legs,
A pot of tea and hard-boiled eggs.'
A bomb disposal engineer
Said, with every sign of fear,
'I've not seen one like that before,'
And rushed out, screaming, through the door.
Everyone became more worried

Till Tom, who seemed to be unflurried,
Asked what was all the fuss about?
'I'll pick it up and take it out.'
He tipped the contents down the drain
And peace and quiet reigned again.
Tom just smiled and shook his head
And quietly to himself he said:
'Excitement's what these people seek.
I'll bring another one next week.'

DAVID HORNSBY

Thinking about the Poem

(1) From your reading of the poem, what did you learn about the personality of Tom?

(2) Did you admire or dislike Tom? Why?

(3) How does the headmaster react to being informed about the bomb?

(4) What comments would you make about the policeman?

(5) How does the bomb-disposal engineer's reaction to the bomb differ from what you might have expected?

(6) What clues tell us that the bomb was quite harmless?

Spelling 5

CLASSROOM UPHEAVAL

companion	academic	contribution	criticism	preferred
expected	deliberately	biology	humiliated	compelled
parallel	dissatisfied	speech	regrettable	compulsory
complaining	opinion	upheaval	miserable	neighbour

Missing Words

Rewrite the following *Upheaval* in your workbook, filling in the blank spaces with words from the spelling box above. Note the helpful letters that are sometimes given.

Upheaval

Mr Chalkley was d.......... with the b.......... class he was teaching. Then he noticed that one student was constantly whispering to his n.........., so Mr Chalkley roared: 'You! The m.......... fellow with the untidy hair. Your behaviour is .... You are making no c.......... whatsoever to the progress of this lesson. In fact, in my ...., you are d.......... disrupting things!'

'He's .... again,' whispered the offending student to his .... 'Yes,' his friend whispered back. 'I p.......... Mr Dustley. Didn't you?' 'Sure. At least he couldn't hear most of what was going on, could he?

'*You* are whispering *again*!' roared Mr Chalkley. 'My recent .... of your behaviour was apparently not sufficient. Well, now I feel c.......... to punish you severely. You will attend my c.......... detention class every week for a month. If you feel h.......... by this punishment — well, that is your own fault.'

Mr Chalkley's s.......... was followed by an .... in the classroom as students leapt to their feet and voiced their discontent with this harsh punishment.

Word Forms

Change each of the words in heavy type into its correct form.

(1) The teacher expressed his **dissatisfied** with the behaviour of the class.

(2) The headmaster was left **speechlessness** with rage at the escape of the rat.

(3) The speaker at the assembly suffered the **humiliated** of having his wig fall off when he nodded too vigorously.

(4) 'If you wish to make a **complaining** you must come and see me in my office.'

(5) Do you have a **preferred** for any particular sport?

(6) The Careers man captured the rat, but **regrettable** it bit him.

(7) 'Now, although you boys may not be **academic** inclined, I believe that all of you have a high **expected** when it comes to the choice of a career.'

(8) The Deputy-Head was very **criticism** of the way the boys had acted during the assembly.

(9) A rat on the loose can cause a lot of **miserable**.

(10) 'Excuse me, but I can **compelled** you to attend my detention class if I so desire.'

Meanings and Words

For each of the meanings below, provide the correct word from the spelling box.

(1) .... is the study of living creatures.

(2) A person who sits near you in the classroom or lives in the house next door is called your ....

(3) An .... is a point of view.

(4) Something that has to be done and cannot be avoided is ....

(5) If two roads run side by side but stay the same distance apart, they are ....

(6) A .... is an offering or a donation.

(7) A noisy disturbance is an ....

(8) Something that is awaited or anticipated is ....

Try Thinking 5

Compounds

Connect words from the column (right) to words in the grid so as to form compound words. Note the example on the first line of the grid.

M	O	O	N	l	i	g	h	t		
R	A	I	L							
W	O	R	K							
R	A	C	E							
U	N	D	E	R						
F	O	O	T							
K	E	T	T	L	E					
S	U	R	F							
W	I	R	E							
A	I	R								
B	U	B	B	L	E					
C	R	A	Y							
W	A	T	E	R						
B	U	L	L							
N	I	G	H	T						

fish

shop

board

<u>light</u>

drum

track

fall

craft

pants

ball

dog

gum

way

less

mare

Are You a Logical Matchmaker?

Carefully study the remarks coming from the respective girls and gents, and then determine which girl would match which gent perfectly. There is only *one* logical solution whereby all the people concerned will be happy. (Answer on p. 258.)

Unit Six

Comprehension 6

This passage is from *The Hiding Place*, an inspiring book by Corrie ten Boom about a Dutch family living and hiding in the very heart of Nazi-occupied Holland during the Second World War.

THE HIDING PLACE

Peter was home, yet he was not safe, any more than any healthy young male was safe. In Germany the munitions factories were desperate for workers. Without warning soldiers would suddenly surround a block of buildings and sweep through them, herding every male between sixteen and thirty into trucks for transport. This method of lightning search and seizure was called 'the razzia', and every family with young men lived in dread of it.

Flip and Nollie had rearranged their kitchen to give them an emergency hiding place as soon as the razzias started. There was a small potato cellar beneath the kitchen floor: they enlarged the trapdoor letting into it, put a large rug on top of it and moved the kitchen table to stand on this spot.

Since Mr Smit's work at the Beje I realized that this hole under the kitchen floor was a totally inadequate hiding place. Too low in the house for one thing, and probably as Mr Smit would say, 'the first place they'd look'. However, it was not a sustained search by trained people it was intended for, but a swoop by soldiers, a place to get out of sight for half an hour. And for that, I thought, it was probably sufficient....

It was Flip's birthday when the razzia came to that quiet residential street of identical attached homes. Father, Betsie, and I had come early with a quarter-pound of real English tea from Pickwick.

Nollie, Annaliese, and the two older girls were not yet back when we arrived. A shipment of men's shoes had been announced by one of the department stores and Nollie had determined to get Flip a pair 'if I have to stand in line all day'.

We were chatting in the kitchen with Cocky and Katrien when all at once Peter and his older brother, Bob, raced into the room, their faces white. 'Soldiers! Quick! They're two doors down and coming this way!'

They jerked the table back, snatched away the rug and tugged open the trapdoor. Bob lowered himself first, lying down flat, and Peter tumbled in on top of him. We dropped the door shut, yanked the rug over it and pulled the table back in place. With trembling hands Betsie, Cocky, and I threw a long tablecloth over it and started laying five places for tea.

There was a crash in the hall as the front door burst open and a smaller crash close by as Cocky dropped a teacup. Two uniformed Germans ran into the kitchen, rifles leveled.

'Stay where you are. Do not move.'

We heard boots storming up the stairs. The soldiers glanced around disgustedly at this room filled with women and one old man. If they had looked closer at Katrien she would surely have given herself away: her face was a mask of terror. But they had other things on their minds.

'Where are your men?' the shorter soldier asked Cocky in clumsy, thick-accented Dutch.

'These are my aunts,' she said, 'and this is my grandfather. My father is at his school, and my mother is shopping, and —'

'I didn't ask about the whole tribe!' the man exploded in German. Then in Dutch: 'Where are your brothers?'

Cocky stared at him a second, then dropped her eyes. My heart stood still. I knew how Nollie had trained her children — but surely, surely now of all times a lie was permissible!

'Do you have brothers?' the officer asked again.

'Yes,' Cocky said softly. 'We have three.'

'How old are they?'

'Twenty-one, nineteen, and eighteen.'

Upstairs we heard the sounds of doors opening and shutting, the scrape of furniture dragged from walls.

'Where are they now?' the solider persisted.

Cocky leaned down and began gathering up the broken bits of cup. The man jerked her upright. 'Where are your brothers?'

'The oldest one is at the Theological College. He doesn't get home most nights because —'

'What about the other two?'

Cocky did not miss a breath.

'Why, they're under the table.'

Motioning us all away from it with his gun, the soldier seized a corner of the cloth. At a nod from him the taller man crouched with his rifle cocked. Then he flung back the cloth.

At last the pent-up tension exploded: Cocky burst into spasms of high hysterical laughter. The soldiers whirled around. Was this girl laughing at them?

'Don't take us for fools?' the short one snarled. Furiously he strode from the room and minutes later the entire squad trooped out — not, unfortunately, before the silent soldier had spied and pocketed our precious packet of tea.

from *The Hiding Place*
by CORRIE TEN BOOM

How Well Did You Understand?

(1) Why was Peter not safe even though he was at home?

(2) What were the Germans in the habit of doing without warning?

(3) What three things had been rearranged in the kitchen to provide for the hiding place?

(4) Give two reasons why the hiding place was inadequate.

(5) What was the hiding place probably sufficient for?

(6) What was special about the day 'the razzia' came to this household?

(7) What was the urgent news brought by Peter and Bob?

(8) How were the boys hidden?

(9) 'If they had looked closer at Katrien she would surely have given herself away . . . .' What would have given her away?

(10) Explain how Cocky tricked the German soldiers.

(11) What caused the soldiers to become angry?

(12) What unfortunate thing happened as the soldiers were leaving?

Dictionary Words

Give the meanings of the following words from the passage. You may like to use the back-of-the-book dictionary.

(a) munitions   (b) sustained   (c) residential   (d) permissible   (e) spasms.

Language 6

Active and Passive Verbs

Look at the two sentences below. They both have the same meaning.

- ACTIVE
  The soldiers **entered** the house.

- PASSIVE
  The house **was entered** by the soldiers.

Notice how the form of the verb is different for each of the sentences. When the subject performs the action (in this case, the action of *entering*), you have the **active** form of the verb. When the action is performed upon the subject, you have the **passive** form of the verb.

Changing from active to passive

Rewrite each of these sentences, changing the form of the verb as necessary to make it passive. (The first sentence will now begin: 'Young Dutchmen ...')

(1) The German soldiers were rounding up young Dutchmen.

(2) Bob and Peter tugged open the trapdoor.

(3) Soldiers would suddenly surround a block of buildings.

(4) Flip and Nollie had rearranged their kitchen to give them an emergency hiding place.

(5) They enlarged the trapdoor.

(6) We pulled the table back into place.

(7) Cocky dropped a teacup.

(8) We heard the sounds of doors opening and shutting.

(9) The man jerked her upright.

(10) The soldier motioned us away with his rifle.

Changing from passive to active

Rewrite each of these sentences, changing the form of the verb as necessary to make it active. (The first sentence will now begin: The munition factories ...')

(1) Workers were needed by the munition factories.

(2) The front door was smashed open by the German soldiers.

(3) A shipment of men's shoes had been announced by one of the department stores.

(4) A long tablecloth was thrown over the table by Betsie, Cocky and me.

(5) The room was filled with women.

(6) A packet of tea was seized by the German soldier.

Missing verbs

Add suitable verbs to each of these subjects so as to make sensible statements. The first one has been done to give you the idea.

(1) Lightning ....*flashes*......
(2) Bees ....
(3) Thunder ....
(4) Leaves ....
(5) Snakes ....
(6) Lions ....
(7) Bells ....

(8) Fire ....
(9) Kings ....
(10) Farmers ....
(11) Rivers ....
(12) Flowers ....
(13) Diamonds ....
(14) Engines ....

(15) Sirens ....
(16) Teeth ....
(17) Chalk ....
(18) Politicians ....
(19) Eyes ....
(20) Clouds ....
(21) Soldiers ....

Choosing verbs

Write out the following sentences, using the most suitable verb from the box in place of the gap left in each one.

darted	stalked	marched	prowled
shuffled	staggered	crawled	sneaked
strutted	jostled	pounced	stamped

(1) The hunter .... the leopard.

(2) The angry teacher .... out of the classroom.

(3) The army .... through the town.

(4) The baby .... across the floor.

(5) The drunken man .... across the street.

(6) The cat .... on the bird.

(7) We were .... by the crowd.

(8) The mouse .... into its hole.

(9) The old man .... along the road.

(10) The vain tournament-winner .... through the clubhouse.

(11) The thief .... into the house.

(12) Many tigers .... through the jungle.

Punctuation 6

Fun with Punctuation

Have some fun with punctuation as you use full stops or question marks to end all of the lines that follow.

(1) *Patient:* Doctor, I hope you'll be able to help me
   Doctor: (soothingly) Well, now, what seems to be the problem
   Patient: I have this terrible feeling I'm a werewolf
   Doctor: How long has this been going on
   Patient: Ever since I was a puppy

(2) *Teacher:* Why are you late for school, Smith
    Pupil: Please, sir, there are only seven people in our house
    Teacher: What's that got to do with being late
    Pupil: Sir, the alarm clock was set for eight

(3) *First vampire:* I just met a fisherman who complained he hadn't had a bite all day
    Second vampire: So, what did you do
    First vampire: What *could* I do
    Second vampire: (stating a fact) You bit him
    First vampire: Exactly

(4) *Question:* What lies at the bottom of the sea and shakes
    Answer: A nervous wreck

(5) *Question:* What is strawberry-flavoured, lies at the bottom of the sea, and shakes
    Answer: A jellyfish

Creative Writing 6

Keeping a Diary

The word 'diary' comes from the Latin word *dies*, meaning 'day'. A diary is, therefore, a book in which daily entries are made. That is why a diary entry is made under a daily date.

Another feature of the diary is that the person who keeps one (called a *diarist*) will often feel inclined to address the diary as 'Dear Diary', and to end an entry with 'Yours ...'. You see, the diary frequently becomes more than just a book — it becomes a friend in whom the writer confides, and whom he or she trusts with secrets.

On the other hand, a typical diary entry will often be concerned with descriptions of the day's weather; of visitors or friends encountered during the day; of meals consumed; and, of course, of anything unusual that happened to make the day different or memorable.

Now let's look at a single diary entry from perhaps the most famous diary in modern times, *The Diary of Anne Frank*. Anne Frank was a thirteen-year-old Jewish girl who was happily living in Amsterdam when the Germans invaded and occupied Holland during the early part of World War II. Anne, her parents, her sister and four other people were forced to go into hiding in sealed-off rooms at the top of an office in an old Amsterdam house when the German invaders began to round up all the Jewish people living in the city to send them to their death.

Anne's first diary entry was for Sunday, 14 June 1942. Her last was on Tuesday, 1 August 1944. In August the Germans burst into the hiding place and took all those living there to concentration camps. Anne Frank died in a concentration camp in March 1945.

Notice as you begin to read how Anne addresses her diary as 'Dear Kitty' — a friend to confide in.

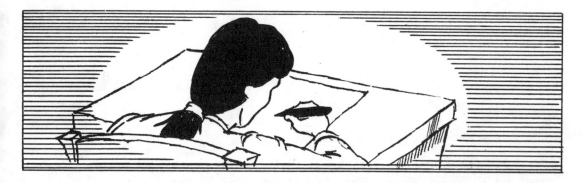

Thursday, 19 November 1942

Dear Kitty,

The first day that Dussel* was here, he immediately asked me all sorts of questions: When does the charwoman come? When can one use the bathroom? When is one allowed to use the lavatory? You may laugh, but these things are not so simple in a hiding-place. During the day we mustn't make any noise that might be heard downstairs; and if there is some stranger — such as the charwoman for example — then we have to be extra careful. I explained all this carefully to Dussel. But one thing amazed me: he is very slow in the uptake. He asks everything twice over and still doesn't seem to remember. Perhaps that will wear off in time, and it's only that he's thoroughly upset by the sudden change.

Apart from that, all goes well. Dussel has told us a lot about the outside world, which we have missed for so long now. He had very sad news. Countless friends and acquaintances have gone to a terrible fate. Evening after evening the green and grey army lorries trundle past. The Germans ring at every front door to inquire if there are any Jews living in the house. If there are, then the whole family has to go at

once. If they don't find any, they go on to the next house. No one has a chance of evading them unless one goes into hiding. Often they go round with lists, and only ring when they know they can get a good haul. Sometimes they let them off for cash — so much per head. It seems like the slave hunts of old times. But it's certainly no joke; it's much too tragic for that. In the evenings when it's dark, I often see rows of good, innocent people accompanied by crying children, walking on and on, in charge of a couple of these chaps, bullied and knocked about until they almost drop. No one is spared — old people, babies, expectant mothers, the sick — each and all join in the march of death.

How fortunate we are here, so well cared for and undisturbed. We wouldn't have to worry about all this misery were it not that we are so anxious about all those dear to us whom we can no longer help.

I feel wicked sleeping in a warm bed, while my dearest friends have been knocked down or have fallen into a gutter somewhere out in the cold night. I get frightened when I think of close friends who have now been delivered into the hands of the cruellest brutes that walk the earth. And all because they are Jews!

Yours, ANNE.

---

* Dussel is a Jewish dentist who has sought refuge with the Frank family.

Your Turn to Write

Use your imagination as you write 'Dear Diary' entries for *one* of these:

(1) Imagine that your country has been defeated in war and occupied by enemy forces. Write a few diary entries showing how your life has changed for the worse.

(2) Imagine that you are a famous person. Write some diary entries for a few of the more interesting days of your life.

(3) Imagine that one of your teachers keeps a diary. Reproduce a few of this teacher's diary entries concerning your class.

Poetry 6

When Adolf Hitler became Chancellor of Germany on 30 January 1933, the Third Reich began. Hitler boasted that it would last for a thousand years. On his way to power, it was the storm troopers (Brownshirts) who especially helped Hitler. Dressed in their brown shirts, and with the dreaded swastika as their emblem, they went around breaking up meetings of Hitler's political opponents and molesting, assaulting or murdering innocent people — including, of course, Jews. 'Song of the Storm Trooper' throws light on the origins and role of Hitler's storm troopers.

SONG OF THE STORM TROOPER

From hunger I grew drowsy
Dulled by my belly's ache.
Then someone shouted in my ear:
Germany awake!

Then I saw many marching
Toward the Third Reich, they said.
Since I had nought to lose
I followed where they led.

And ,as I marched, there marched
Big Belly at my side.
When I shouted 'Bread and jobs',
'Bread and jobs,' he cried.

The leaders wore high boots,
I stumbled with wet feet.
Yet all of us were marching
To the selfsame beat.

I wanted to march leftward,
Squads right, the order was.
I blindly followed orders
For better or for worse.

And toward some new Third Reich,
But scarcely knowing whither,
Pale and hungry men
And well fed marched together.

They gave me a revolver
And said: now shoot our foe!
But as I fired on his ranks
I laid my brother low.

It was my brother, hunger
Made us one I know.
And I am marching, marching
With my own and my brother's foe.

So I have lost my brother,
I wove his winding sheet.
I know now by this victory
I wrought my own defeat.

BERTOLT BRECHT
Translated by H.R. Hays

Thinking about the Storm Troopers

(1) Why did the speaker in the poem join the storm troopers?

(2) What clues tell you that the speaker lost his independence and individuality when he joined the storm troopers?

(3) What evidence can you find to show that the Nazis relied on violence to achieve their aims?

(4) How do you know that the speaker regretted becoming a storm trooper?

(5) What do you think the poet is trying to tell the reader in 'Song of the Storm Trooper'?

All people who are involved in war suffer. But, as Herbert Read's 'The Refugees' shows, the people who seem to suffer most are the innocent civilians.

THE REFUGEES

Mute figures with bowed heads
they travel along the road:
old women, incredibly old
and a hand-cart of chattels.

They do not weep:
their eyes are too raw for tears.

Past them have hastened
processions of retreating gunteams
baggage-wagons and swift horsemen.
Now they struggle along
with the rearguard of a broken army.

We shall hold the enemy towards nightfall
and they will move
mutely into the dark behind us,
only the creaking cart
disturbing their sorrowful serenity.

HERBERT READ

Thinking about Refugees

(1) The word 'mute' means 'not making a sound'. Why do you think the figures are mute?

(2) What is 'a hand-cart of chattels'?

(3) What does the poet mean by 'their eyes are too raw for tears'?

(4) What words of the poet reveal that an army has been defeated?

(5) What are your feelings towards the refugees?

(6) Why do you think Herbert Read wrote this poem?

Spelling 6

THE HIDING PLACE

tyranny	hesitation	uniformed	tension	perceived
soldiers	emergency	disgustedly	laughter	inadequate
officer	seized	hysterical	unfortunately	residential
sufficient	permissible	precious	terrified	opportunity

Missing Words

Read through *The Search*, below, and then write into your workbook the spelling-box words that correctly fill the blanks. Note the helpful letters.

The Search

During the t.......... of Hitler, Holland was invaded by the German armies. Since young men living in the .... areas of Holland were likely to be s.......... and taken to the munition factories in Germany, the ten Boom family constructed a hiding place in case an e.......... arose. It was i.......... against a sustained search by trained people, but it was s.......... to withstand a swoop by s.......... . One day the ten Boom brothers Peter and Bob p.......... the Germans searching a house two doors away; they immediately dived into the hiding place. Suddenly, after crashing through the front door, two u.......... Germans rushed through the ten Boom house. Katrien was t.......... . When the German o.......... asked Cocky where her brothers were, she told him without .... that they were under the table. As the tablecloth was flung back, Cocky burst into spasms of high h.......... l.......... . The t.......... was broken. The soldiers, thinking they were being mocked by Cocky, turned away d.......... . U.........., one of the German soldiers, as he departed, took the o.......... to steal a p.......... packet of tea that was on the table.

Using the Clues

Using the following clues, write down the appropriate words from the spelling box.

(1) A word opposite in meaning to 'luckily'.

(2) A word meaning 'with a sickening dislike'.

(3) A word meaning 'of great value'.

(4) A word opposite in meaning to 'sufficient'.

(5) A word meaning 'allowable'.

(6) A word meaning 'members of an army'.

(7) A word meaning 'greatly frightened'.

(8) An adjective derived from 'hysteria'.

(9) A word opposite in meaning to 'democracy'.

(10) A word meaning 'a favourable chance'.

Word Forms

Complete each of these sentences by using the correct form of the word given in brackets.

(1) The German soldier showed his .... [**disgustedly**].

(2) The situation at the ten Booms' house was very .... [**tension**].

(3) The German method of lightning search and .... [**seize**] was called 'the razzia'.

(4) Hitler was a .... [**tyranny**].

(5) Cocky's .... [**terrified**] caused her to .... [**laughter**] .... [**hysteria**].

(6) The German soldiers were not very .... [**perception**].

(7) All the .... [**residential**] were terrified.

(8) The soldier did not have .... [**permissible**] to take the tea.

Try Thinking 6

Gear Up!

Items of clothing or footwear, described on the left, are to be found in the wardrobe on the right. Gear up by bringing together each description and item described. The answer to the first one is underlined to give you an example.

(1) A loose-fitting woollen jacket buttoned down the front.

(2) A big, broad-brimmed Mexican hat.

(3) A pleated tartan skirt.

(4) A sleeping-suit, often striped.

(5) A blanket with an opening for the head.

(6) Wooden shoes.

(7) A loose-fitting shirt.

(8) Rubber overshoes to keep out the rain.

(9) Stout leg-protectors.

(10) A neck and chest warmer, often long and made of wool.

(11) Snug-fitting hand-coverings.

(12) A strong head-protector used in motorbike riding.

sombrero   crash-helmet

pyjamas

gloves

cardigan

scarf

clogs

kilt

blouse

galoshes   poncho

gaiters

Letter Shuffle

Shuffle the letters in each of the opening words to arrive at a new word suggested by the clue. Note your example.

(1) PIN becomes the sharp bite of a dog: NIP

(2) LOAF becomes the young of a horse: ....

(3) LAMP becomes the flat part of the hand: ....

(4) RAIL becomes the den of an animal: ....

(5) MUG becomes something a tooth is set in: ....

(6) LEAF becomes a tiny biting creature: ....

(7) PART becomes something that might catch you: ....

(8) BRUSH becomes a kind of bush: ....

(9) LOPE becomes a long, rounded piece of timber: ....

(10) POSH becomes a place that sells things: ....

(11) RIPE becomes a kind of wharf: ....

(12) LEMON becomes a large juicy fruit: ....

(13) PAGE becomes an open-mouthed stare: ....

(14) SAG becomes an American word for petrol: ....

(15) TIME becomes a very small insect: ....

About Symbols

A symbol is a sign or emblem which, by general usage, is recognized to stand for something: a product, a warning, a political organization — the possibilities are endless.

Look at and think about each of the symbols below, and then decide what it stands for or represents. (Answers on p. 258.)

Unit Seven

Comprehension 7

Carl is a fourteen-year-old boy who works on a farm for his foster-parents Ray and Ena. He becomes a very keen observer of dingoes. But one night he is faced with a brutal decision. . . .

THE TRAP

That night, after Ray and Ena had gone to bed, Carl once more made the journey from the farmhouse to the top fenceline. Once more he positioned himself amongst the scrub, looking up into the gully.

Tonight there was no howling from the hills, but still the boy waited. He could sense that the dingoes were in the gully waiting to make their futile nightly reconnaissance of the fenceline.

He had been waiting more than an hour before he saw them swoop down from the gully. This time they came even nearer to the fence and he had a close view of their lean bodies as they whirled past him.

He stood to watch them as they ran along the fenceline. Suddenly something was wrong. There was a sharp yelp of pain. The pack slowed, looking behind. Then, without finishing its course, the pack turned straight back into the gully. From half way along the fence came the sound of moaning.

Carl raced along the inside of the fence. One of the dingoes was hunched on the ground. As he drew close he saw that its hind leg was caught in a trap.

The dingo traps! On his first day at the farm Ray had shown them to him. He had

looked at their savage metal teeth and imagined the pain if one of his own legs were caught in one.

That was what Ray must have been doing two days ago while Carl had been helping Ena in the garden — putting those savage-looking traps along the outer fenceline. Now Ray had got what he wanted.

Not knowing quite what he was doing, Carl began climbing the dog-proof fence. Once he had reached the top he vaulted onto the ground on the far side.

He approached the dingo warily. Perhaps he could set it free and re-set the trap so it would look as if it had never been used.

As he drew nearer, the dingo turned on him, baring its teeth and snapping. From its mouth came a dribble of white foam.

It thinks I'm its enemy too, Carl realised. It thinks I'm just like Ray, out to kill the lot of them.

He tried talking gently to the dingo as one talks to a pet dog, but the animal showed no sign of understanding and only increased its ferocity whenever the boy tried to approach it.

Carl stood as near as he dared. The dingo was desperately trying to tear its leg away from the trap but the teeth of the trap had caught it too high on the leg to make that possible.

Blood poured from the dingo's wound, matting in its coat around the leg and covering the frame of the trap. It was obvious that there was no way that Carl could free the dingo from the trap without being savagely bitten.

There were tears in his eyes as he stared at the stricken animal. He couldn't just leave it to struggle all night in agony. Even death, if it were quick, would be better than that.

He would fetch Ray. He would be glad that one of his traps had worked and would come up and shoot the dingo. It was all that he could do.

He climbed back over the fence and ran all the way back to the farmhouse. Panting and perspiring he reached the kitchen door.

'Ray,' he called out, 'come quickly!'

There were sounds from inside and Ray stumbled to the door in his pyjamas. He was only half awake.

'What's the matter? What's happened?' Ena's face peered anxiously from the door behind him.

'A dingo,' gasped Carl, 'caught in one of the traps. You'll have to come and shoot it.'

'Why wake me up about it?' said Ray crossly. 'I'll knock it off in the morning if its still alive.'

'But it's in pain,' said Carl. 'You can't leave it like that all night.'

'I don't care how much pain it's in,' said Ray. 'I'm not going to walk all that way up the hill just to put a bloody dingo out of its misery. If it's in pain it bloody well deserves it.'

Carl just stood there. He had no idea what to do. He couldn't believe that Ray

would let the animal writhe in pain all night.

Ray seemed to sense his criticism.

'If it's so important to you, you can go up and shoot it,' he said. 'There's a loaded twelve-bore in the shed. Just release the safety catch, aim at the dingo's head and pull the trigger. It won't be the last time you'll have to do it, if you're going to feel sorry for every damn dingo that gets caught in a trap.'

'I'll go,' said Carl.

'Be careful,' said Ena. 'You shouldn't let him go, Ray. Or at least go with him.'

'He'll be right,' said Ray. 'Or if he isn't he's a fool. I'm not having my sleep disturbed for any dingo.'

He closed the kitchen door. Carl ran to the shed. He knew the gun stood in a corner near the door. He checked the safety catch was on and began half running, half walking up the hill.

After what seemed an age he reached the fence. Throwing the gun over, he climbed after it. The dingo rose to its feet as much as its condition allowed and snarled at him.

Carl picked up the gun, set its butt against his shoulder as he had seen Ray do,

released the safety catch and aimed at the dingo's head. With a trembling finger he pulled the trigger.

The blast threw him backwards to the ground. All the breath was knocked from his body.

He dragged himself to his feet and looked down. The dingo's head had been blown apart. Its body still twitched. Blood and bits of flesh were scattered about the trap.

Carl leaned on the fence and turned away from the sight. His stomach was churning and he suddenly vomited against the fence. He moved away and just stood, gulping in great breaths of air.

He supposed he should go back. Mecha-nically he picked up the gun, fastened the safety catch and dropped it back over the fence. He climbed over himself and in a dazed state walked slowly back to the house. He replaced the gun in the shed, let himself into his room, tore off his clothes and climbed into bed. His whole body was shaking and his stomach still churned.

Gradually the shaking ceased, but his weary body now heaved with sobs. He cried in a way he hadn't cried since he was a small child. With images of the wounded dingo and the body with its shattered head sharp in his mind, he cried himself to sleep.

from *Dingo Boy*
by MICHAEL DUGAN

How Well Did You Understand?

(1) Why was it important for Carl to position himself so that he could look up into the gully?

(2) What sounds did Carl hear after the dingoes had passed by?

(3) Why was one of the dingoes hunched on the ground?

(4) What did Carl think he might be able to do for the injured animal?

(5) Why was he unable to do anything?

(6) How did Carl try to calm the dingo?

(7) Why couldn't the dingo get its leg out of the trap?

(8) What two decisions did Carl come to as he stared, with tears in his eyes, at the stricken animal?

(9) How did Ray react to the news that a dingo had been caught in one of his traps?

(10) How did Ray shift responsibility for the dingo from himself onto Carl?

(11) How did Carl put the dingo out of its misery?

(12) How did Carl suffer for what he had to do?

(13) *Discuss*: Was it right or wrong for Carl to take the dingo's life? Try to give convincing reasons for your point of view.

Dictionary Words

Give the meaning of each of these words from the passage. You might like to use the back-of-the-book dictionary.

(a) futile (b) reconnaissance (c) writhe (d) butt (e) churn.

Language 7

Present Participles

Present participles always end with 'ing' — e.g. moving, singing, running, hitting. They often help to form verbs:

> Carl had been **waiting** for more than an hour.

Sometimes they are used as adjectives:

> With a **trembling** finger he pulled the trigger.

Present participles can also be used to begin phrases:

> The pack slowed, **looking** behind.

Identifying present participles

Write down the following sentences and underline the present participles.

(1) Once more he positioned himself amongst the scrub, looking up into the gully.

(2) That was what Ray must have been doing two days ago while Carl had been helping Ena in the garden.

(3) As he drew nearer the dingo turned on him, baring its teeth and snapping.

(4) The dingo was desperately trying to tear its leg away from the trap.

(5) Blood poured from the dingo's wound, matting in its coat around the leg and covering the frame of the trap.

(6) Planting and perspiring he reached the kitchen door.

(7) His stomach was churning and he suddenly vomited against the fence.

Forming present participles

The usual way of forming a present participle is to add 'ing'. However, words ending with a single 'e' usually drop the 'e' before adding 'ing'.

love/loving   decide/deciding   please/pleasing

Verbs that end with a single consonant preceded by a single vowel, and have a stress on the final syllable, usually double the final consonant before adding 'ing'.

stab/stabbing   refit/refitting   occur/occurring

Now, keeping in mind these rules, change the following verbs into present participles.

(1) contain ……….   (7) expel …………   (13) choose ……….   (19) receive ……….

(2) live ……………   (8) travel ……….   (14) prefer ……….   (20) copy …………

(3) submit ……….   (9) provide ………   (15) run ………….   (21) cancel ……….

(4) guess …………   (10) compel ………   (16) freeze ……….   (22) rob …………..

(5) approach ……..   (11) occur …………   (17) forget ……….   (23) patrol ……….

(6) admit …………   (12) begin …………   (18) refer …………   (24) knit …………..

Using present participles to join sentences

Present participles can be used to link sentences together. Combine each pair of sentences into a single sentence by changing the verb (in heavy type) into a present participle. Look at the boxed example:

The dingo turned on Carl. It **bared** its teeth.
becomes
Baring its teeth, the dingo turned on Carl.

(1) Carl **looked** at the savage metal teeth.
    He imagined the pain if one of his own legs were caught in the trap.

(2) Carl stood to watch the dingoes.
    They **ran** along the fenceline.

(3) Carl **stared** at the stricken animal.
    He could feel tears in his eyes.

(4) Ray would **be** glad that one of his traps had worked.
    He would come up and shoot the dingo.

(5) Ray **stumbled** to the door in his pyjamas.
He was only half awake.

(6) Carl just stood there.
He **had** no idea what to do.

(7) Carl **leaned** on the fence.
He turned away from the sight of the dead dingo.

(8) Carl cried himself to sleep.
He **thought** of the wounded dingo.

Appropriate present participles

Select from the box the most appropriate present participle for each of the nouns.

twinkling	glaring	hissing	croaking
sparkling	bleating	rumbling	dripping
bellowing	galloping	glowing	babbling
whistling	whirring	creaking	chiming
rattling	droning	screeching	splintering

(1) .... kettle   (11) .... brook

(2) .... stars   (12) .... bulls

(3) .... frogs   (13) .... headlights

(4) .... sheep   (14) .... diamonds

(5) .... fire   (15) .... helicopters

(6) .... horses   (16) .... door

(7) .... chains   (17) .... brakes

(8) .... bells   (18) .... plane

(9) .... tap   (19) .... wood

(10) .... volcano   (20) .... steam

Punctuation 7

The Exclamation Mark

The exclamation mark is used at the end of a word or sentence to indicate a command, to express some powerful surge of emotion, or to convey urgency.

EXAMPLES: Watch out for the trap!   Look out!   Help me!   Quick!

Make your mark!

Select an exclamation mark, a question mark or a full stop to end each of the following sentences.

(1) Run for your life

(2) Will the dingoes come tonight

(3) The boy waited to see the dingoes

(4) Ray, come quickly

(5) What's happened

(6) Hurry, it's urgent

(7) Where are the pups

(8) Carl returned to the farmhouse

(9) Don't shoot

(10) Why did you wake me up

Creative Writing 7

More on the Writer's Technique

The following description of the appearance of a monstrous bear is taken from *Shardik* by Richard Adams. Read through it carefully, and then answer the questions that follow.

THE BEAR

A little distance away, something unimaginably heavy was moving and this movement was beating the ground like a drum. The vibration grew until even a human ear could have heard the irregular sounds of ponderous movement in the gloom. A stone rolled downhill through fallen leaves and was followed by a crashing of undergrowth. Then, at the top of the slope beyond the red rock, the thick mass of branches and creepers began to shake. A young tree tilted outwards, snapped, splintered and pitched its length to the ground, springing up and down in diminishing bounds on its pliant branches, as though not only the sound but also the movement of the fall had set up echoes in the solitude.

In the gap, half-concealed by a confused tangle of creepers, leaves and broken flowers, appeared a figure of terror, monstrous beyond the nature even of that dark, savage place. Huge it was — gigantic — standing on its hind legs more than twice as high as a man. Its shaggy feet carried great, curved claws as thick as a man's fingers, from which were hanging fragments of torn fern and strips of bark. The mouth gaped open, a steaming pit set with white stakes. The muzzle was thrust forward, sniffing, while the blood-shot eyes peered short-sightedly over the unfamiliar ground below. For long moments it remained erect, breathing heavily and growling. Then it sank clumsily upon all fours, pushed into the undergrowth, the round claws scraping against the stones — for they could not be retracted — and smashed its way down the slope towards the red rock. It was a bear — such a bear as is not seen in a thousand years — more powerful than a rhinoceros and heavy as eight strong men.

from *Shardik* by RICHARD ADAMS

Some questions

(1) Sometimes a writer will choose to describe in detail a *setting* that will form a background for action — rather like the stage props or scenery in a play. What particular setting is described in detail in this piece of writing?

(2) Often a piece of descriptive writing is designed to appeal to one or more of a reader's *senses* (which comprise *smell, hearing, touch, sight* and *taste*). Which of the reader's senses is mainly appealed to in the first paragraph?

(3) In the second paragraph the appeal switches to a different sense. Which of the senses is particularly appealed to now?

(4) The writer, Richard Adams, uses *suspense* to great effect in this passage. Suspense is the feeling of expectancy that something dramatic — or even dreadful — is going to happen. How does the writer build up the suspense in the first paragraph?

(5) In the second paragraph, the writer uses a variety of effective *words* to convey the idea of the power and size of the creature that appears in the forest. Find four words that effectively convey the power and size of the creature.

(6) *Comparisons* are also used to give an idea of size. Find two comparisons the writer has employed.

(7) 'The mouth gaped open, a steaming pit set with white stakes.' Look more closely at this comparison and explain in your own words what is actually being compared.

(8) The last sentence of the description finally tells us that the creature is a bear. Why do you think the writer has left it until the very end to reveal this information?

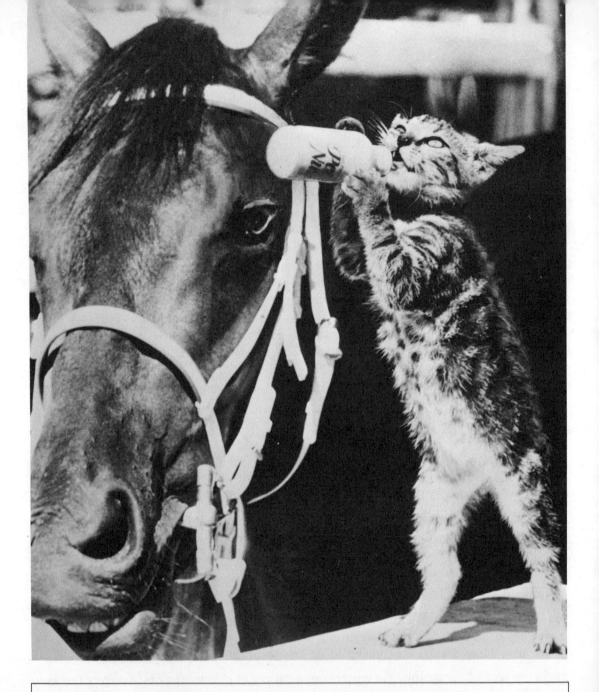

Your Turn to Write

See how well you can write using *one* of these ideas:

(1) Imagine that the two animals in the picture can talk. Reproduce one of their amusing or serious conversations.

(2) A Day in the Life of a . . .   [*Select an animal*]

(3) 'Animals that I am afraid of.'

(4) 'My favourite animal book or story.'

Poetry 7

'The Trap' depicts a fox's struggle for survival after being caught in a hidden trap. As you read, think whether anything else is being depicted by the poet.

THE TRAP

'That red fox,
Back in the furthest field,
Caught in my hidden trap,
Was half mad with fear.
During the night
He must have ripped his foot
From the cold steel.
I saw him early this morning,
Dragging his hurt leg,
Bleeding a path across the gold wheat,
Whining with the pain;
His eyes like cracked marbles.
I followed as he moved,
His thin body pulled to one side
In a weird helplessness.
He hit the wire fence,
Pushing through it
Into the deep, morning corn,
And was gone.'
The old man looked around the kitchen
To see if anyone was listening.
'Crazy red fox,
Will kill my chickens no longer.
Will die somewhere in hiding.'
He lit the brown tobacco carefully,
Watching the blue smoke rise and disappear
In the movement of the air.
Scratching his red nose slowly,
Thinking something grave for a long moment,
He stared out of the bright window.
'He won't last long with that leg,' he said.
The old man turned his head
To see if his wife was listening.
But she was deep in thought,
Her stained fingers

Pressing red berries in a pie.
He turned his white head
Toward the open window again.
'Guess I'll ride into the back field, first thing.
Some mighty big corn back there this year.
Mighty big corn.'
His wife looked up from her work,
Smiled almost secretly to herself,
And finished packing the ripe berries
Into the pale crust.

WILLIAM BEYER

Thinking about the Poem

(1) What did the fox do when he was caught in the trap?

(2) 'His eyes like cracked marbles.' Why do you think the poet compares the fox's eyes to cracked marbles?

(3) Why had the farmer set the trap?

(4) What does the farmer suggest is likely to happen to the fox?

(5) 'Guess I'll ride into the back field, first thing.' Why do you think the farmer is going into the back field?

(6) After reading the poem what feelings do you have towards (a) the fox, and (b) the farmer?

(7) Do you think the title 'The Fox' would have been better than 'The Trap'? Give a reason for your opinion.

(8) Did you enjoy this poem? Why or why not?

Spelling 7

DINGO BOY

anxiety	journey	argument	released	struggle
ferocity	misery	safety	pyjamas	stomach
reconnaissance	benefit	disturbance	angrily	approached
perspiration	argue	agony	mechanically	gradually

Missing Words

Fit the correct words from the spelling box into the spaces left blank in the passage below.

An Act of Mercy

As the dingoes made their nightly .... of the fenceline, Carl saw one of them collapse in a.......... . Its leg was caught in a trap. Because of its f.........., Carl a.......... the dingo warily. He was so filled with a.......... concerning the dingo's s.......... to free itself that he decided to j.......... to the farmhouse to fetch Ray. When Carl, bathed in ...., reached the kitchen, Ray came to the door in his .... An a.......... took place and Ray a.......... told Carl to kill the dingo himself. Returning to the trap with a loaded shotgun, Carl prepared to put the dingo out of its m.......... . He released the .... catch on the gun, aimed, and blew the dingo's head apart. Carl's s.......... was churning as he m.......... picked up the gun. G.......... he stopped shaking, but his body now heaved with sobs. He eventually cried himself to sleep.

Word Forms

Complete these sentences by using the correct form of each of the words given in brackets.

(1) The dingo was a .... [**ferocity**] animal.

(2) It was an .... [**agony**] decision for Carl to kill the dingo.

(3) Carl looked .... [**anxiety**] at the trapped dingo.

(4) Ray was greatly .... [**angrily**] by Carl's request.

(5) Carl was .... [**misery**] after he had killed the dingo.

(6) The dog-proof fence was .... [**benefit**] to the farm.

(7) Carl was greatly .... [**disturbance**] by the death of the dingo.

(8) .... [**perspiration**], Carl reached the farmhouse door.

Completing Words

Complete the words by filling in the blanks.

(1) approach _ b _ _   (4) graduat _ o _   (7) anxiou _ _ y   (10) struggl _ n _

(2) argument _ t _ _ e   (5) miser _ _ _ _ y   (8) journ _ _ s   (11) mechan _ _ m

(3) disturb _ nc _   (6) agon _ _ s   (9) benefit _ _   (12) safel _

Try Thinking 7

Name Knowledge

Try thinking of the right name for each of the following. Note your clues.

(1) The name for an underwater vessel: s _ _ _ _ _ _ _ _

(2) The name for the bone framework that supports the body: s _ _ _ _ _ _ _ _

(3) The name for a machine that calculates and remembers: c _ _ _ _ _ _ _ _

(4) The name for a place where films are shown: c _ _ _ _ _ _

(5) The name for a book that lists the meanings of words: d _ _ _ _ _ _ _ _ _

(6) The name for a place where grain is stored: s _ _ _

(7) The name for a song for two people: d _ _ _ _

(8) The name for a kind of small cave: g _ _ _ _ _ _

(9) The name for a person who plays games of chance for money: g _ _ _ _ _ _ _

(10) The name for a boat that carries passengers across a waterway: f _ _ _ _ _

(11) The name for a platform from which ships may be loaded: w _ _ _ _ _

(12) The name for idle talk about other people: g _ _ _ _ _ _

(13) The name for an exact copy of something: d _ _ _ _ _ _ _ _

(14) The name for a large spoon with a long handle: l _ _ _ _ _

Compound Words

Complete the following groups of words by choosing a word from the box for each group. The first one has been done to show you the way.

sun	foot	play	news	rain	land	dead	book	butter	hand

(1) ..*news*.. agent

...*news*... paper

..*news*.. cast

..*news*.. reader

(2) .... fall

.... bow

.... coat

.... drop

(3) .... lock

.... end

.... heat

.... pan

(4) .... mark

.... end

.... case

.... keeping

(5) .... scotch

.... fly

.... cup

.... milk

(6) .... scape

.... mark

.... lady

.... slide

(7) .... bag

.... rail

.... cuffs

.... writing

(8) .... mate

.... ground

.... wright

.... thing

(9) .... ball

.... path

.... step

.... hold

(10) .... rise

.... glasses

.... shade

.... shine

Common Sense on the Highway

Only one lane of a highway being available, how would you go about organizing the movements of the black cars and the white cars so that all four can continue in their respective directions? Take coins or rubbers to represent the cars, and experiment with shifting them in as few moves as possible. (Seven-move answer on p. 259.)

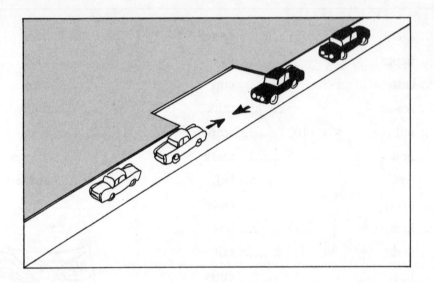

Unit Eight

Comprehension 8

The sports journalist Ian Wooldridge wrote the following account of the incredible Olympic achievement of Mary Peters.

AN INCREDIBLE ACHIEVEMENT

Mary Peters, late on a September afternoon in Munich in 1972, was acclaimed the greatest all-round woman athlete in the world. Against most predictions and all current form statistics she won the pentathlon at the XXth Olympic Games with what, even when the sports-watching days are over, I shall still probably recall as the ultimate example of the triumph of a single human will.

Her motive was that she was running for the people of Northern Ireland. On the eve of this most punishing of women's competitive events she was astoundingly relaxed.

'For me,' she told me, 'the bronze or silver medals would be worthless. Back home they have had nothing to cheer about for years. I am going to win the gold.'

A fair comparison would be the third seed at Wimbledon announcing in advance neither Borg nor Connors had a chance. Ranged against her, to name but two, were Burglinde Pollak and Heide Rosendahl. Miss Pollak, very blonde, very Iron Curtain–trained, looked like the sort of woman the average truck-driver would think twice about before engaging in a fist fight. She was also the world-record holder.

Miss Rosendahl, in contrast, was given to blinking disarmingly behind steel-rimmed spectacles, but her sprinting and long-jumping were legendary. Also, as a West German, she was the local girl performing before an idolatrous home crowd and those acquainted with the deep-throated roars of Germans urging other Germans to supreme effort never underestimate the high-octane content of such passionate support.

Mary Peters obliterated them both from her mind. The long Veronica Lake hairstyle, the soft, gentle voice, the concern for humanity, the self-deprecating humour conceal in her what sportswriters, for want of a precise psychological definition, call the 'killer streak'.

It was there, all right. We were about to stand witness to what, in athletics terms, amounted to cold-blooded murder.

The women's pentathlon comprises five disciplines: the 100-metres hurdles, shot, high-jump, long-jump and 200-metres curved sprint. Now it is mostly completed in a day.

In the 1972 Olympics it was spread over two days and, by the heaviest irony, the real agony for Mary Peters was the night in between. After the first three events she was leading the field. The hated long-jump and the 200 metres were still to come.

All night, in her room in the tower blocks of the Olympic Village, she turned and sweated and made coffee and read magazines with eyes that registered nothing.

Dawn didn't break at all.

It began seeping in down the sides of the curtains. Mary watched it thankfully. She had not slept for a single minute. By the time she went down in the lift the sun was already glinting off the dragon's-back roof of Munich's extraordinary stadium.

The longest day was about to follow the longest night of her life. We met and talked briefly. She did not mention the horrendous attack of nervous insomnia, as if to have done so would have been acknowledging a weakness on this, the day she was going to dedicate to Northern Ireland.

Throughout the entire Province, she knew, the Catholics and the Protestants and the godless alike would be watching her on television, and she was about to show them that someone cared.

So help me, defeat never entered her mind.

Relatively, in the athletics stratosphere in which she was competing, Miss Peters was a bad long-jumper. Rosendahl immediately hit her with a colossal 22 ft 5 in. [6.83 m], and Pollak jumped 20 ft 4½ in. [6.21 m].

Mary never expected better than 19 ft 6 in. [5.94 m]. She fractionally overstepped on the first of her three jumps and thus wasted a leap of just over 20 feet. She had to settle for a best of 19 ft 7½ in. [5.98 m].

It meant that with only the 200 metres to come the three of them were almost deadlocked. Peters still just led with 3871 points, Pollak had closed up to 3824

points, and Rosendahl's amazing jump had brought her up to 3750 points.

It was a bad moment for Britons, like me, who were unashamedly willing Mary to win. She didn't have to be first in the 200 metres to win the overall gold medal, but she had to be so damn close to whoever did that it made little difference.

And the respective fastest ever times did not inspire the faint-hearted: 24.2 secs by Peters, 23.8 by Pollak, 23.1 by Rosendahl.

Mostly the sportswriter can watch dispassionately, insulated by the knowledge that provided he can avoid air crashes and sign a non-proliferation treaty with drink, his career could span six, seven, even eight Olympiads. One athlete, he could say, matters neither here nor there. This day it did.

The pistol fired.

Mary, in lane three, made the classically perfect start, driving low into the curve at the top of the stadium before she straightened. At 80 metres, running now into a solid wall of *Deutschland, Deutschland Über Anyone*,[1] she had a metre on Pollak, immediately to her left. But out there, three lanes to her right, Rosendahl was running like the wind, three metres clear of the entire field, a superb athlete now supercharged by national fervour.

Each one-tenth of a second that separated them, under pentathlon rules, was going to pull Rosendahl 10 points closer to Peters. Mary had to stay in touch. But at 130 metres something feeling very like Nemesis[2] struck.

For a split second she faltered, almost staggered. 'It was almost,' she recalled later, 'as though someone had thrown a

---

1 *Germany, Germany Above Anyone.*
2 Divine vengeance; fate.

switch and cut the power off. I could sense my body getting more and more upright, which means disaster.'

It was then that years of remorseless bullying by her coach, Buster McShane, paid off. 'Arms, arms,' he used to scream at her in bleak fields on damp, cold afternoons in Northern Ireland.

The litany flooded through the assembling mists into what was left of her brain. She got the arms moving once again and, somehow, her legs came tumbling after. Thus, reeling, she crossed the finish line, and fell into oblivion.

The scores were eventually flashed up: Rosendahl 22.96 seconds, Peters 24.08 seconds. For both women it was the fastest 200 metres they had ever run. But for Mary Peters it was gibberish. Her mind could not handle the mathematics.

Had she won the pentathlon or not?

It was then Heide Rosendahl came up to Mary and put an arm round her shoulders. Mary saw the answer in Heide's face. 'Congratulations,' said Heide in English. The gold medal was on its way to Northern Ireland.

Mary had won it by exactly one-tenth of a second. In four of her five events in Munich she had established personal bests. Her total of 4801 points was a new world and Olympic record. The only moment she doubted herself was when the final race was done.

from *Mary Peters* by IAN WOOLDRIDGE

How Well Did You Understand?

(1) What, in Munich in 1972, was Mary Peters acclaimed as?

(2) What did she win?

(3) How do we know that the sports journalist was very impressed by her achievement?

(4) What clue indicates that Burglinde Pollak, one of Mary's opponents, was physically very strong?

(5) Her other opponent, Heide Rosendahl, could look forward to passionate support from the crowd. Why?

(6) What was concealed behind Mary Peters's rather mild manners?

(7) Why would it have been better for Mary Peters if the pentathlon had been scheduled for completion in one day instead of being spread over two?

(8) What did she suffer from during 'the longest night of her life'?

(9) Why were the three women 'almost deadlocked' with only the 200-metres event to go?

(10) What happened to Mary Peters at the 130-metre mark?

(11) How did she avoid disaster?

(12) When was the only moment that Mary doubted herself?

Dictionary Words

Write down the meaning of each of the following words from the passage. You might like to use the back-of-the-book dictionary to help you.

(a) acclaimed   (b) disarmingly   (c) idolatrous   (d) self-deprecating   (e) insomnia.

Language 8

Past Participles

Like the present participle, the past participle can be used as part of a verb.

> The coach had **trained** an Olympic champion.

And again, the past participle too can be used as an adjective.

> The **trained** runner performed well.

The past participle usually ends with 'ed'. But it can end in other ways — e.g. forbidden, drunk, sworn, blown, fallen, swum, hung.

A good way of working out the form of the past participle of a verb is to imagine that 'I have' comes in front of it. Thus, to work out the past participle of the verb *spring*, for instance, you think to yourself, 'I have sprung'; so *sprung* is the past participle.

Forming past participles

Complete these sentences by changing the words in brackets into past participles.

(1) Mary Peters had .... [**win**] the gold medal for Northern Ireland.

(2) The race was .... [**see**] by a large crowd.

(3) The runners had .... [**speed**] along the track.

(4) Even though at one stage she had .... [**lose**] some of her confidence, she had still .... [**seek**] to win the gold medal.

(5) Another world record was .... [**break**].

(6) The sportswriter could have been .... **[forgive]** for thinking Mary Peters wouldn't win.

(7) She had .... **[swear]** to win the gold medal.

(8) The runner had .... **[fling]** herself onto the turf.

(9) Mary Peters had .... **[show]** what could be .... **[do]** if one were determined.

(10) After her win, she was .... [**smite**] with exhaustion.

Verb table

Complete this verb table by filling in the missing parts. The first one has been done to help you.

Present Tense	Present Participle	Past Tense	Past Participle
fly	flying	flew	flown
drink			
	ringing		
		swam	
			shaken
sing			
	blowing		
		stood	
			fought
take			
	sinking		
		began	
			thrown

Past participles used as adjectives

Change the verbs in brackets into past participles. The first one has been done to help you.

(1) a ...*fallen*... tree [fall]

(2) a .... nail [bend]

(3) a .... few [choose]

(4) a .... team [beat]

(5) a .... drug [forbid]

(6) a .... friend [forget]

(7) a .... car [steal]

(8) a .... sheep [shear]

(9) a .... account [pay]

(10) a .... child [spoil]

(11) a .... criminal [know]

(12) the .... sun [rise]

(13) a .... arm [swell]

(14) a .... enemy [swear]

(15) a .... report [write]

(16) a .... garment [tear]

(17) a .... baby [wake]

(18) a .... cardigan [knit]

(19) a .... name [give]

(20) the .... cattle [drive]

(21) the .... logs [saw]

(22) the .... snow [melt]

(23) an .... cake [eat]

(24) the .... lake [freeze]

Combining sentences by the use of past participles

Link these pairs of sentences together using the past participles (in heavy type).

(1) The child was **injured** by the car. The child did not move.

(2) The high mountains gleamed in the sunlight. They were **capped** with snow.

(3) The cowboy was approaching the ranch. He was **mounted** on a beautiful white horse.

(4) The manager was **annoyed** by the speech. He left the room immediately.

(5) The footballer kicked a goal. He was **covered** with mud.

(6) His house was **built** near the beach. It was sheltered by palm-trees.

Punctuation 8

The Comma

The comma is used to mark a natural pause in a sentence — at the place where a person, if reading aloud, would pause momentarily or take a breath.

EXAMPLE: Although she was tired, defeat never entered her mind.

Supply the comma

In each of the following sentences, supply a comma where a pause would naturally occur.

(1) Taking a deep breath the gymnast began her superb performance on the parallel bars.

(2) While the crowd held its breath the great Don Bradman swung his bat at the hurtling ball.

(3) The sprinters sprang from the starting-blocks feet pounding the cinders.

(4) As John McEnroe tenses for his serve the umpire watches intently.

(5) Hooves drumming the horses galloped past the winning-post.

(6) When the rain began to fall in torrents the golfers and the spectators dashed for cover.

(7) Exhausted and almost out of breath the swimmer touched the side of the pool a split second before her rival.

(8) The football crowd was deliriously happy even though the home team had lost.

(9) There I was the javelin poised in my hand.

(10) Without any doubt this athlete would be the next world marathon champion.

Creative Writing 8

The passage following is from the book *This Sporting Life* by David Storey. It deals with football, describing action situations in which a feverish exhilaration grips both the players and the spectators. First read about some of the team action; then answer the questions on the writer's technique that follow.

FOOTBALL ACTION

We made a scrum over the spot, the short piston limbs interlocking, then straining. A movement began across the field and young Arnie ran in with an ankle tap and the player crumbled. The ball rolled free and the boy scooped it up alertly with one hand and side-stepping started to run down the field. He found Frank with a long pass coming up laboriously in support. The great bulk of Frank, his lessened speed, drew the opposing forwards magnetically. They leapt wildly at his slow procession through them. Before he fell under their simultaneous attacks he flicked the ball expertly into the gap he'd deliberately created. Maurice, waiting in receipt, didn't hear the oppressive noise that came from Frank as he hit the ground; he took the ball one-handed and with short precise steps cut his way through to the full-back, and was almost on the line when the winger, coming across with a greater and more famous speed, knocked him over like a stalk.

The two teams shot into position in the thick din of excitement. Frank stood behind Maurice and took the ball as it came between the scrum-half's legs. I started running up from behind, Frank held the ball, then slipped it to me as I passed in full stride. I hit the wall of waiting men like a rock. For a second they yielded, drew together, and held. A dull pain shot from the top of my skull. I struggled into a position I knew would ease the impact and give me more chance with any excited fist. I heard through compressed ears the screams and groans of the crowd, almost the individual voices of agony, before I was flung down.

I rose with the same motion and played the ball. Young Arnie had it. I'd never realized how popular he was with the crowd. When, with an apparently casual blow, he was banged down, I was vaguely satisfied at his indiscretion. I took the ball as he played it and sent it to the centres. It passed straight to the super-protected wingman. He gathered cleanly and bustled up the field only to be shoved into touch. The crowd disapproved.

We folded down to the scrum, panting with the first breathlessness, steam rising from the straining 'backs. I saw the damp shape roll between my legs and Maurice snatched it up impatiently. With an extravagant dummy he shot by the still dazed captain and was caught by the winger. He kicked out, lashed out, contorted, and threw himself over the line.

The crowd screamed and surged like penned animals, like a suddenly disturbed pool. Whistles, bells, and trumpets crashed and soared on the animal roar. I ran to him, banged his back, and we walked back in pleased groups.

from *This Sporting Life*
by DAVID STOREY

The Writer's Technique — Powerful Words

The strength and power of this football action-writing is created largely through the writer's deliberate use of the *strong* and *unusual* word or phrase in preference to the more usual and obvious one. *Powerful* comparisons contribute to the reader's involvement in the hard-hitting action.

Read the following descriptions and answer the accompanying questions, each of which concerns an underlined word, phrase or comparison.

(1) the <u>short piston</u> limbs interlocking

- Why do the legs of the players in the scrum resemble short pistons?

(2) the player <u>crumbled</u>

- The writer could have used a word such as 'fell'. Why didn't he?

(3) the boy <u>scooped</u> it up alertly

- Why not simply 'picked it up'?

(4) drew the opposing forwards <u>magnetically</u>

- What does this colourful word do for its verb 'drew'?

(5) they leapt wildly at his <u>slow procession</u> through them

- What do these words vividly portray about the progress of Frank's great bulk through the forwards?

(6) with short precise steps [he] <u>cut his way</u> through to the full-back

- What comparison is being made here? Why is it a strong one?

(7) the winger knocked him over <u>like a stalk</u>

- This is a clear and straightforward comparison. Explain why it is a good one.

(8) the two teams shot into position in the thick <u>din</u> of excitement

- This is a very expressive word. See if you can think up an alternative word to describe a concentrated sound.

(9) 'I hit the <u>wall</u> of waiting men like a <u>rock</u>

- What quality do these two words share? Why are they apt (fitting) words to use here?

(10) with an apparently casual blow he was <u>banged</u> down

- This word is expressive because it combines which *two* of the following qualities: weakness, skill, sound, force?

(11) he gathered cleanly and <u>bustled up</u> the field

- What kind of progress do you see in your mind's eye as you read this?

(12) I saw <u>the damp shape</u> roll

- Why not just say 'the ball'?

(13) he <u>kicked out, lashed out, contorted,</u> and threw himself over the line

- The word 'kicked' refers to legs. What bodily actions do the other two words suggest?

(14) whistles, bells, and trumpets <u>crashed</u> and <u>soared</u> on the animal <u>roar</u>

- Why are these words good to use for sounds linked with a crowd gone wild?

Your Turn to Write

Try your hand at writing about *one* of the following:

(1) 'A sportsperson I admire very much.'

(2) 'A sportsperson I dislike intensely.'

(3) Write a description beginning, 'This was the moment for which we had all been waiting. As the cheering swelled to a roar, I leaned forward to see ...'

(4) Dangerous Sports.

Poetry 8

In 'Sports Field' the poet, Judith Wright, not only describes a sportsground and the children who use it, but also anticipates some of the difficulties they will face in life.

SPORTS FIELD

Naked all night the field
breathed its dew until
the great gold ball of day
sprang up from the dark hill.

Now as the children come
the field and they are met.
Their day is measured and marked,
its lanes and tapes are set;

and the children gilt by the sun
shoulder one another;
crouch at the marks to run,
and spring, and run together —

and the children pledged and matched,
and built to win or lose,
who grow, while no one watches,
the selves in their sidelong eyes.

The watchers love them in vain.
What's real here is the field,
the starter's gun, the lane,
the ball dropped or held;

and set towards the future
they run like running water,
for only the pride of winning,
the pain the losers suffer,

till the day's great golden ball,
that no one ever catches,
drops; and at its fall
runners and watchers

pick up their pride and pain
won out of the measured field
and turn away again
while the star-dewed night comes cold.

So pride and pain are fastened
into the heart's future,
while naked and perilous
the night and the field glitter.

JUDITH WRIGHT

Thinking about the Poem

(1) What is 'the great gold ball of day'? Why is 'ball' an appropriate word?

(2) What does the poet mean by 'Their day is measured and marked'?

(3) What does the poet mean when she refers to the runners' and watchers' 'pride and pain'?

(4) What does Judith Wright show us about life itself?

(5) Did you like or dislike the poem? Why?

Spelling 8

OLYMPICS

atmosphere	competitive	endurance	technique	triumph
strength	passionate	acquainted	vigorous	personality
spectacular	witness	psychological	incredible	congratulations
prediction	difference	strenuous	victorious	eventually

Word Forms

Complete each of the following sentences by using the correct form of the word in brackets.

(1) Exercise helps to .... [strength] the muscles.

(2) Each girl longed for .... [victorious].

(3) I .... [prediction] that the Irish girl will win.

(4) We would like to .... [**congratulations**] the winner.

(5) Now a .... [**difference**] girl has taken the lead.

(6) As usual, the .... [**competitive**] is fierce.

(7) The study of the mind is called .... [**psychological**].

(8) I would like to .... [**acquainted**] you with the latest methods.

(9) The parade around the Olympic Stadium was a magnificent .... [**spectacular**].

(10) The gold medal is reserved for the .... [**triumph**] winner.

Missing Words

Rewrite *The Olympic Runners*, inserting the appropriate word from the spelling box into each blank place.

The Olympic Runners

An i........... a........... surrounded the women runners at the Olympics. Each contestant was putting forth all her s........... and each one was possessed by a ps........... need to finish .... It was a s........... performance by all the women runners, but even at the halfway mark it was apparent that the leading runner was displaying a d........... in t..........., and also a c........... awareness that would help her to t........... in the end. Nevertheless it was a s........... run for all the women. When it .... ended, hearty .... were showered on the winner by the immense crowd. Later, when the sportswriter became better a........... with the winner, he found that her will to win was an important part of her p........... .

Working with List-words

(1) Give the *person* for each of the following. (E.g. 'sail' would become 'sailor'.)
   (a) competitive   (b) acquainted   (c) victorious.

(2) Give one list-word for each of the following:
   (a) one who has seen or watched something happen: ....
   (b) dominated by very strong feelings: ....
   (c) a forecast or foretelling of what will happen in the future: ....

(3) For each of the following, give a list-word that is opposite in meaning.
   (a) similarity   (b) weakness   (c) defeated   (d) believable.

Try Thinking 8

What AGE Am I?

The answers to the clues below all end with AGE. Note the example.

(1) I am a vegetable: c <u>a</u> <u>b</u> <u>b</u> AGE

(2) I am something actors perfom on: s__AGE

(3) I am a long journey: v_ _ AGE

(4) I am quite fierce: s_ _ AGE

(5) I am tied up with brown paper and string: p_ _ _ AGE

(6) I am carried around by travellers: l_ _ _ AGE

(7) I am a legal union between man and woman: m_ _ _ _ _ AGE

(8) I am the place where a car is kept: g_ _ AGE

(9) I am the result of a crash: w_ _ _ _ _ AGE

(10) I am water that has got away: l_ _ _ AGE

(11) I am chopped meat stuffed in a skin: s_ _ _ AGE

(12) I am something a train traveller uses: c_ _ _ _ _ AGE

(13) I am electrical: v_ _ _ AGE

(14) I am a dressing for a wound: b_ _ _ _ AGE

Little Bits and Things

Things sometimes come in little bits. There's a small quantity on the left that will match with an item on the right. See if you can make the correct matches.

LITTLE BITS	SOME THINGS
a crumb of	water
a speck of	flowers
a grain of	butter
a puff of	paper
a lock of	bread
a splinter of	wood
a pat of	hair
a scrap of	sand
a blade of	glass
a gleam of	oil
a chip of	dirt
a sip of	wind
a posy of	light
a smear of	grass

Mayday!

See whether you can solve this puzzle. (The solution is on p. 259.)

Transfer the data gleaned from the clues into the grid...using a tick to indicate a positive assumption and a cross for a negative one. You will then be able to cross-refer data inside this grid with the aid of logical deduction.

Five families, each with a different type of house and a different number of children, have different ways of spending their May School Holidays. Can you work out which is which?

1. The Mayday family (with 1 child) doesn't live in a cottage.
2. The family which lives in a semi spends the day gardening; they have as many children as the flat-dwellers and the Fundays together.
3. The cinema-going family has 2 children and doesn't live in a terrace or cottage. The Mundays, who go for a bush walk, don't live in a cottage either.
4. The 4-child family (not the Freedays) goes to the beach; and it's the Heydays who have the largest family.

	Occupation					House					Children				
	Cinema	Bush walk	Gardening	Beach	Television	Cottage	Townhouse	Flat	Semi	Terrace	1	2	3	4	5
Freeday															
Funday															
Heyday															
Mayday															
Munday															
1															
2															
3															
4															
5															
Cottage															
Townhouse															
Flat															
Semi															
Terrace															

Unit Nine

Comprehension 9

An interstellar gangster, the vile and monstrous Jabba the Hutt, has hurled Luke Skywalker, the Jedi Knight, into the lair of the monstrous Rancor. Princess Leia, a captive of Jabba, watches in agony — but the creatures of Jabba's court caper in anticipation. Now read on....

LUKE AND THE RANCOR

The floor suddenly dropped away, sending Luke and his guard crashing into the pit below. The trapdoor immediately closed again. All the beasts of the court rushed to the floor-grating and looked down.

'Luke!' yelled Leia. She felt part of her self torn away, pulled down into the pit with him. She started forward, but was held in check by the manacle around her throat.

In the pit below, Luke picked himself up off the floor. He found he was now in a large cavelike dungeon, the walls formed of craggy boulders pocked with lightless crevices. The half-chewed bones of countless animals were strewn over the floor, smelling of decayed flesh and twisted fear.

Twenty-five feet above him, in the ceiling, he saw the iron grating through which Jabba's repugnant courtiers peered.

The guard beside him suddenly began to scream uncontrollably, as a door in the side of the cave slowly rumbled open. With infinite calm, Luke surveyed his surroundings as he removed his long robe down to his Jedi tunic, to give him more freedom of movement. He backed quickly to the wall and crouched there, watching.

Out of the side passage emerged the giant Rancor. The size of an elephant, it was somehow reptilian, somehow as unformed as a nightmare. Its huge screeching mouth was asymmetrical in its head, its fangs and claws set all out of proportion. It was clearly a mutant, and wild as all unreason.

The guard picked up the pistol from the dirt where it had fallen and began firing laser bursts at the hideous monster. This only made the beast angrier. It lumbered toward the guard.

The guard kept firing. Ignoring the laser blasts, the beast grabbed the hysterical guard, popped him into its slavering jaws, and swallowed him in a gulp. The audience above cheered, laughed, and threw coins.

The monster then turned and started for Luke. But the Jedi Knight leaped eight meters straight up and grabbed onto the overhead grate. The crowd began to boo. Hand over hand, Luke traversed the grating toward the corner of the cave, struggling to maintain his grip as the audience jeered his efforts. One hand slipped on the oily grid, and he dangled precariously over the baying mutant.

Two jawas ran across the top of the grate. They mashed Luke's fingers with their rifle butts; once again, the crowd roared its approval.

The Rancor pawed at Luke from below, but the Jedi dangled just out of reach. Suddenly Luke released his hold and dropped directly onto the eye of the howling monster; he then tumbled to the floor.

The Rancor screamed in pain and stumbled, swatting its own face to knock away the agony. It ran in circles a few times, then spotted Luke again and came at him. Luke stooped down to pick up the long bone of an earlier victim. He brandished it before him. The gallery above thought this was hilarious and hooted in delight.

The monster grabbed Luke and brought him up to its salivating mouth. At the last moment, though, Luke wedged the bone deep in the Rancor's mouth and jumped to the floor as the beast began to gag. The Rancor bellowed and flailed about, running headlong into a wall. Several rocks were dislodged, starting an avalanche that nearly buried Luke, as he crouched deep in a crevice near the floor. The crowd clapped in unison.

Luke tried to clear his mind. Fear is a great cloud, Ben used to tell him. It makes the cold colder and the dark darker; but let it rise and it will dissolve. So Luke let it rise past the clamor of the beast above him, and examined ways he might turn the sad creature's rantings on itself.

It was not an evil beast, that much was clear. Had it been purely malicious, its wickedness could easily have been turned on itself — for pure evil, Ben had said, was always self-destructive in the end. But this monster wasn't bad — merely dumb and mistreated. Hungry and in pain, it lashed out at whatever came near. For Luke to have looked on that as evil would only have been a projection of Luke's own darker aspects — it would have been false, and it certainly wouldn't have helped him out of this situation.

No, he was going to have to keep his mind clear — that was all — and just outwit the savage brute, to put it out of its misery.

Most preferable would have been to set it loose in Jabba's court, but that seemed unlikely. He considered, next, giving the creature the means to do itself in — to end its own pain. Unfortunately, the creature was far too angered to comprehend the solace of the void. Luke finally began studying the specific contours of the cave, to try to come up with a specific plan.

The Rancor, meanwhile, had knocked the bone from its mouth and, enraged, was scrabbling through the rubble of fallen rocks, searching for Luke. Luke, though his vision was partially obscured by the pile that still sheltered him, could see now past the monster, to a holding cave beyond — and beyond that, to a utility door. If only he could get to it.

The Rancor knocked away a boulder and spotted Luke recoiling in the crevice. Voraciously, it reached in to pluck the boy out. Luke grabbed a large rock and smashed it down on the creature's finger as hard as he could. As the Rancor jumped, howling in pain once more, Luke ran for the holding cave.

He reached the doorway and ran in. Before him, a heavy barred gate blocked the way. Beyond this gate, the Rancor's two keepers sat eating dinner. They looked up as Luke entered, then stood and walked toward the gate.

Luke turned around to see the monster coming angrily after him. He turned back to the gate and tried to open it. The keepers poked at him with their two-pronged spears, jabbed at him through the bars, laughing and chewing their food, as the Rancor drew closer to the young Jedi.

Luke backed against the side wall, as the Rancor reached in the room for him. Suddenly he saw the restraining-door control panel halfway up the opposite wall. The Rancor began to enter the holding room, closing for the kill, when all at once Luke picked up a skull off the floor and hurled it at the panel.

The panel exploded in a shower of sparks, and the giant iron overhead restraining door came crashing down on the Rancor's head, crushing it like an axe smashing through a ripe watermelon.

Those in the audience above gasped as one, then were silent. They were all truly stunned at this bizarre turn of events. They all looked to Jabba, who was apoplectic with rage. Never had he felt such fury. Leia tried to hide her delight, but was unable to keep from smiling, and this increased Jabba's anger even further. Harshly he snapped at his guards: 'Get him out of there. Bring me Solo and the Wookiee. They will all suffer for this outrage.'

In the pit below, Luke stood calmly as several of Jabba's henchmen ran in, clapped him in bonds, and ushered him out.

The Rancor keeper wept openly and threw himself down on the body of his dead pet. Life would be a lonely proposition for him from that day.

from *Return of the Jedi*
by JAMES KAHN

How Well Did You Understand?

(1) How were Luke and his guard delivered to the pit below?

(2) Why couldn't Leia throw herself into the pit with Luke?

(3) What was horrible about the dungeon's floor?

(4) Why did Luke remove his long robe?

(5) How big was the beast that emerged from the side passage?

(6) The monster 'was somehow reptilian, somehow as unformed as a nightmare'. What kind of an image does this description call up in your imagination?

(7) How did the guard react towards the monster?

(8) What happened to the guard?

(9) How did Luke first manage to escape from the monster?

(10) 'The Rancor screamed in pain . . . .' What had happened to it?

(11) What action did Luke take to avoid being eaten after the Rancor had grabbed him?

(12) In your own words, briefly sum up what Luke really thought of the Rancor.

(13) How did Luke escape from the Rancor as it reached in to pluck him from his hiding-place in the rubble of fallen rocks?

(14) How did Luke get the great iron restraining door to come crashing down?

(15) How was the Rancor finally killed?

(16) How did Jabba feel about Luke's victory?

(17) Why did the Rancor's keeper weep for his dead pet?

Dictionary Words

Give the meanings of the following words. Use the back-of-the-book dictionary for any help you need.

(a) manacle   (b) courtiers   (c) asymmetrical   (d) slavering   (e) precariously
(f) apoplectic.

Language 9

Adjectives

An adjective adds colour, shape, size, strength, feeling or some other quality to a noun. Good writers use adjectives to make their writing come alive. Look at these phrases from *Return of the Jedi*. The adjectives are in heavy type.

craggy boulders	**lightless** crevices	**repugnant** courtiers	**salivating** mouth

Adjectives are found everywhere. Look at the 'Garfield' cartoon and see how many adjectives you can discover.

Identifying adjectives

Remembering that adjectives add meaning to nouns, identify the adjectives in these sentences based on the passage.

(1) Luke found he was now in a large cavelike dungeon.

(2) In the ceiling, he saw the iron grating through which Jabba's repugnant courtiers peered.

(3) Out of the side passage emerged the giant Rancor.

(4) With infinite calm, Luke surveyed his surroundings as he removed his long robe down to his Jedi tunic, to give him more freedom of movement.

(5) The guard began firing laser bursts at the hideous monster.

(6) The beast grabbed the hysterical guard and popped him into its slavering jaws.

(7) Luke stooped down to pick up the long bone of an earlier victim.

(8) Life would be a lonely proposition for him.

Forming adjectives

Fill the blank spaces by converting the nouns (in heavy type) into adjectives. The first one has been done to help you.

(1) Luke was in great **danger**.
Luke's situation was ......*dangerous*...... .

(2) Luke displayed great **courage**.
Luke was ....

(3) Luke never lost **confidence**.
Luke always remained ....

(4) The guard was filled with **terror**.
It was a .... experience for the guard.

(5) Jabba was a **villain**.
Jabba was a .... creature.

(6) Princess Leia was a woman of great **beauty**.
Princess Leia was a very .... woman.

(7) Never had Jabba felt such **fury**.
Never had Jabba been so ....

(8) Luke displayed great **ingenuity** in disposing of the Rancor.
Luke's plan for disposing of the Rancor was ....

(9) The Rancor showed great **hostility** towards Luke and the guard.
The Rancor was .... to Luke and the guard.

(10) Luke's fight with the Rancor provided a great spectacle for the courtiers.
Luke's fight with the Rancor was .... for the courtiers.

(11) *Return of the Jedi* stirs the **imagination**.
Return of the Jedi is an .... story.

(12) Luke always displayed **optimism**.
Luke always remained ....

(13) The Rancor died in an **instant**.
The Rancor's death was ....

(14) The Rancor displayed **antagonism** towards Luke.
The Rancor was .... towards Luke.

(15) Luke achieved a **miracle** in defeating the Rancor.
Luke's defeat of the Rancor was ....

(16) There was a great **number** of courtiers in attendance.
There were .... courtiers present.

Adjectives and their opposites

Write down adjectives opposite in meaning to the adjectives in italics. For instance, 'a *crooked* stick' would become 'a *straight* stick'.

(1) a *new* watch	(9) a *cruel* remark	(17) an *inferior* product
(2) a *deceitful* politician	(10) a *busy* secretary	(18) a *difficult* problem
(3) a *clever* student	(11) a *fertile* land	(19) a *deep* pool
(4) a *humble* man	(12) a *narrow* street	(20) a *guilty* prisoner
(5) a *distant* relative	(13) a *tame* horse	(21) a *shiny* coin
(6) a *courageous* deed	(14) a *rough* edge	(22) a *future* happening
(7) a *full* tank	(15) a *sweet* fruit	(23) a *sharp* instrument
(8) a *peaceful* crowd	(16) a *front* entrance	(24) a *different* answer

Missing adjectives

Some of the adjectives from the passage below have been placed in the box. Insert them in their appropriate places in the passage.

harmless	mild	firm	good	clever	tall
quiet	handsome	beloved	mischievous	eighteen	strapping
	broad-shouldered	little	other	fourteen	

Jack and Peterkin

Jack Martin was a t.........., s.........., b.......... youth of e.......... years, with a h.........., good-humoured, f.......... face. He had had a g.......... education, was c.......... and hearty and lion-like in his actions, but m.......... and q.......... in disposition. My .... companion was Peterkin Gay. He was l.........., quick, funny, m.........., and about .... years old. But Peterkin's mischief was almost always ...., else he could not have been so much b.......... as he was.

from *Coral Island* by R.M. BALLANTYNE

Punctuation 9

The Comma Again

Commas are used to mark off introductory expressions such as *therefore, however, indeed, nevertheless, on the other hand, meanwhile.*

EXAMPLE: However, the Rancor was not an evil beast.

Another use of the comma is to mark off a participial phrase at the beginning of a sentence.

EXAMPLE: Screaming in pain, the Rancor ran around in a circle.

Inserting commas

Correctly insert commas to mark off introductory words or participial phrases in the following sentences:

(1) Picking up the pistol the guard began firing laser bursts at the hideous monster.

(2) Nevertheless Luke never gave up hope.

(3) Meanwhile the Rancor had knocked the bone from its mouth.

(4) Fighting the monster Luke was in great danger.

(5) Grabbing Luke the monster brought him up to its salivating mouth.

(6) Therefore Luke decided to use a new approach.

(7) Trying to hide her delight Leia was unable to keep from smiling.

(8) However Jabba was very angry.

Creative Writing 9

Technique, Purpose and the Reader

Here is a description of the alien creature Jabba the Hutt, from *Return of the Jedi* by James Kahn. Read through it carefully and then answer the questions on the writer's technique that follow.

JABBA THE HUTT

His head was three times human size, perhaps four. His eyes were yellow, reptilian — his skin was like a snake's, as well, except covered with a fine layer of grease. He had no neck, but only a series of chins that expanded finally into a great bloated body, engorged to bursting with stolen morsels. Stunted, almost useless arms sprouted from his upper torso, the sticky fingers of his left hand languidly wrapped around the smoking-end of his water-pipe. He had no hair — it had fallen out from a combination of diseases. He had no legs — his trunk simply tapered gradually to a long, plump snake-tail that stretched along the length of the platform like a tube of yeasty dough. His lipless mouth was wide, almost ear to ear, and he drooled continuously. He was quite thoroughly disgusting.

Questions on the Writer's Technique

(1) A writer may choose to try to arouse a strong response in the reader in the very opening sentences of a description. What were your feelings towards Jabba after you had read the first two sentences?

(2) What is the writer's purpose in using such words as 'bloated', 'engorged' and 'bursting' when describing the size and habits of Jabba?

(3) Part of the writer's purpose in the description of Jabba is to show us how horribly alien this creature was. What words and phrases tell us that Jabba's limbs were far from human?

(4) Writers often use comparisons to make their descriptions vivid. Do you think that the comparison of Jabba's tail to a tube of yeasty dough is an apt one? Give a reason for your answer.

(5) 'He was quite thoroughly disgusting.' This simple sentence concludes the passage about Jabba. Would you say that it adequately sums up a reader's likely reaction to Jabba? Give a reason for your answer.

Your Turn to Write

See how well you can write using *one* of these topics:

(1) Write an essay beginning, 'It was the greatest movie I'd ever seen'.

(2) The Time Machine.

(3) The Lost World.

(4) Prehistoric creatures, trapped beneath the ice for millions of years, suddenly come to life when the ice is melted by a nuclear explosion. They are heading towards your city. What happens?

Poetry 9

In 'Solar Travel' the poet, Maurice Carpenter, dreams that he is a space pilot, pioneering the planets of the solar system. But sinister undertones soon come to the surface....

SOLAR TRAVEL

I lay asleep on a clear bright night;
The moon filled my room with a flood of light;
I dreamed I was sailing the seas of space
And my ship bore the badge of the human race.

We are the pilots of sunlit space,
The new pioneers of the human race
With eight new planets to be won
Under the Empire of the sun.

I was the first to land on Mercury
Hot as a cinder dry as a quarry;
I planted my flag and did my duty
Boarded my ship and left in a hurry.

We are the pilots of sunlit space
Leaving our terrestrial base
With seven new planets to be won
Under the Empire of the sun.

I was the first on dusty Venus
To stand and gaze in those hot arenas,
The hills shifted and metals boiled
As fetid smokes around me coiled.

I was the first on frozen Mars
In this last act of the human farce
To gaze on a place where the seas are dry
And motor-bike moons chug round the sky.

I was the first on giant Jupiter
To know the human race grow stupider,
Gravity made me dull as lead,
I choked on a methane and ammonia bed.

We are pilots of the black and blazing
Spaces that keep our minds amazing
With four new planets to be won
Under the Empire of the sun.

I was the first on the ring of Saturn
To see the earth an attractive slattern
We'd raped and wronged and left to die.
I hardly dared look her in the eye.

I was the first on far Uranus
To know no golden age could save us,
No Titn come to break our chains
And save us from our lives' sweet pains.

We are the pilots of our shining dreams
Riding the solar system's seams,
Never to find, though space bend and twist
An inn we could call 'Space Traveller's rest'.

I stood on Neptune's enormous belly
Coughing clouds, knee deep in jelly
And thought of Adam and his fall,
The aberration that foxed us all.

I stood on Pluto's absolute zero
Knowing at last I was no hero,
Uttermost darkness closing in,
No more planets for me to win.

We are the pilots of space returned
Sun-drenched to the earth we spurned,
Pilots of the brimming ether
Daring the interstellar weather,
Exploring the Empire of the sun
To rule all planets but our own.

MAURICE CARPENTER

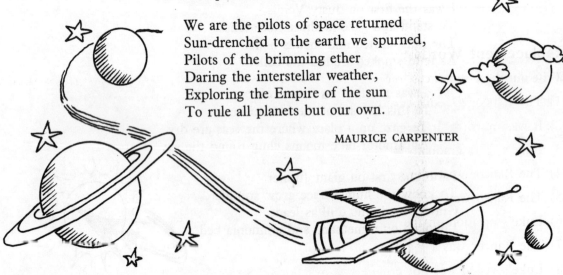

Thinking about Solar Travel

(1) Why were the space pilots 'The new pioneers of the human race'?

(2) 'I planted my flag ....' Why did the space pilot do this?

(3) Why would Mercury have been unsuitable for human habitation?

(4) In what ways were the planets Venus and Mars different from each other?

(5) Why was Jupiter an unpleasant planet?

(6) According to the space pilot, how had mankind treated Earth?

(7) What impression did the space pilot give you of the planets of the solar system?

(8) Do you think 'Solar Travel' is a suitable title for the poem? Why? What other title could you suggest?

Spelling 9

RETURN OF THE JEDI

repugnant	examined	emerged	crevice	gallery
ceiling	preferable	screeching	maliciously	uncontrollably
precarious	comprehend	partially	avalanche	surveyed
dissolve	voraciously	hilarious	specific	hideous

Replacement Words

Write out these sentences, replacing the words or phrases (in heavy type) with list-words.

(1) The Rancor **greedily** ate the guard.

(2) It was **more desirable** for Luke to set the Rancor loose in Jabba's court.

(3) Luke's fears gradually began to **melt away**.

(4) The Rancor was uttering **shrill, high-pitched** sounds.

(5) The Rancor ran around the pit **without restraint**.

(6) Luke's position on the grating was **insecure**.

(7) The Rancor was a **loathsome** creature.

(8) Luke's vision was **not completely** obscured by the pile of rocks.

Missing Words

Use words from the spelling box to fill in the blanks and complete the story.

In the Lair of the Rancor

After Luke and the guard had fallen through the trapdoor, Luke could see in the c.......... above him the iron grating through which Jabba's r.......... courtiers were now peering. When the .... monster, the Rancor, appeared, the guard beside Luke began to scream u.......... . Luke calmly s.......... his surroundings as he .... ways of dealing with the s.......... Rancor. Although the guard was desperately firing laser bursts at the Rancor, it v.......... consumed him with its slavering jaws. Then the Rancor m.......... turned its attention towards Luke. The s.......... thought Luke was h.......... when he brandished before the Rancor the long bone of an earlier victim.

Luke, having narrowly escaped being buried in an .... of falling rocks, devised a s.......... plan of action. When he e.......... from his c.........., Luke accomplished what he had planned. All the courtiers and Jabba were unable to c.......... the violent death of the monster after the restraining door of the holding room crashed onto the Rancor's head.

Fun with Clues

Keep your wits about you as you track down the list-words by using the clues.

(1) This word ends with an insect.

(2) This word has a very cold ending.

(3) This word has all five vowels in it.

(4) These words end with the plural of 'me'.

(5) This word has a car near its middle.

(6) This word has an organ of sight in it.

(7) This word ends with a finish.

(8) This word has a female bird in it.

Try Thinking 9

Odd Word Out

In each of the following there is one word that does not belong. See if you can pick it out.

 (1) rice   wheat   syrup   barley   corn

 (2) cheese   tea   coffee   milk   water

 (3) car   bicycle   truck   taxi   bus

 (4) cap   helmet   sombrero   balaclava   sock

 (5) saw   knife   hammer   scissors

 (6) table   chair   stool   pew   throne

 (7) book   newspaper   radio   magazine   journal

 (8) dog   rabbit   lion   elephant   snake

 (9) wave   pool   pond   breeze   lake

(10) violin   flute   whistle   trumpet   bugle

(11) stone   tree   bush   shrub   hedge

(12) shark   cod   salmon   stingray   octopus   seal

Body Language

Each of the words on the left goes with a word on the right to form a part or a function of the body. See if you can pair up the words correctly.

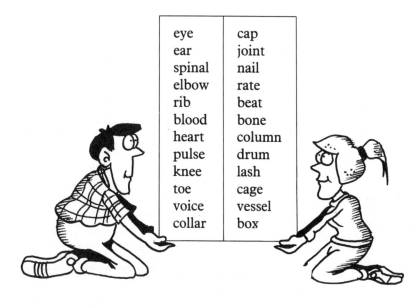

eye	cap
ear	joint
spinal	nail
elbow	rate
rib	beat
blood	bone
heart	column
pulse	drum
knee	lash
toe	cage
voice	vessel
collar	box

Build-A-Word

Use the two clues to construct two words, in such a way that the second word builds on the first. An example is provided to give you the idea.

(1) (a) the past tense of 'eat'

(b) a friend

	A	T	E
M	A	T	E

(2) (a) a deep hole

(b) to throw in baseball

(3) (a) a tablet of medicine

(b) for resting the head on

(4) (a) opposite of day

(b) armoured warrior on horseback

(5) (a) to run away

(b) sheep's wool

(6) (a) worn on the head

(b) a small axe

(7) (a) an adult male

(b) a large luxury home

Unit Ten

Comprehension 10

James Herriot, the vet, is looking forward to getting home. It is getting late and he is feeling very tired. In addition, he has badly cut his left forefinger and is driving with a huge bandage wrapped round it. Just then a man, waving frantically, pulls him up.

ARE YOU THE VET?

He pushed his head in at the window. 'Are you the vet?' His voice was breathless, panic-stricken.

'Yes, I am.'

'Oh thank God! We're passing through on the way to Manchester and we've been to your surgery ... they said you were out this way ... described your car. Please help us!'

'What's the trouble?'

'It's our dog ... in the back of the car. He's got a ball stuck in his throat. I ... I think he might be dead.'

I was out of my seat and running along the road before he had finished. It was a big white saloon and in the darkness of the back seat a wailing chorus issued from several little heads silhouetted against the glass.

I tore open the door and the wailing took on words.

'Oh Benny, Benny, Benny ...!'

I dimly discerned a large dog spread over the knees of four small children. 'Oh Daddy, he's dead, he's dead!'

'Let's have him out,' I gasped, and as the young man pulled on the forelegs I supported the body, which slid and top-pled on to the tarmac with a horrible limpness.

I pawed at the hairy form. 'I can't see a bloody thing! Help me pull him round.'

We dragged the unresisting bulk into the headlights' glare and I could see it all. A huge, beautiful collie in his luxuriant prime, mouth gaping, tongue lolling, eyes staring lifelessly at nothing. He wasn't breathing.

The young father took one look then gripped his head with both hands. 'Oh God, oh God....' From within the car I heard the quiet sobbing of his wife and the piercing cries from the back. 'Benny ... Benny....'

I grabbed the man's shoulder and shouted at him. 'What did you say about a ball?'

'It's in his throat ... I've had my fingers in his mouth for ages but I couldn't move it.' The words came mumbling up from beneath the bent head.

I pushed my hand into the mouth and I could feel it all right. A sphere of hard solid rubber not much bigger than a golf ball and jammed like a cork in the pharynx, effectively blocking the trachea.

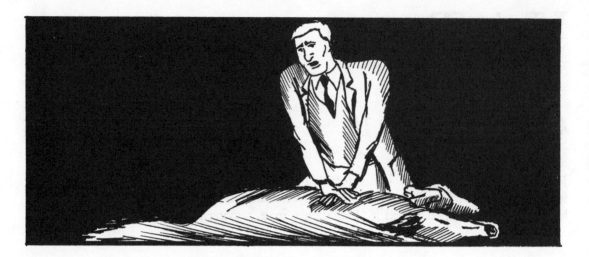

I scrabbled feverishly at the wet smoothness but there was nothing to get hold of. It took me about three seconds to realize that no human agency would get the ball out that way and without thinking I withdrew my hands, braced both thumbs behind the angle of the lower jaw and pushed.

The ball shot forth, bounced on the frosty road and rolled sadly on to the grass verge. I touched the corneal surface of the eye. No reflex. I slumped to my knees, burdened by the hopeless regret that I hadn't had the chance to do this just a bit sooner. The only function I could perform now was to take the body back to Skeldale House for disposal. I couldn't allow the family to drive to Manchester with a dead dog. But I wished fervently that I had been able to do more, and as I passed my hand along the richly coloured coat over the ribs the vast bandaged finger stood out like a symbol of my helplessness.

It was when I was gazing dully at the finger, the heel of my hand resting in an intercostal space, that I felt the faintest flutter from below.

I jerked upright with a hoarse cry. 'His heart's still beating! He's not gone yet!' I began to work on the dog with all I had. And out there in the darkness of that lonely country road it wasn't much. No stimulant injections, no oxygen cylinders or intra-tracheal tubes. But I depressed his chest with my palms every three seconds in the old-fashioned way, willing the dog to breathe as the eyes still stared at nothing. Every now and then I blew desperately down the throat or probed between the ribs for that almost imperceptible beat.

I don't know which I noticed first, the slight twitch of an eyelid or the small lift of the ribs which pulled the icy Yorkshire air into his lungs. Maybe they both happened at once but from that moment everything was dreamlike and wonderful. I lost count of time as I sat there while the breathing became deep and regular and the animal began to be aware of his surroundings; and by the time he started to look around him and twitch his tail tentatively I realized suddenly that I was stiff-jointed and almost frozen to the spot.

With some difficulty I got up and watched in disbelief as the collie staggered to his feet. The young father ushered him round to the back where he was received with screams of delight.

The man seemed stunned. Throughout the recovery he had kept muttering, 'You just flicked that ball out . . . just flicked it out. Why didn't I think of that . . .?' And when he turned to me before leaving he appeared to be still in a state of shock.

'I don't . . . I don't know how to thank you,' he said huskily. 'It's a miracle.' He leaned against the car for a second. 'And now what is your fee? How much do I owe you?'

I rubbed my chin. I had used no drugs. The only expenditure had been time.

'Five bob,' I said. 'And never let him play with such a little ball again.'

He handed the money over, shook my hand and drove away. His wife, who had never left her place, waved as she left, but my greatest reward was in the last shadowy glimpse of the back seat where little arms twined around the dog, hugging him ecstatically, and in the cries, thankful and joyous, fading into the night.

'Benny . . . Benny . . . Benny. . . .'

from *Vets Might Fly*
by JAMES HERRIOT

How Well Did You Understand?

(1) 'Are you the vet?' What two things about the man's voice tell the vet that the matter is urgent?

(2) What has happened to the dog?

(3) Why are the children in the back of the car wailing?

(4) What method fails to remove the ball from the dog's throat?

(5) How *does* the vet succeed in getting the ball free?

(6) How does the vet test the dog for a sign of life?

(7) What suddenly gives him hope that the dog might yet be saved?

(8) Why is the vet limited to old-fashioned methods to bring the dog back to life?

(9) What actions does the vet take to bring the dog back to life?

(10) What happens to make the author say that 'from that moment everything was dreamlike and wonderful'?

(11) How is the collie welcomed back to the car by the children?

(12) Why was the father stunned and in a state of shock throughout the collie's recovery?

(13) What was the vet's greatest reward?

Dictionary Words

Look up these words from the passage in the dictionary at the back of the book.

(a) silhouetted (b) discern (c) pharynx (d) trachea (e) corneal (f) intercostal
(g) tentatively (h) ecstatically.

Language 10

Comparison of Adjectives

Look at these three sentences:

- That is an **old** house.
- The house next door is **older**.
- The house down the street is the **oldest** of the three houses.

The first sentence is a simple statement about *one* house. The second sentence makes a comparison between *two* houses. The third sentence compares *more than two* houses. Thus, adjectives have three degrees of comparison:

1 POSITIVE (one thing)	*old*
2 COMPARATIVE (two things)	*older*
3 SUPERLATIVE (more than two things)	*oldest*

The comparative degree is formed by adding 'r' or 'er'. The superlative degree is formed by adding 'st' or 'est'.

sweet	sweeter	sweetest	late	later	latest
high	higher	highest	tall	taller	tallest

When the positive form ends with 'y' preceded by a consonant, the 'y' is changed to 'i' before the 'er' or 'est' is added:

easy	easier	easiest	lovely	lovelier	loveliest

When the positive form has only one syllable, and that syllable ends with a consonant preceded by a single vowel, the consonant is doubled before the 'er' or 'est' is added.

wet	wetter	wettest	big	bigger	biggest

When adjectives have more than two syllables, their comparative and superlative degrees are usually formed by addition of the words 'more' and 'most'.

beautiful	more beautiful	most beautiful
affectionate	more affectionate	most affectionate

Some adjectives do not follow the rules just outlined. You should learn the exceptions shown in the table below.

Positive	Comparative	Superlative
good	better	best
many	more	most
little	less	least
bad	worse	worst

Table of adjectives

Copy the following table into your workbook and fill in the blanks. The first one has been done to help you.

Positive	Comparative	Superlative
large	larger	largest
	tinier	
cautious		
		best
sad		
		youngest
	more comfortable	
helpful		
		farthest
	wetter	
friendly		
		worst
	heavier	

Comparative or superlative?

Complete each of the following sentences by inserting either the comparative or the superlative form of the word in brackets.

(1) She is the .... runner in the school. [**good**]

(2) He is the .... student in the class. [**conscientious**]

(3) James is the .... of the twins. [**tall**]

(4) Of the three sisters, Rebecca is the .... [**slim**]

(5) That was the .... thing you could have done. [**bad**]

(6) His right arm is the .... one. [**strong**]

(7) Who is the ...., Jennifer or Allison? [**fast**]

(8) It was the .... examination I had ever attempted. [**easy**]

(9) Duncan is .... than Trent. [**lazy**]

(10) He is the .... of the three sons. [**young**]

Completing the comparisons

Correctly insert the positive, comparative or superlative form of each of the missing adjectives. The first one has been done to help you.

(1) Hot is to ...*hotter*... as ....*cold*.... is to colder.

(2) Good is to .... as .... is to worse.

(3) .... is to prettiest as lovelier is to ....

(4) Thin is to .... as .... is to fatter.

(5) .... is to least as more is to ....

(6) .... is to highest as wide is to ....

(7) Healthy is to .... as .... is to sicker.

(8) Glad is to .... as .... is to happier.

(9) .... is to cleaner as dirty is to ....

(10) Bigger is to .... as .... is to greatest.

Punctuation 10

The Comma Continued

A comma is used to separate the name of the person addressed, or spoken to, from the rest of the sentence.

EXAMPLES:
- Mr Herriot, this dog is sick.
- Is that you, doctor?
- Come on, Benny, everything is going to be all right.

Inserting commas

Mark off with a comma or commas the name of the person addressed or spoken to in each of the following.

(1) The collie has a ball stuck in his throat Mr Herriot.

(2) Doctor please come quickly!

(3) Tell us about your collie Mrs Alexander.

(4) You just plucked that ball out of his throat Geoff.

(5) Daddy I think he's just a wonderful dog.

(6) Thank you Mr Herriot for everything you've done.

(7) Here's a ball for you to catch Benny.

(8) Nurse how is the patient coming along?

(9) I need a second opinion Professor Lawrence on this urgent case.

(10) Doctor Morton I would like to make veterinary medicine my career.

Creative Writing 10

The passage that follows is from *The Slum Cat* by Ernest Thompson Seton and is notable for the way in which the writer uses words and phrases with great care and precision. Because of this, the actions and ideas are always interesting and full of vitality. Let's look at the way the writer chooses words and phrases to gain the interest and involvement of the reader. But first of all, read and enjoy the passage.

KITTY HEADS FOR HOME

Her sense of direction was clear; it said, 'Go south', and Kitty trotted down the foot-path between the iron rails and the fence.

Cats can go very fast up a tree or over a wall, but when it comes to the long steady trot that reels off mile after mile, hour after hour, it is not the cat-hop, but the dog-trot, that counts.

. . . She was tired and a little foot-sore. She was thinking of rest when a Dog came running to the fence near by, and broke out into such a horrible barking close to her ear that Pussy leaped in terror. She ran as hard as she could down the path, at the same time watching to see if the Dog should succeed in passing the fence. No, not yet! but he ran close by it, growling horribly, while Pussy skipped along on the safe side. The barking of the Dog grew into a low rumble — a louder rumble and roaring — a terrifying thunder. A light shone. Kitty glanced back to see, not the Dog, but a huge Black Thing with a blazing red eye coming on, yowling and spitting like a yard full of Cats. She put forth all her powers to run, made such time as she had never made before, but dared not leap the fence. She was running like a Dog, was flying, but all in vain; the monstrous pursuer overtook her, but missed her in the darkness, and hurried past to be lost in the night, while Kitty crouched gasping for breath, half a mile nearer home since that Dog began to bark.

This was her first encounter with the strange monster, strange to her eyes only; her nose seemed to know him and told her this was another landmark on the home trail. But Pussy lost much of her fear of his kind. She learned that they were very stupid and could not find her if she slipped quietly under a fence and lay still. Before morning she had encountered several of them, but escaped unharmed from all.

About sunrise she reached a nice little slum on her home trail, and was lucky enough to find several unsterilized eatables in an ash-heap. . . .

from *The Slum Cat*
by ERNEST THOMPSON SETON

Probing the Writer's Technique

(1) Look at the opening sentence. Another way this sentence could be begun is, 'Her sense of direction was clear and it told her to go south'.

Why does the original version strike the reader as more vital and interesting than the second one?

(2) Compare these two sentences:

(a) She was tired and a little foot-sore.

(b) She was suffering from fatigue and found that walking was a somewhat painful process.

Decide which of the two is the better description and explain why you think so.

(3) 'Rumble' is a word that echoes the very sound it stands for. This kind of word often adds to the vitality and excitement of the action being described.

See if you can find at least two other words in the passage which have sound-qualities and add to the vitality and excitement of the writing.

(4) Where is the climax or high point in this piece of writing?

(5) In a piece of writing, it is necessary to lead up to a climax by clear steps obvious to a reader. What two or three clear steps lead up to the climax in this piece of writing?

(6) What is the Black Thing that pursues Kitty? What clues provided by the writer led you to your answer?

(7) In this piece of writing, the reader is given a cat's-eye view of Kitty's experiences. Keeping this in mind, can you suggest why the writer uses capital letters for the various animals mentioned?

(8) The last sentence of the passage contains some rather gentle humour. In your own words, say what this humour consists of.

Your Turn to Write

Try your hand at writing about *one* of these topics:

(1) Imagine you are the boy in the picture. What are your feelings towards your dog?

(2) Imagine you are the dog in the picture. How do you feel about your master? Do you enjoy being a dog?

(3) 'It is wrong to keep pets when so many humans in the world are starving.' What are your views on this?

(4) Imagine you are a vet. Write down some of your unusual experiences, as though for a book soon to be published.

(5) Write an essay with the title 'It's a Dog's Life'.

Poetry 10

'Cat!' is an unusual poem: it presents us with a dog's thoughts as it unsuccessfully attempts to catch a cat.

CAT!

Cat!
Scat!
Atter her, atter her,
Sleeky flatterer,
Spitfire chatterer,
Scatter her, scatter her,
Off her mat!
Wuff!
Wuff!
Treat her rough!
Git her, git her,
Whiskery spitter!
Catch her, catch her,
Green-eyed scratcher!
Slathery
Slithery
Hisser,
Don't miss her!
Run till you're dithery,
Hithery
Thithery
Pfitts! Pfitts!
How she spits!
Spitch! Spatch!
Scritching the bark
Of the sycamore-tree,
She's reached her arc
And's hissing at me
Pfitts! Pfitts!
Wuff! Wuff!
Scat,
Cat!
That's
That!

ELEANOR FARJEON

Cat Questions

(1) Why is 'Cat!' a better title than 'Cat'?

(2) Why is the cat called a 'Sleeky flatterer'?

(3) What is the cat doing when it becomes a 'Spitfire chatterer'?

(4) 'Scatter her, scatter her, / Off her mat!' What do you think the dog is in the process of doing?

(5) Why is the cat called a 'Whiskery spitter'?

(6) Why is the cat referred to as a 'Green-eyed scratcher'?

(7) 'Pfitts! Pfitts! / Wuff! Wuff!' What are these sounds?

(8) What is the cat doing when 'She's reached her arc'?

(9) What words tell you that the poem has been written from a dog's point of view?

(10) The poet uses many sound-words in the poem. Jot down two or three that you liked and explain why you liked them.

(11) Briefly outline what happens in the poem.

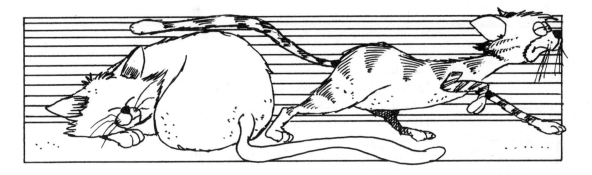

CATALOGUE

Cats sleep fat and walk thin.
Cats, when they sleep, slump;
When they wake, stretch and begin
Over, pulling their ribs in.
Cats walk thin.

Cats wait in a lump,
Jump in a streak.
Cats, when they jump, are sleek
As a grape slipping its skin —
They have technique.
Oh, cats don't creak.
They sneak.

Cats sleep fat.
They spread out comfort underneath them
Like a good mat,
As if they picked the place
And then sat;
You walk around one
As if he were the City Hall
After that.

If male,
A cat is apt to sing on a major scale;
This concert is for everybody, this
Is wholesale.
For a baton, he wields a tail.

(He is also found,
When happy, to resound
With an enclosed and private sound.)

A cat condenses.
He pulls in his tail to go under bridges,
And himself to go under fences.
Cats fit
In any size box or kit,
And if a large pumpkin grew under one,
He could arch over it.

When everyone else is just ready to go out,
The cat is just ready to come in.
He's not where he's been.
Cats sleep fat and walk thin.

ROSALIE MOORE

Catalogue Questions

(1) 'Cats sleep fat and walk thin.' What does the poet mean by these words?

(2) To what does the poet compare cats' sleek jumping? Do you think this is a good comparison? Why?

(3) What is the main point the poet makes about a cat's singing?

(4) What would you call the 'enclosed and private sound' of a cat?

(5) 'A cat condenses.' When does this happen?

(6) 'When everyone else is just ready to go out, / The cat is just ready to come in.' What do these words suggest about a cat's nature?

(7) A catalogue is a complete list. Can you suggest two reasons why the poet called her poem 'Catalogue'?

(8) Which stanza of the poem did you like best? Explain why.

Spelling 10

ARE YOU THE VET?

veterinarian	description	persevered	miracle	impossible
supported	symbol	recovery	miraculous	wonderful
horrible	hoarse	disbelief	satisfaction	received
tongue	injection	realized	oxygen	delightfully

Missing Words

As you read through *Vet on the Job*, decide which words from the spelling box will fit the blank spaces. Write these words into your workbook. Note the clue-letters given.

Vet on the Job

When the .... looked in d........... at the dog, he noticed that its .... was enlarged and the poor creature had a .... wound. He r........... that it would take a .... to save its life. The owner s........... the animal on the operating table while the vet gave it an .... and administered .... through a face-mask. The dog's r........... seemed i..........., but everyone r........... a w........... feeling of s........... when it walked again after a week's recuperation. The .... cure had been accomplished.

Word Forms

Rewrite the following sentences in your workbook, changing each word given in brackets into its correct form.

(1) The vet showed great [**persevere**] in his treatment of the sick cat.

(2) At first I [**disbelief**] him when he told me his dog had survived the accident.

(3) An adequate supply of hay will [**satisfaction**] a horse.

(4) What a [**delightfully**] puppy!

(5) Imagine my [**horrible**] when I heard the screech of the car's brakes.

(6) According to the vet, there was a certain amount of [**hoarse**] in the dog's bark.

(7) The vet prepared to [**injection**] the horse with an antibiotic.

(8) Herriot's novels are very [**description**].

(9) The [**realized**] that her pet was cured came suddenly to the girl.

Share-A-Letter

The shared letters shown in the following pairs will enable you to find the right words in the spelling box.

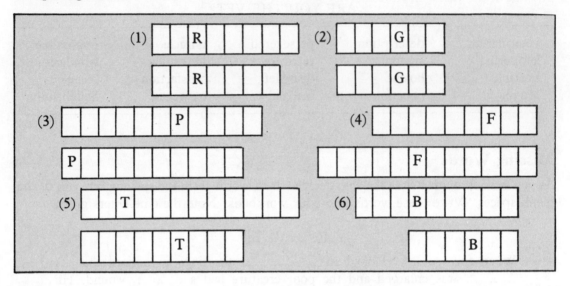

Try Thinking 10

Rearrangements

Rearrange the items in each of the following groups so that each group begins with the smallest item and grades to the largest. (For example: SLICE LOAF CRUST CRUMB *would become* CRUMB CRUST SLICE LOAF.)

(1) body   hand   finger   arm

(2) adolescent   adult   baby   child

(3) sentence   syllable   letter   word

(4) village   room   city   town   house

(5) lake   ocean   drop   sea   pool

(6) tree   stick   log   forest   splinter

(7) mountain   universe   planet   solar system   continent

(8) sergeant   captain   private   lieutenant   corporal

(9) tree   seed   apple   orchard   core

(10) fowl   elephant   bee   mouse   horse

Bye Buy

The two pictures show the shelves of the shop before and after a customer has been in to buy one of the vases. In choosing his vase, he's had the manager show him every one, and the remaining vases have been put back in a different order. Which vase did the customer buy? (Answer on p. 259.)

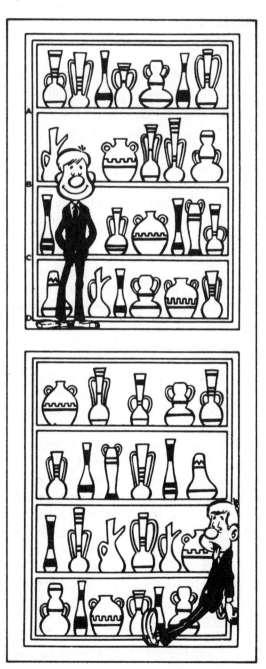

Unit Eleven

Comprehension 11

Dr Howard Florey was one of the men who gave the world the wonder-drug penicillin. Here is the story of the first test of penicillin on a human being.

THE FIRST TEST

At Oxford, Florey had put his entire department on penicillin. Now he was getting penicillin infinitely more pure than the earlier batches, and the power of this concentrated stuff was staggering — diluted a million to one it could still kill microbes!

Early in February of 1941, after nearly two years of hard work, the pile of penicillin seemed large enough to treat one human patient.

Dr Charles Fletcher was selected to give the first treatment. When he took his vial of penicillin over to the Radcliffe Infirmary, the doctors there picked out their man — an Oxford policeman, forty-three years old, who had been in the hospital for four months. He had come in with a little sore at the corner of his mouth — a sore that stubbornly refused to heal and instead began to spread. Sulfa drugs did him no good; his was a breed of germs which were resistant to sulfas. Now he was dying from a combined staphylococcus and streptococcus infection of his face, scalp, both eyes, lungs, bones, and blood.

Fletcher examined the policeman. He was emaciated, moaning in pain, too weak even to lift an arm. He was coughing up pus. In spite of blood transfusions, his blood count was almost at rock bottom.

Fletcher took two hundred milligrams — less than one hundredth of an ounce — of his white powder, dissolved it in water, sucked up the clear liquid in a syringe, and then injected it into the policeman's arm muscles. Three hours later he put a shot of one hundred milligrams into the policeman's veins. All through the day, every three hours, another tiny dose of penicillin was injected. After the first twelve hours the patient was still alive — but that was the best you could say.

'We'll keep it up all night, every three hours,' Fletcher said.

The next day a nurse, hardly believing it herself, wrote on the policeman's chart: 'Striking improvement.'

The policeman was not merely alive — he was getting better! His temperature was down a little, his pain was disappearing, his lungs sounded better, and the laboratory sent back an encouraging report on his blood count. Here, for the first time, penicillin was bringing a man back from the grave.

It was a Wednesday when they started the treatment. By Friday, even the regular

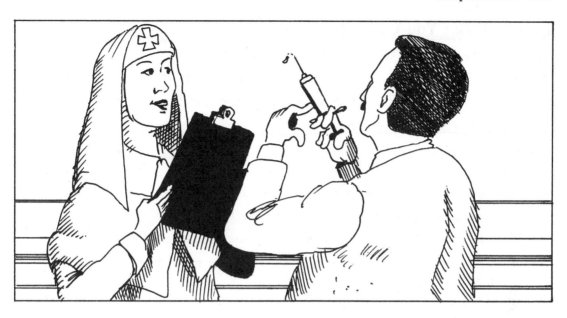

hospital doctor was beaming.

They were by no means through. The policeman was amazingly better, but he was not cured, and the little stockpile of penicillin was almost exhausted. The scientists rushed back to the patient's bedside. 'Collect every ounce of this man's urine and send it over to the laboratory,' they directed. 'He's excreting a lot of penicillin through his kidneys. Maybe we can get some of it back.'

Now they began a desperate attempt to get penicillin out of the policeman's urine, purify it, concentrate it again, and inject it back into him.

For a while this grotesque routine seemed to work. On Saturday the nurse jotted down again, 'Continued improvement'. On Sunday they had to interrupt treatment from noon to six o'clock at night until they could recapture more penicillin from the urine bottles, but the policeman was improving steadily, his blood count was climbing back, and one infected eye was practically normal.

On Monday the nurse greeted the doctors with cheering news. 'He's much better this morning,' she announced. 'What about the injections today? Do we continue the usual ...'

'No,' said the doctors. 'No injections today. We've run out of penicillin.'

'But he's been doing so well! Can't you make some more?'

'It would take weeks, and he'll be dead by then.'

He was.

'The attempt to treat this forlorn case was chiefly valuable in that it showed that penicillin could be given over a period of five days without significant toxic effect,' Florey and his group reported. 'Later experience showed that the dose of penicillin employed was too small, and the period of administration too short.'

One vital lesson came out of the dramatic case of the dying policeman: *Give enough penicillin, and give it long enough, or you'll lose your patient.*

from *Magic in a Bottle*
by MILTON SILVERMAN

How Well Did You Understand?

(1) Why was the power of pure penicillin 'staggering'?

(2) Why had it become possible to treat one human patient by early February 1941?

(3) A policeman was chosen for treatment with penicillin. Why was he chosen?

(4) How sick was the policeman?

(5) How was the penicillin given to him?

(6) How did the nurse describe the policeman's condition after he had been treated with penicillin for a day and a night?

(7) What signs of improvement could be seen in the policeman?

(8) How did the scientists try to increase their stock of penicillin?

(9) What crisis occurred on the Monday on which the nurse greeted the doctors with cheering news?

(10) What was the tragic result of the lack of penicillin?

(11) 'Later experience showed that the dose of penicillin employed was too small, and the period of administration too short.' Explain this statement in your own words.

(12) What vital lesson was learnt from the case of the dying policeman?

Dictionary Words

Give the meanings of the following words from the passage. You may like to refer to the back-of-the-book dictionary.

(a) infinitely   (b) emaciated   (c) excreting   (d) grotesque   (e) forlorn   (f) toxic.

Language 11

Adverbs

As their name suggests, adverbs add to the meaning of verbs. They tell *how, when, where* or *why* the action of the verb takes place. Look at the adverbs in heavy type in the following sentences. The adverbs add to the meaning of the verbs, which are in italics. As you can see, adverbs often end with 'ly'.

- The sore **stubbornly** *refused* to heal.
- The policeman *was improving* **steadily**.
- The little stockpile of penicillin *was* **almost** *exhausted*.

As well as adding to the meaning of verbs, adverbs can add to the meaning of adjectives. In the following, the adjectives are in italics.

* One infected eye was **practically** *normal*.
* The policeman was **amazingly** *better*.
* The dose of penicillin employed was **too** *small* and the period of administration **too** *short*.

Finally, adverbs can even add to the meaning of other adverbs. The adverbs being added to in the following example are in italics.

* Now he was getting penicillin **infinitely** *more* pure and responding **surprisingly** *fast*.

Selecting adverbs

Insert the appropriate adverbs from the box into the spaces below. Use each adverb only once.

cheaply	daily	stealthily	sweetly	nostalgically	contentedly
fiercely	lazily	secretly	mortally	wildly	carefully

(1) The fire burnt ....

(2) The cattle grazed ....

(3) The soldier was .... wounded.

(4) The conspirators plotted ....

(5) The newspaper was printed ....

(6) The army charged ....

(7) The old man .... remembered his childhood.

(8) The shop-owner sold the goods ....

(9) The sleepy cat stretched ....

(10) The young woman sang ....

(11) The doctor .... examined the wound.

(12) The burglar crept .... through the warehouse.

Forming adverbs

Form adverbs from these words. The first one has been done to help you.

(1) grateful ....*gratefully*....   (5) drowsy ....   (9) gradual ....

(2) busy ....   (6) brutal ....   (10) poetic ....

(3) accurate ....   (7) hungry ....   (11) guilty ....

(4) useful ....   (8) sympathetic ....   (12) responsible ....

(13) respectful .... (17) necessary .... (21) frantic ....

(14) happy .... (18) sincere .... (22) conscious ....

(15) lawful .... (19) honourable .... (23) cruel ....

(16) personal .... (20) courteous .... (24) sensible ....

Adverbs and their opposites

Write down adverbs that are opposite in meaning to the adverbs in heavy type.

(1) The manager spoke **angrily**.

(2) The driver was **slightly** injured.

(3) The train arrived **late**.

(4) The criminal answered **falsely**.

(5) A noise was heard **above**.

(6) The footballer **deliberately** tripped his opponent.

(7) The children were playing **outside**.

(8) The sounds of birds were **often** heard.

(9) The motorist drove the car **recklessly**.

(10) The traveller **wearily** climbed the hill.

(11) The principal **hurriedly** left the hall.

(12) The girl spoke **clearly**.

(13) The light shone **brightly**.

(14) The storeman **clumsily** packed the boxes.

(15) The student addressed the teacher **respectfully**.

Adverbs and adjectives

Insert the appropriate adverbs and adjectives from the box into the spaces provided in the passage at the top of the page opposite.

cunning	flat	across	always	noiseless
intently	down	more	few	deep
silently	loathsome	glassy	hideous	least
so	wide	quickly	mercilessly	there

A Most Dangerous Creature

There is nothing that one comes .... in hunting m.......... horrible and l.......... than the crocodile; nothing that s.......... surely and q.......... gives the sensation of 'creeps in the back' as the n.......... sight of one in the water just where you l.......... expected it, or the discovery of one s.......... and i.......... watching you, with its head resting .... on the sand-spit. A.......... there is the feeling of horror that this h.........., cowardly, cruel thing — the enemy of man and beast alike — with its look of a c.......... smile in its green, g.......... eyes and its great w.......... mouth, will m.......... drag you down — down — down to the bottom of some d.........., still pool, and hold you t.......... till you drown. It is all done in silence: a .... bubbles come up where a man went ....; and that is the end of it.

Adapted from *Jock of the Bushveld* by SIR PERCY FITZPATRICK

Punctuation 11

More Fun with Punctuation

Have fun using the comma, the full stop, the question mark and the exclamation mark as you correctly punctuate each of the following humorous items.

(1) *Question:* What ghost haunts an educational building
   Answer: The school spirit

(2) *Teacher:* Only an idiot would say that he was absolutely certain about anything
   Student: Are you sure about that Miss
   Teacher: Of course I am

(3) *Question:* What usually runs in families
   Answer: Noses

(4) *Question:* What has fifty heads but can't think
   Answer: A box of matches

(5) *Teacher (to a little girl crying bitterly):* What's the matter
   Little girl: My shoes are hurting me
   Teacher (exclaiming): Well you've got them on the wrong feet
   Little girl (loudly and fearfully): These are the only feet I've got

(6) *Question:* Why didn't the worms go into the Ark in pairs
   Answer: Because they went in apples

Creative Writing 11

The Climax, or High Point of Action

In a piece of creative writing intended to tell a story, the writer often leads up to a climax or high point of the action. The following piece is from the horror story *Dracula* by Bram Stoker, and it contains a definite climax!

GORGED

Then a wild desire took me to obtain that key at any risk and I determined then and there to scale the wall again and gain the Count's room. He might kill me, but death now seemed the happier choice of evils. Without a pause I rushed up to the east window and scrambled down the wall, as before, into the Count's room. It was empty, but that was as I expected. I could not see a key anywhere, but the heap of gold remained. I went through the door in the corner and down the winding stair and along the dark passage to the old chapel. I knew now well enough where to find the monster I sought.

The great box was in the same place, close against the wall, but the lid was laid on it, not fastened down, but with the nails ready in their places to be hammered home. I knew I must search the body for the key, so I raised the lid and laid it back against the wall; and then I saw something which filled my very soul with horror. There lay the Count, but looking as if his youth had been half-renewed, for the white hair and moustache were changed to dark iron grey; the cheeks were fuller, and the white skin seemed ruby-red underneath; the mouth was redder than ever, for on the lips were gouts of fresh blood, which trickled from the corners of the mouth and ran over the chin and neck. Even the deep, burning eyes seemed set amongst swollen flesh for the lids and pouches underneath were bloated. It seemed as if the whole awful creature were simply gorged with blood; he lay like a filthy leech, exhausted with his repletion. I shuddered as I bent over to touch him, and every sense in me revolted at the contact; but I had to search, or I was lost. The coming night might see my own body a banquet in a similar way to those horrid three. I felt all over the body, but no sign could I find of the key. Then I stopped and looked at the Count. There was a mocking smile on the bloated face which seemed to drive me mad. This was the being I was

helping to transfer to London, where, perhaps for centuries to come, he might amongst teeming millions satiate his lust for blood, and create a new, and ever widening circle of semi-demons to batten on the helpless. The very thought drove me mad. A terrible desire came over me to rid the world of such a monster. There was no lethal weapon at hand, but I seized a shovel which the workmen had been using to fill the cases, and lifting it high, struck, with the edge downward, at the hateful face. But as I did so the head turned, and the eyes fell full upon me, with all their blaze of basilisk horror. The sight seemed to paralyse me, and the shovel turned in my hand and glanced from the face, merely making a deep gash above the forehead. The shovel fell from my hand across the box, and as I pulled it away the flange of the blade caught the edge of the lid, which fell over again, and hid the horrid thing from my sight. The last glimpse I had was of the bloated face, bloodstained and fixed with a grin of malice which would have held its own in the nethermost hell.

from *Dracula* by BRAM STOKER

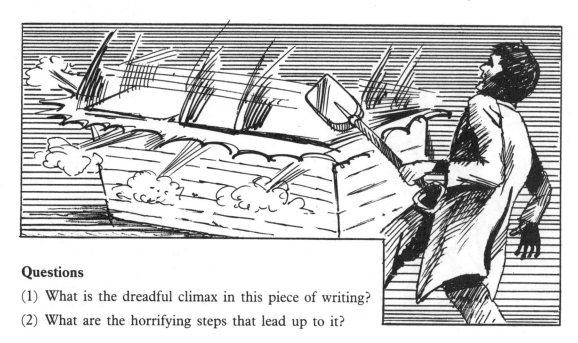

Questions

(1) What is the dreadful climax in this piece of writing?

(2) What are the horrifying steps that lead up to it?

The piece of creative writing that follows is from *The Hound of the Baskervilles* by Sir Arthur Conan Doyle and contains the climax of the story. Read — and tremble!

HOUNDED

'Hist!' cried Holmes, and I heard the sharp click of a cocking pistol. 'Look out!' It's coming!'

There was a thin, crisp, continuous patter from somewhere in the heart of that crawling bank. The cloud was within fifty yards of where we lay, and we glared at it, all three, uncertain what horror was about to break from the heart of it. I was at Holmes's elbow, and I glanced for an instant at his face. It was pale and exultant, his eyes shining brightly in the moonlight. But suddenly they started forward in a rigid, fixed stare, and his lips parted in amazement. At the same instant Lestrade gave a yell of terror and threw himself face downwards upon the ground. I sprang to my feet, my inert hand grasping my pistol, my mind paralysed by the dreadful shape which had sprung out upon us from the

shadows of the fog. A hound it was, an enormous coal-black hound, but not such a hound as mortal eyes have ever seen. Fire burst from its open mouth, its eyes glowed with a smouldering glare, its muzzle and hackles and dewlap were outlined in flickering flame. Never in the delirious dream of a disordered brain could anything more savage, more appalling, more hellish, be conceived than that dark form and savage face which broke upon us out of the wall of fog.

With long bounds the huge black creature was leaping down the track, following hard upon the footsteps of our friend. So paralysed were we by the apparition that we allowed him to pass before we had recovered our nerve. Then Holmes and I both fired together, and the creature gave a hideous howl, which showed that one at least had hit him. He did not pause, however, but bounded onwards. Far away on the path we saw Sir Henry looking back, his face white in the moonlight, his hands raised in horror, glaring helplessly at the frightful thing which was hunting him down.

But that cry of pain from the hound had blown all our fears to the winds. If he was vulnerable he was mortal, and if we could wound him we could kill him. Never have I seen a man run as Holmes ran that night. I am reckoned fleet of foot, but he outpaced me as much as I outpaced the little professional. In front of us as we flew up the track we heard scream after scream from Sir Henry and the deep roar of the hound. I was in time to see the beast spring upon its victim, hurl him to the ground and worry at his throat. But the next instant Holmes had emptied five barrels of his revolver into the creature's flank. With a last howl of agony and a vicious snap in the air it rolled upon its back, four feet pawing furiously, and then fell limp upon its side. I stooped, panting, and pressed my pistol to the dreadful, shimmering head, but it was useless to press the trigger. The giant hound was dead.

from *The Hound of the Baskervilles*
by SIR ARTHUR CONAN DOYLE

Questions

(1) Our attention is immediately gripped in the opening sentence. What technique is used by the writer to achieve this?

(2) How is our interest sustained and kept at a high level as we approach the moment of climax?

(3) In your own words, say at what point in the action the climax actually comes.

The next passage is from *I Can Jump Puddles* by Alan Marshall. It deals with a crisis and a climax in a young boy's life — an operation on his legs.

SCARED

Nurse Conrad wheeled me down a long corridor and through glass doors into the theatre in the centre of which stood a high table with thin, white legs.

Sister Cooper and a nurse were standing near a bench upon which steel instruments lay on a white cloth.

'Well, here you are!' exclaimed the sister walking over to me and stroking my head.

I looked into her eyes, seeking assurance there.

'Feeling frightened?' she asked.
'Yes.'
'You silly boy. There's nothing to be frightened of. In a minute you'll go to sleep and after a little while you'll wake up in your bed again.'

I could not understand how this was possible. I was certain I would wake up from any sleep if the nurses tried to move me. I wondered whether they were just saying this to fool me and that, instead of

waking up in my bed, something painful was going to happen to me. But I believed Nurse Conrad.

'I'm not frightened,' I said to the sister.

'I know you're not,' she said confidentially as she lifted me on to the table and placed a low pillow beneath my head. 'Now don't move or you'll roll off.',

Dr Robertson entered briskly and stood smiling down at me as he massaged his fingers.

'"Sh! Sh! Go out black cat", so that's the song you sing, is it?'

He patted me and turned away.

'Abbot buggies and black cats, eh!' he murmured as a nurse came forward and helped him into a white gown. "Abbot buggies and black cats! Well! Well!'

Dr Clarke, a grey-haired man with a tight-lipped mouth, walked in.

'The Council hasn't filled in that hole near the gate yet,' he said, turning to face a nurse holding his white gown up in front of her ready for him to slip it on. 'I don't know ... Can you rely on any man's word these days? This gown seems too big ... No, it's mine all right.'

I looked at the white ceiling and thought of the puddle near our gate that always came after rain; I could jump it easily but Mary couldn't. I could jump any puddle.

Dr Clarke had moved round to my head where he stood holding a hollowed, white pad like a shell, above my nose.

At a sign from Dr Robertson he saturated the pad with liquid he poured from a little blue bottle and I gasped as I drew a laden breath. I jerked my head from side to side but he followed my nose with the pad and I saw coloured lights, then clouds came and I floated away upon them.

from *I Can Jump Puddles*
by ALAN MARSHALL

Questions

(1) Even in the first sentence, the impending climax is suggested by Alan's surroundings. How do his surroundings set the tone for the climax?

(2) As Alan is being prepared for the trial ahead, he finds that other members of the hospital staff do not share his anxiety. How is this indicated?

(3) How does Alan mentally prepare *himself* for the operation?

(4) What does he *really* mean when he thinks to himself that he 'could jump any puddle'?

(5) In your own words, say what the climax is in this piece of writing.

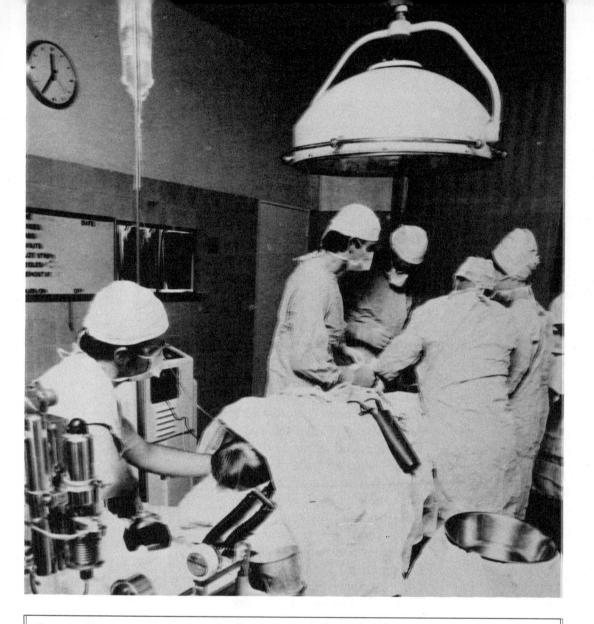

Your Turn to Write

See how well you can write using *one* of these topics:

(1) Write a composition beginning, "Emergency! Emergency!"

(2) Write a story entitled 'The Time I Went into Hospital'.

(3) Imagine you are a nurse in a busy public hospital. Write some diary entries for two or three of your busier, more dramatic days.

(4) A Day in the Life of a Doctor.

(5) You are going to have an operation. What are your thoughts as you are being wheeled into the operating theatre?

Poetry 11

Even when she is dealing with such a serious subject as someone's operation, Pam Ayres's flair for humour still manages to come to the fore.

EVER SINCE I HAD ME OP

Hello, it's nice to see you looking well,
What? How am I?
I haven't been so good myself
But I've been getting by,
Yes, I've had a bit of trouble
Well, I wouldn't bore a friend
But if you knew how much I'd suffered
Well, your hair would stand on end.

No, I'm not one to complain
And we all have our cross to bear,
And I wouldn't even tell you
What they did to me in there.
If you asked how many stitches
I wouldn't let it cross my lips,
Well all right then, twenty-seven
And that's not including clips.

Course, it was only fifty-fifty,
On the drip all night and day.
Oh they gave me all the lot
And then they took it all away.
You wouldn't have recognized me
And I'm glad I never seen ya
And the doctor on the case
Gave up and went back home. To Kenya.

Well, I know you're in a hurry
And you haven't time to stop,
And I've just seen Deirdre,
She'll want to know about me op.
And there's always someone worse off
Than youself, without a doubt,
In my case I haven't met him
But I'm sure that he's about.

And you're healthy dear, enjoy it
For it fades away so soon,
Now I've got me eighteen pills
So I'll get through this afternoon.
Don't give a thought to how I've suffered
I'm the last one to complain,
And I'll keep on smiling through it all
Until we meet again.

PAM AYRES

Probing the Poem for Details

(1) Jot down some of the words and phrases the main character uses to try to prove to her friend that she was very sick in hospital.

(2) What clues tell you that the speaker enjoys describing her operation?

(3) Why does she say 'I'm glad I never seen ya'?

(4) What happened to her doctor?

(5) 'Well, I know you're in a hurry / And you haven't time to stop, . . .' Why does the main character suddenly say this to her friend?

(6) Why is the poem's title a better one than the title 'Ever Since I Had My Operation' would be?

(7) Did you find the poem humorous or serious? Give a reason for your viewpoint.

(8) What kind of person do you think the speaker is?

Spelling 11

PENICILLIN

scientist	infection	laboratory	disappearing	purify
dissolve	illness	vein	exhausted	practically
interrupt	thermometer	emergency	administration	individual
valuable	deteriorate	encouragement	hygiene	penicillin

Missing Words

As you read through *Penicillin*, decide on the words from the spelling box which will fit the blank spaces. Write down these words in your workbook. Note that some clue-letters are given to help you.

Penicillin

Before the discovery of .... an i............... that was basically caused by an i............... could cause a person to d............... in health until there was .... no hope left. However, in an Oxford l............... a most w............... wonder drug was developed which would not only i............... the progress of a disease but also cure it. Another advantage was that it could be given by mouth instead of having to be injected into a .... This was the kind of e............... that was needed to make penicillin available world-wide.

Using the Clues

Go to words in the spelling box for answers to the following.

(1) Another word for 'sickness' is ....

(2) An artery is one kind of blood vessel. Another kind is a ....

(3) An instrument for measuring temperature is a ....

(4) The opposite of 'improve' is ....

(5) Another word for 'vanishing' is ....

(6) If you feel worn out, you feel ....

(7) Every person is an ....

(8) A place where scientific experiments are carried out is a ....

Jumbled Words

Unjumble the spelling-box words given in brackets.

(1) Her .... [snelisll] is not serious.

(2) These tablets will .... [odsivels] in water.

(3) This is an .... [gemreeync]!

(4) The needle entered the .... [neiv] without difficulty.

(5) In our fitness course, health and .... [nigeyeh] are important subjects.

(6) Every .... [lauidvindi] is treated differently.

(7) The hospital .... [toniratsindiima] gave Florey several patients to care for.

(8) Always shake down the mercury in a .... [mommrhteeet] before taking a patient's temperature.

(9) The microscope is a .... [lavbaleu] item of .... [robroylaat] equipment.

Try Thinking 11

Contagious Disease!

Examine the clues to find the words numbered 1–7 across. Then read down to discover the name of a contagious disease.

Clues

1 Worn on the face by a doctor or nurse at an operation.

2 The sharp cutting instrument used by a surgeon.

3 The room where an operation is performed.

4 The name for the sign of a disease or illness.

5 Florence Nightingale was called "The lady with the .....".

6 The female or male assisting member of a medical team.

7 A short word for 'painful'.

Arrow Words

In this puzzle, all you have to do is use the clues to find the nine words. Each word contains the letter 'n'.

Clues

1 The darkness that comes when the sun sets.

2 Another word for 'beneath'.

3 A pair of .... hose.

4 To say numbers in sequence.

5 A form of transport that runs on lines.

6 Lean to one side.

7 Useful and convenient.

8 An unusual trick or way of behaving.

9 A running loop in the end of a cord or rope.

1	N				
2		N			
3			N		
4				N	
5					N
6				N	
7			N		
8		N			
9	N				

Decoding

Each of the nine letters in the grid below is represented by the shape formed by the lines around the letter. For examples, R = ⌐¬ .

Key:	M	U	P
	A	C	L
	E	R	H

Decode the following and discover the names of four fruits.

(1) ∟ ¬ ⊐ ☐ Γ   (2) ∟ ⊏ ⊔ ⌐   (3) ⊐ ∟ ∟ ⊏ ¬

(4) ∟ ¬ ⊐ ⊓

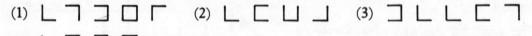

Signing On

Each of the following word-signs hints at a familiar saying or phrase. See if you can decipher them. (Answers on p. 259.)

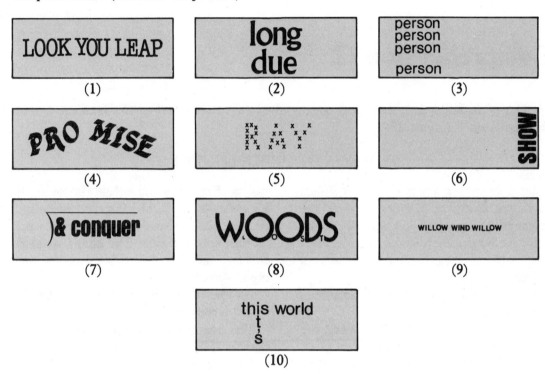

(1) LOOK YOU LEAP

(2) long due

(3) person person person / person

(4) PRO MISE

(5)

(6) SHOW

(7))& conquer

(8) W.O.O.D.S

(9) WILLOW WIND WILLOW

(10) this world / t's

Unit Twelve

Comprehension 12

The Day of the Bomb describes the dropping of the first atom bomb on the Japanese city of Hiroshima on 6 August 1945.

THE DEATH OF HIROSHIMA

Colonel Tibbets, captain of the B29, *Enola Gay*, was flying at 31 600 feet over the centre of the town of Hiroshima. In the hold, the bombardier, Major Ferebee, was busy with the mechanism that was to release the bomb.

Now Ferebee took aim at his objective. The bomb dropped.

With a diabolical whistling scream, the monster hurtled downwards.

The crew of the *Enola Gay* pulled dark glasses over the eyepieces in their oxygen masks, as they had been told to do. None of the flyers knew the point of wearing these dark glasses. None of them knew what would happen in the next few minutes. They were merely carrying out strict instructions.

And all of them waited, all of them numb. And they listened, and thought they could hear the whine of the falling bomb. But it was not the whining they could hear, it was the rush of blood which their wildly beating hearts sent pounding through their veins. And all of them, with stony faces, stared blankly into space, motionless, paralysed by the faint inkling of a disaster such as the world had never known.

The watch on Colonel Tibbets's wrist was unaffected by the violent throbbing of his pulse. Inside it, tiny cogs were turning, each revolution sending one second after another into the past. The hands stood at fourteen minutes, thirty-five seconds past eight o'clock.

On the bomb, an ingenious device released a parachute.

The bomb drifted downwards on its parachute.

The hands on the watch pointed to fourteen minutes and fifty seconds past eight o'clock.

At that moment the bomb was 2000 feet above the ground.

And when, at fifteen minutes past eight, it had dropped a further 500 feet, a scientific device lit a fuse inside the bomb. Neutrons split the atomic nucleus of the heavy metal, uranium 235, and this splitting continued in a series of unbelievably rapid chain reactions.

In the millionth part of a second, a new sun flamed in the sky, a glaring white light.

A hundred times brighter than the heavenly sun.

And this ball of fire radiated several million degrees of heat on to the city of Hiroshima.

At that moment 86 100 people were burned to death.

At that moment 72 000 people were severely injured.

At that moment 6820 houses were blown to pieces, and the vacuum thus created sucked them several miles into the air as particles of dust.

At that moment, too, 3750 buildings collapsed, and the ruins began to burn.

At that one moment deadly neutrons and gamma-rays bombarded the site of the explosion over an area of three-quarters of a mile.

At that moment man, made in God's image, had used his powers of scientific invention to make his first attempt to destroy himself.

The attempt succeeded.

The *Enola Gay* had made a half-turn south-westwards. Soon after dropping the bomb, the crew had seen a flash of light that dazzled them for several seconds, despite their dark glasses. The glaring, sudden flash was followed by a roll of thunder that drowned even the noise of the engines. Immediately afterwards the plane was shaken as if it had suddenly run into a storm zone. At first the flyers could not believe that all these phenomena were the consequence merely of the bomb explosion. They had neither expected nor ever experienced such monstrous repercussions. At first they thought the bomb must have hit a large ammunition dump; but now they saw a gigantic mushroom of smoke rearing up more than half a mile above the spot where the bomb had been dropped. And they saw that the head of this sinister mushroom was composed of balls of fire, surpassing any human notion of the fires of Hell. There was something so diabolical about this fire incarnate that the watchers remained motionless in their seats, as if paralysed.

Colonel Tibbets stared wildly at the dreadful mushroom of smoke and flame. With a faint conception of the most colossal disaster ever to have struck a human community, he was the first to pull off his dark glasses and look down. But instead of the sea of houses that composed Hiroshima he saw only swirling brown smoke. He tried to account for what had happened. The *Enola Gay* had carried a bomb. Only one! He had seen it. It had been scarcely bigger than any of the many thousand-pound bombs dropped on enemy objectives in earlier attacks. It had only been a different shape. And it had been attached to a parachute instead of hurtling freely down. Was it possible for a bomb of only average size to annihilate a whole town? No; it was impossible. It could not be. Because it would be inhuman. And because such a devilish invention could not have been thought of by men in their right minds. Yes, the answer was that such a thing was impossible.

But what his eyes showed him was no imagination. The city of Hiroshima was almost completely enveloped in smoke from the explosion.

from *The Day of the Bomb*
by KARL BRUCKNER

How Well Did You Understand?

(1) 'Diabolical' means 'of the devil'. Why is this a good word to use to describe the scream of the bomb?

(2) 'None of the flyers knew the point of wearing these dark glasses'. Why had the flyers been instructed to wear them?

(3) What does the writer aim to show the reader by his use of statistics?

(4) The bomb killed people and destroyed buildings. What other horrors did it produce?

(5) Why do you think the writer has used the words 'made in God's image' in referring to the inventors of the atomic bomb?

(6) What evidence can you find to show that the crew had no idea of the destruction the bomb would bring to Hiroshima?

(7) How do you know that the noise of the bomb exploding was extremely loud?

(8) What effect did the exploding of the bomb have on the plane?

(9) What effect did the sight of the fireballs in the mushroom cloud have upon the flyers?

(10) In what way was the bomb's descent different from that of other bombs?

(11) Why was Colonel Tibbets so amazed that the bomb he had dropped was able to annihilate a whole town?

(12) What clues tell you that the writer does not approve of the dropping of the first atom bomb?

Dictionary Words

Give the meaning of each of the following words. You might like to use the back-of-the-book dictionary.

(a) phenomena   (b) surpassing   (c) incarnate   (d) conception   (e) annihilate.

Language 12

Meaning and Context

When you consult a dictionary to learn the meaning of a word, you often find that a word does not have just one meaning but a number of meanings. The numerous meanings that a word may possess help to enrich our language. One invaluable aid to determining a word's meaning is the *context* in which the word is used. The context is the surrounding words and ideas. Look carefully at the following two sentences in which the word 'boil' is used.

- The doctor lanced the **boil**.
- The water had started to **boil**.

In the first sentence we quickly recognize that the word 'boil' is used to denote *a sore* of a kind most of us have seen — an inflamed pus-filled swelling of the skin. In the second sentence we can readily deduce from the context that the word 'boil' is used in relation to *water* changing from a liquid to a vapour.

Defining the meanings

Look at these groups of sentences. Each group contains a word (in heavy type) used in a number of ways — its meaning changes according to its context. Your task is to write down the various meanings of the words in heavy type.

(1) (a) The groom placed the **ring** on the bride's finger.
    (b) She will **ring** later in the week to make an appointment.
    (c) The **ring**leader was sent to gaol.

(2) (a) The mechanic was able to **fit** new wheels on the car.
    (b) A good sportsman needs to keep **fit**.
    (c) That bread is not **fit** to be eaten.
    (d) In a **fit** of temper, the producer stormed out of the room.

(3) (a) Please don't get **cross** with me.
    (b) Sign the document where it's marked with a **cross**.
    (c) Don't **cross** the road till the traffic stops.
    (d) Have you finished the **cross**word puzzle?

(4) (a) The champion tennis player had a good **service**.
    (b) There is a church **service** twice on Sundays.
    (c) The millionaire owned a silver dinner-**service**.
    (d) The **service** station sold diesel oil as well as petrol.

(5) (a) The **sack** was full of potatoes.
    (b) The manager decided to **sack** the drunken worker.
    (c) Because we were tired, we decided to hit the **sack** earlier than usual.
    (d) After their victory, the Vandals began to **sack** the city.

(6) (a) The bride wore a dress with a long **train**.
    (b) The players needed to **train** two nights a week for the grand final.
    (c) The **train** arrived late.

Selecting the most appropriate words

The English language has many words that are similar in meaning yet do not mean exactly the same thing. In the following exercises, you need to select from the boxes the most appropriate words to fit in the spaces. Each word is to be used only once.

(1) | archaic ancient obsolete antique old senile |

    (a) The .... Egyptians designed their own alphabet.
    (b) The Spitfire fighter plane of World War II is now ....
    (c) Their grandmother is now so .... that she has to be cared for like a baby..
    (d) .... furniture is often very valuable.
    (e) 'Methinks' is an .... word.
    (f) When P.G. Wodehouse wrote his last book he was a very .... man.

(2) | friend ally neighbour companion associate acquaintance |

    (a) Her mother was her travelling ....
    (b) Italy had been an .... of Germany in World War II.
    (c) He proved himself a true .... by helping me when I was in need.
    (d) The executive received financial assistance from a business ....
    (e) Her next-door .... helped her with the children.
    (f) She was no more than an ....

(3) | evil vicious naughty injurious corrupt |

    (a) Smoking is considered .... to one's health.
    (b) The child was extremely ....
    (c) Hitler was an .... man.
    (d) The policeman who took a bribe was ....
    (e) The bank-robber felled the teller with a .... blow..

Shades of meaning

Explain the differences in the meanings of the words in each of these twelve groups.

(1) small tiny microscopic

(2) wanderer explorer adventurer

(3) murder manslaughter genocide

(4) drowsy weary exhausted

(5) snack meal banquet

(6) annoyed angry furious

(7) look stare glance

(8) breeze wind cyclone

(9) hop leap spring

(10) stool chair bench

(11) murmur growl scream

(12) flicker sparkle flash

Using better words

In your writing, always strive to use the best words you can. In the following exercises, replace each 'nice' with a more expressive word from the box.

interesting	affectionate	chivalrous	picturesque
accomplished	elegant	refreshing	friendly
comfortable	melodious	delicious	fragrant

(1) a *nice* armchair   (4) a *nice* scene   (7) a *nice* neighbour   (10) a *nice* pianist

(2) a *nice* perfume   (5) a *nice* tune   (8) a *nice* shower   (11) a *nice* dog

(3) a *nice* meal   (6) a *nice* knight   (9) a *nice* gown   (12) a *nice* book

Punctuation 12

The Colon

A colon is often used to introduce a list of things or people.

EXAMPLE: The following men were in the crew: a captain, a major, a colonel, a technical expert and a bomb-aimer.

Note the way commas are used to separate each item from the next. Also, note the way 'and' is used to add on the last item.

Inserting colons

In each of the following sentences, put in the colon, the necessary commas and the full stop.

(1) There are various kinds of aircraft trainers fighters transports seaplanes and bombers

(2) The bomb has many horrible effects devastation fear injury and destruction

(3) Here is a list of urgently needed medical supplies antibiotics bandages splints surgical instruments and blood plasma

(4) The living creatures worst affected by the blast are men women children animals and birds

(5) These were the dangers shock waves searing light flying glass falling debris and radioactive dust

(6) The bomb victims were treated by various people doctors nurses nuns priests ambulance attendants and social workers

Creative Writing 12

Living in a valley that has miraculously escaped contamination, sixteen-year-old Ann Burden believes she is the only survivor of a nuclear holocaust — until a stranger, completely enveloped in an anti-radiation suit, enters the valley.

SURVIVORS

'You're better,' I said.

'For the moment,' he said. 'At least I think I can eat something.'

I put the tray down in front of him and he stared at it.

'Amazing,' he said. He just whispered it.

'What?'

'This. Fresh eggs. Toast. Coffee. This valley. You, all by yourself. You are all by yourself?'

It was sort of a key question and he looked a little suspicious as he asked it, as if I, or someone, might be playing a trick on him. Still, there wasn't any use pretending anything else.

'Yes.'

'And you managed to stay alive, and raise chickens and eggs and cows?'

'It hasn't been so hard.'

'And the valley. How did it escape?'

'I don't really understand that. Except that people always used to say the valley had its own weather.'

'A meteorological enclave. Some kind of an inversion. I suppose that's a theoretical possibility. But the odds —'

I said: 'You'd better eat. It will all get cold.'

If he was going to be too sick to eat later, he had better eat now, and build up his strength. As for the valley, I had wondered enough about it, especially in the first few months, when I was still expecting the deadness to creep in from outside. But it did not, and there was not much sense calling it a theoretical possibility when we were in it. At that point I did not know yet that he was a chemist, a scientist. And scientists won't just accept things — they always have to try to figure them out.

He ate his breakfast. Then, still sitting up, he told me his name. And, of course, I told him mine.

'Ann Burden,' he said. 'But weren't there other people living in the valley?'

'My family,' I said. 'And the people who owned the store, Mr and Mrs Klein.'

And I told him about how they drove away and never came back. Also about the Amish, and what my father had seen in Ogdentown.

'I suppose they kept going too long,' he said. 'It's hard not to, especially at first. I know. You keep hoping. And of course, so soon after the war there was still the nerve gas.'

'Nerve gas?'

'That's what killed most of the people. In a way it's better. They just went to sleep and never woke up.'

It had taken him ten weeks to get from Ithaca to the valley, and all that way, all that time, he had seen no living thing — no people, no animals, no birds, no trees, not even insects — only grey wasteland, empty highways and dead cities and towns. He had been ready to give up and turn back when he finally came over the ridge and saw, in the late evening, the haze of blue-green. At first he thought it was a lake, and, like all the other lakes he had come upon, dead. But the next morning by better light he saw that this green was different, a colour he had almost forgotten.

As I had suspected, he still did not believe it, but came on to investigate anyway. Not until he came over Burden Hill did he know that he had finally found life.

from *Z for Zachariah*
by ROBERT C. O'BRIEN

Considering the Writer's Technique

(1) How does the writer create the impression that fresh eggs, toast and coffee have become scarce items of food?

(2) What clues tell us that the man has been affected by radiation?

(3) The author uses the colours *green* and *grey* in his description of the landscape. What does green signify? What does grey signify?

(4) What effect does the writer achieve by his repetition of the word 'no' in 'he had seen no living thing — no people, no animals, no birds, no trees, not even insects'?

(5) How does the writer suggest that there may be some hope for Ann and the newcomer?

Your Turn to Write

Gather your thoughts together as you write on *one* of these topics:

(1) There has been a nuclear war. You are one of the few surviving people on Earth. Describe your situation. What kind of new world would you try to build?

(2) 'Ban the Bomb!' Put forward arguments for or against the possession of nuclear weapons by your country.

(3) "Science has gone too far." What do *you* think?

(4) If you were a world leader, how would you try to ensure peace in the world?

Poetry 12

'Your Attention Please' gives a dramatic picture of what the moments before a nuclear missile strike might be like.

YOUR ATTENTION PLEASE

The Polar DEW has just warned that
A nuclear rocket strike of
At least one thousand megatons
Has been launched by the enemy
Directly at our major cities.
This announcement will take
Two and a quarter minutes to make,
You therefore have a further
Eight and a quarter minutes
To comply with the shelter
Requirements published in the Civil
Defence Code — section Atomic Attack.
A specially shortened Mass
Will be broadcast at the end
Of this announcement —
Protestant and Jewish services
Will begin simultaneously —
Select your wave length immediately
According to instructions
In the Defence Code. Do not
Take well-loved pets (including birds)
Into your shelter — they will consume
Fresh air. Leave the old and bed-
ridden, you can do nothing for them.
Remember to press the sealing
Switch when everyone is in
The shelter. Set the radiation
Aerial, turn on the geiger barometer.
Turn off your Television now.
Turn off your radio immediately
The Services end. At the same time
Secure explosion plugs in the ears
Of each member of your family. Take
Down your plasma flasks. Give your children
The pills marked one and two

In the C.D. green container, then put
Them to bed. Do not break
The inside airlock seals until
The radiation All Clear shows
(Watch for the cuckoo in your
perspex panel), or your District
Touring Doctor rings your bell.
If before this, your air becomes
Exhausted or if any of your family
Is critically injured, administer
The capsules marked 'Valley Forge'
(Red Pocket in No.1 Survival Kit)
For painless death. (Catholics
Will have been instructed by their priests
What to do in this eventuality.)
This announcement is ending. Our President
Has already given orders for
Massive retaliation — it will be
Decisive. Some of us may die.
Remember, statistically
It is not likely to be you.
All flags are flying fully dressed
On Government buildings — the sun is shining.
Death is the least we have to fear.
We are all in the hands of God,
Whatever happens happens by His Will.
Now go quickly to your shelters.

PETER PORTER

Thinking about the Poem

(1) Why is the announcement urgent?

(2) What clues tell you that the nuclear attack has been expected for some time?

(3) Why do you think the religious services are to be held?

(4) When will the airlock seals be able to be broken?

(5) What instructions are given concerning children?

(6) Why would some people need to take the capsules marked 'Valley Forge'?

(7) Why do you think the instruction to leave the old and bed-ridden is given? Do you agree with it or not? Why?

(8) 'Our President / Has already given orders for / Massive retaliation . . . .'
Do you agree with the President's orders? Why or why not?

(9) 'All flags are flying fully dressed / On Government building . . . .'
Why do you think the announcer is concerned to make this statement?

(10) 'We are all in the hands of God, / Whatever happens happens by His Will.'
What comment would you make on these lines?

(11) In the light of 'Your Attention Please', what are your feelings about nuclear warfare?

(12) What other title can you suggest for this poem?

Spelling 12

THE DAY OF THE BOMB

disaster	parachute	vacuum	consequence	annihilated
disastrous	ingenious	experiences	immediately	account
instructions	injured	continued	violent	community
surpassed	explosion	device	ammunition	scarcely

Missing Words

Read through *The Bomb* and decide on words from the spelling box which will fit the blank spaces. Write the words into your workbook. Note clue-letters.

The Bomb

In his book *The Day of the Bomb*, Karl Bruckner describes how the first atom bomb a........... an entire c........... . In one part of his a.......... he relates the e........... of the American bomber crew, who, acting under ...., were responsible for the dropping of the bomb. When Major Ferebee, the bombardier, sent the bomb hurtling downward, an i.......... d.......... released a .... to slow down the bomb's descent. The atomic .... that followed was the most v.......... that had ever occurred. It killed 86 100 people and severely i.......... 72 000, and the v.......... sucked 6820 houses several miles into the air as particles of dust. Another c.......... was the bombardment of the site by deadly neutrons and gamma-rays. The members of the bomber crew were s.......... able to believe their eyes. They thought they had hit an immense a.......... dump. Indeed, Colonel Tibbets sensed that this d.......... s.......... any others that a human community had ever known.

Match the Meanings

Match the list-words in the first column with their meanings in the second column.

WORDS	MEANINGS
injured	directions
consequence	clever
scarcely	lasted
annihilated	straight away
ingenious	exceeded
continued	hurt
immediately	result
surpassed	hardly
disastrous	destroyed entirely
instructions	catastrophic

Completing Words

Complete the words by filling in the blanks.

(1) scarc_t_

(2) explos__e

(3) consequent__l

(4) immed__cy

(5) continuat___

(6) account_b_l_t_

(7) ingenu__y

(8) commun_l

(9) annihil_t_o_

(10) injur__s

(11) surpassi__

(12) instructi__

(13) viol___e

(14) disastrous_y

(15) exp_r_enc__

Try Thinking 12

Who Should Survive?

To solve this problem, the class divides into small groups; each group elects a discussion leader and a secretary. The discussion leader goes to each group-member in turn for ideas, and the secretary records these. Then each group produces its solution and presents it — in a persuasive way — to the class. Here is the situation:

> There has been a nuclear holocaust. The only survivors left on earth are twelve persons in an anti-nuclear bomb shelter. One month must elapse before the level of radiation in the outside atmosphere falls sufficiently for life to be possible on the earth's surface. However, even with rigid rationing, there is food and water for only *seven* persons for a month. So, only seven out of the twelve can possibly survive. Which ones? Give your reasons. Here are the twelve persons:

1   **John White**, 37, is a manual worker. Does not believe in God. He was in good health. He was married — no children. Enjoys sport.

2   **Mrs Wharton**, 38, has been a counsellor in mental health and social problems. She is in good health. Was married with one child (Andy). She has always been active in community work.

3   **Andy Wharton**, 10, has been in a special school for three years because he does not seem to be able to cope with ordinary schoolwork. He is in good health and enjoys keeping pets.

4   **Mrs Robinson**, 23, was a waitress in a bistro but she never seemed able to keep a job for long. She was married at 18 but later divorced and has one child (Hilda), who is only a baby.

5   **Hilda Robinson**, 3 months old. In good health. Still being nursed.

6   **Joanne Brown**, 8, is in good health and was in primary school. Her parents were Chinese.

7   **Mr Randolph**, 25, is African. He was in his last year of medical school. Was active in demonstrations against the bomb. In good health. Wears trendy clothes.

8   **Mrs Symonds**, 28, was an engineer and lived in Poland. She was married but had no children. She is in good health. Enjoys reading rather than sport of any kind.

9   **Mr Crabtree**, 55, a musician. Average health. Was married with two children. Enjoys woodworking and metalworking.

10   **Father Broadhurst**, 37, priest. He is in good health and has been an athlete. Enjoys stamp-collecting.

11   **Dr Snape**, 70, Austrian, doctor in general practice. Has had heart attacks in the past five years but continued to practise.

12   **Nick Wood**, 48, has criminal record but is now reformed. Was married with three children. He smokes and drinks heavily.

Unit Thirteen

Comprehension 13

Nino Culotta, an Italian recently arrived in Australia, decides to go for a swim at a Sydney beach. His lack of understanding of the Australian surfing scene creates problems for him — and for the lifesavers on surf patrol.

JUST KEEP BETWEEN THE FLAGS

There were many people in the water, but they all seemed to be gathered together in big groups. This, I thought, was no doubt because of the sharks. I do not like to swim in very uncrowded waters, a shark would have no difficulty in finding me. But the young man had said they were nothing to worry about. So I determined that I would show these Australians that an Italian from the North was not afraid of their sharks. I entered the water where no one else was swimming. When I was about waist deep, I heard a whistle blow on the shore. I turned to see why, as it sounded like a police whistle. A young man with a close-fitting cap on his head, tied on with white strings, was waving to me. I waved to him. I had seen these young men on the news-reels at home. It was they they called lifesavers.. They were very brave young men. No doubt he was saluting my own courage. At that moment, it seemed that the whole of the Pacific Ocean fell on the back of my neck. I was knocked down, and found myself on the bottom of the ocean, with my face in the sand. I got up with difficulty, in time to see another bank of water attacking me. I fought through it, and could see that there was calmer water further out in the sea. Once out there, I started swimming. It was very pleasant. The water was not too cold, and the sun was very bright. I floated on my back, enjoying very much the sensation of being lifted up and down by the waves.

Presently I saw another man swimming out towards me. And when a wave lifted me up, I saw three others on the beach, with their hands above their heads. 'Ah,' I thought, 'the lifesavers. They practise. They too are not afraid of the sharks. I will congratulate this man on his courage, and he will congratulate me. We will be comrades in danger.' The man reached me, and he appeared to be very irritable. He said, 'What the bloody hell d'yer think you're doing?'

I said, 'I am swimming. It is very pleasant.'

He said, 'Get over between the flags.'

'I do not see any flags.'

'Get over there with the crowd.'

'I do not like crowds.'

'New Australians. I've had 'em. You're in a rip, here. D'you want to finish up in New Zealand?'

'It is a nice place, this New Zealand?'

'You're goin' the right way to find out. Now get over there with the mob.'

'I like swimming here. I am not afraid of the sharks.'

'They're not afraid of you either. S'pose I'll have to haul you in for your own protection, you silly mutt.'

'What, please, is a mutt?'

'Look in the mirror some day. Come on, grab hold of the line.'

'I am sorry. I do not wish to play.'

'We're not playing. You're in a rip. Grab the line.'

'No.'

'D'you want me to use force?'

'If you attempt the use of force, I shall be forced to bump you on the head.'

He swam closer to me. I raised my fist to bump him. But I did not bump him. I did not know how he defended himself, but I found myself turned around, and he had gripped me under the armpits, and I realised we were being towed towards the shore. No matter how I struggled, I could not get away. So I soon ceased to struggle. I said, 'You are taking me to the shore?'

He said, 'Yes.'

I said, 'When we reach the shore I will bump you on the head.'

He said, 'We'll see about that.'

He took one hand away from me, and made some sort of signal. Before I could take any advantage of the situation, his hand was back again under my arm. Then water was crashing all around us, and I had trouble keeping it out of my mouth and nose. Then I felt that he was standing. I put my feet down, and touched hard sand. I stood up and said to myself, 'Now I will bump him.' He said, 'Grab him. He's trying to turn on a blue.' Three other lifesavers, whom I had not seen arrive, suddenly lifted me into the air. There were

two at my head end, and one at my feet. My feet were higher than my head. They began to carry me through the shallow water to the beach. It was most undignified. I said so. They did not answer. I told them to put me down, and I would fight them all. Still they did not answer. They carried me up the beach, and the first lifesaver said, 'Take him into the club'. Despite my protests, and the curious people who were gathered around, they carried me right off the beach, and into this club. There, in the centre of a large expanse of floor, they sat me down. But they still held me too tightly for me to move. I was very irritable. The first lifesaver stood in front of me, and said, 'Can you understand plain English?'

I said, 'Is it plain English when I say I will bump you on the head?'

'Yeah, that's plain enough.'

'Then I understand English.'

He said, 'Good. Hold him while I read the riot act.'

He then proceeded to explain to me why it was necessary to swim only in certain areas, because of these 'rips'. He explained what a 'rip' was, and how he had brought me in because I refused to leave this 'rip', and soon I would have been far out, and the line would not have reached me, and there would have been much trouble. He was very polite, and I stopped being irritable. I said, 'I am sorry. I did not understand.'

He said, 'That's all right. Just keep between the flags. Everything all clear now?'

I said, 'Yes, everything is all clear.'

He said, 'Good. Tell your New Australian mates, will yer? They're a bloody nuisance.'

'I have no New Australian mates. I am only two days in Sydney.'

'Okay. See you around.'

'Thank you. I will see you around.'

from *They're a Weird Mob*
by NINO CULOTTA (JOHN O'GRADY)

How Well Did You Understand?

(1) Why did Nino think people were swimming together in big groups?

(2) Why did he decide to swim where no one else was swimming?

(3) How did Nino know what lifesavers were?

(4) What happened when Nino first entered the water?

(5) What opinion did he have of lifesavers?

(6) Why did Nino think the lifesaver was waving to him?

(7) Why had the lifesaver swum out to Nino?

(8) What was the lifesaver's attitude towards him?

(9) What was Nino's attitude to the lifesaver?

(10) Why wasn't Nino able to 'bump' the lifesaver?

(11) Why did the lifesavers carry Nino into the clubhouse?

(12) Why did Nino finally stop being 'irritable'?

(13) Nino's speech-pattern reveals that he is a New Australian. How would an 'old' Australian have expressed the following?
(a) 'It is a nice place, this New Zealand?'
(b) 'I am only two days in Sydney.'

(14) John O'Grady, the author of *They're a Weird Mob*, is an Australian. How, other than through Nino's speech, does O'Grady convey the impression that Nino is new to this country?

Dictionary Words

Give the meanings of the following words. You might like to use the back-of-the-book dictionary.

(a) sensation   (b) mutt   (c) expanse   (d) irritable   (e) undignified.

Language 13

Effective Communication

Communication may be described as an exchange of ideas and feelings, and as the successful giving and receiving of information. The choice of words and their arrangement in sentences are very important if effective communication is to be achieved. Look at this amazing sentence:

> Hastily summoning an ambulance, the corpse was taken to the morgue.

It's certainly not easy to imagine any corpse calling for an ambulance! The writer has failed to communicate to the reader the meaning intended, by forgetting to put in an appropriate subject. The sentence should have been written something like this:

> Hastily summoning an ambulance, the police ordered that the corpse be taken to the morgue.

Avoiding communication breakdown

Clarity in speech and writing is essential for successful   ..nication. Rewrite the following sentences so that they properly communicate the intended meaning in each case.

(1) She spoke to her friend, who had been ill by telephone.

(2) Walking across the paddock, there were dead birds all around us.

(3) This is a quiet, happy neighbourhood with dogs and children riding bicycles.

(4) People with relatives buried in this cemetery should keep them in order.

(5) An umbrella was lost by a young lady with silver ribs.

(6) The young man had his arm tattooed in the Navy, but now that he's getting married he'd like it taken off.

(7) Be sure to try Sanderson's Savoury Sausages. You'll never get better.

(8) After working all day, the job was finished.

(9) The students observed the aeroplanes flying in formation through the window.

(10) If the milk does not agree with the baby, boil it.

(11) The salesgirl unpacked the stockings from their boxes and threw them in the waste bin.

(12) All meat in this window is from local farmers killed on the premises. [*Sign in a butcher's window*]

(13) Reports have been made about these cars that are quite ridiculous.

(14) Strolling across the farm the view was magnificent.

(15) For a delicious baked custard — in a bowl, mix three eggs, a quarter of a cup of sugar and warm milk. Cook standing in boiling water.

Misused words

Our language contains many words that people often confuse. When words are misused, communication is hindered. Write out each of the following sentences, selecting the correct word from the brackets.

(1) He is determined to [**precede/proceed**] with his coaching.

(2) [**Whose/who's**] taken my lunch?

(3) If you need glasses you should consult an [**optimist/optometrist**].

(4) The winner of the contest received two [**complimentary/complementary**] tickets.

(5) Her writing was so untidy that it was almost [**eligible/illegible**].

(6) Diabetes is often a [**heredity/hereditary**] disease.

(7) [**Your/You're**] not leaving the country.

(8) The novelist had an [**imaginative/imaginary**] mind.

(9) The [**personal/personnel**] manager was responsible for helping the staff.

(10) She was [**beside/besides**] herself with anger.

Faulty sentences

Faulty expression in your writing also leads to communication breakdown. Correct the faults in the following sentences.

(1) She performed real good.

(2) He was that surprised that he could not reply.

(3) Neither Mark or John are going to the cinema.

(4) Drake was the most bravest captain of the fleet.

(5) They swam faster than him.

(6) She couldn't find her brother nowhere.

(7) The tourist asked them both did they speak French?

(8) We knew you would be pleased by this most perfect copy.

(9) The taxi-driver should have drove to where you and he was waiting.

(10) We must learn him to behave himself.

(11) The coach, as well as the players, were pleased by the victory.

(12) The reason I won was because I had a new racquet.

(13) He got real angry when he seen me win the game.

(14) Between you and I, I believe Trent and Allison must of quarrelled.

(15) There are less people here today than there was yesterday.

Needless repetition

Rewrite each of these sentences, omitting unnecessary words.

(1) In my opinion, I think you'll win the race.

(2) The two countries were united together by their allegiance to the king.

(3) He hurried into the room in great haste.

(4) The lifeboat was a necessary essential.

(5) I will repeat again the instructions I gave you yesterday.

(6) When the soldiers finished their leave, they returned back to their camp.

(7) In spite of interjections he continued on with his speech.

(8) In his report, the pilot reported that the plane's radio was faulty.

Punctuation 13

The Apostrophe — To show possession

The apostrophe is used to show possession in the following ways:

- If the noun that possesses is *singular*, add **'s**.
  EXAMPLE: The insect's eyes. (The eyes of the insect.)

- If the noun that possesses is *plural* and already ends with 's', simply add an apostrophe.
  EXAMPLE: The birds' feathers. (The feathers of the birds.)

- If the noun that possesses is *plural* but does not end with 's', add **'s**.
  EXAMPLE: The men's hats. (The hats of the men.)

An exercise

Change each of the following so that an apostrophe is used to show possession. The first is done for you as an example.

(1) the school of the girls — the girls' school

(2) the tails of the sheep

(3) the car of the teacher

(4) the book of the children

(5) the handlebars of the bicycle

(6) the dresses of the ladies

(7) the egg of the duck

(8) the cheering of the crowd

(9) the point of the pencil

(10) the exercises of the pupils

Another exercise

Correctly insert the apostrophe into each of the following.

(1) the mans coat

(2) childrens books

(3) the babies toys

(4) a cats whiskers

(5) two dogs tails

(6) a heros welcome

(7) the geeses feathers

(8) the womens meeting

(9) the thieves hoard

(10) the pianos tone

Creative Writing 13

Descriptions of People

The description of a person's appearance and habits is often meant to suggest certain facts about his or her character to the reader. Here is the famous description of the old sea-dog Billy Bones, from *Treasure Island* by Robert Louis Stevenson. Billy Bones is seen through the eyes of young Jim Hawkins, whose father keeps the 'Admiral Benbow' inn.

The description has been placed on the left; while certain things about the character of Billy Bones, as suggested to the reader by aspects of his appearance and habits, have been placed in italics on the right. As you read, see if you agree with the facts that have been deduced.

BILLY BONES

I take up my pen in the year of grace 17–, and go back to the time when my father kept the 'Admiral Benbow' inn, and the brown old seaman, with the sabre-cut, first took up his lodging under our roof.

I remember him as if it were yesterday, as he came plodding to the inn door, his sea-chest following behind him in a hand-barrow, a tall, strong, heavy, nut-brown man; his tarry pigtail falling over the shoulders of his soiled blue coat; his hands ragged and scarred, with black broken nails and the sabre-cut across one cheek, a dirty livid white. I remember him looking round the cove and whistling to himself as he did so, and then breaking out in that old sea-song that he sang so often afterwards:

'Fifteen men on a dead man's chest —
　　Yo-ho-ho, and a bottle of rum!'

in the high, old tottering voice that seemed to have been tuned and broken at the capstan bars. Then he rapped on the door with a bit of stick like a handspike that he carried, and when my father appeared, called roughly for a glass of rum. This, when it was brought to him, he drank slowly, like a connoisseur, lingering on the taste, and still looking about him at the

DEDUCTIONS

Our first impression is of an outdoor type of man whose past life has been brutal. He no longer seems to care about how he looks to others. He is a rather frightening figure.

Obviously he is rude, and accustomed to his commands being obeyed. The writer stresses his taste for strong drink — as if this were one of the few delights left to him.

cliffs and up at our signboard.

'This is a handy cove,' says he, at length; 'and a pleasant sittyated grog-shop. Much company, mate?'

My father told him no, very little company, the more was the pity.

'Well, then,' said he, 'this is the berth for me. Here you, matey,' he cried to the man who trundled the barrow; 'bring up alongside and help up my chest. I'll stay here a bit,' he continued. 'I'm a plain man; rum and bacon and eggs is what I want, and that head up there for to watch ships off. What you mought call me? You mought call me captain. Oh, I see what you're at — there'; and he threw down three or four gold pieces on the threshold. 'You can tell me when I've worked through that,' says he, looking as fierce as a commander.

And, indeed, bad as his clothes were, and coarsely as he spoke, he had none of the appearance of a man who sailed before the mast; but seemed like a mate or skipper, accustomed to be obeyed or to strike. The man who came with the barrow told us the mail had set him down the morning before at the 'Royal George'; that he had inquired what inns there were along the coast, and hearing ours well spoken of, I suppose, and described as lonely, had chosen it from the others for his place of residence. And that was all we could learn of our guest.

He was a very silent man by custom. All day he hung round the cove, or upon the cliffs, with a brass telescope; all evening he sat in a corner of the parlour next the fire, and drank rum and water very strong.

from *Treasure Island*
by ROBERT LOUIS STEVENSON

The reader is a little tantalized by the way the old sea-dog is attracted by the lack of company at the inn.

The fact that the inn is a lonely place suggests that the old sea-dog has gone out of his way to avoid people.

And now comes a real hint of mystery — the old skipper is haunted by some fear and must be constantly on the watch.

For our second description we turn to Doctor No, from the book of the same name by Ian Fleming. As before, read the description on the left and the deductions suggested to the reader on the right.

DOCTOR NO

Doctor No came slowly out from behind the desk and moved towards them. He seemed to glide rather than take steps. His knees did not dent the matt, gunmetal sheen of his kimono and no shoes showed below the sweeping hem.

Bond's first impression was of thinness and erectness and height. Doctor No was at least six inches taller than Bond, but the straight immovable poise of his body made him seem still taller. The head also was elongated and tapered from a round, completely bald skull down to a sharp chin so that the impression was of a reversed raindrop — or rather oildrop, for the skin was of a deep almost translucent yellow.

It was impossible to tell Doctor No's age: as far as Bond could see, there were no lines on the face. It was odd to see a forehead as smooth as the top of the polished skull. Even the cavernous indrawn cheeks below the prominent cheekbones looked as smooth as fine ivory. There was something Dali-esque about the eyebrows, which were fine and black and sharply upswept as if they had been painted on as make-up for a conjurer. Below them, slanting jet-black eyes stared out of the skull. They were without eyelashes. They looked like the mouths of two small revolvers, direct and unblinking and totally devoid of expression. The thin fine nose ended very close above a wide compressed wound of a mouth which, despite its almost permanent sketch of a smile, showed only cruelty and authority. The chin was indrawn towards the neck. Later Bond was to notice that it rarely

DEDUCTIONS

The reader quickly deduces that there is something unusual and even sinister about Doctor No. The words 'gunmetal sheen' even point to a deadly quality.

The impression of oddity is reinforced by the tallness of Doctor No and by the reversed-raindrop shape of his head — and by the fact that the head is hairless and oil-like in colour.

The eyes — without eyelashes and as direct as revolvers — reinforce our first feeling of deadliness. The mouth is like a wound. Thus, there is a quality of horror and rigidity about the head and face of this person. The smile lacks humour.

moved more than slightly away from centre, giving the impression that the head and the vertebra were in one piece.

The bizarre, gliding figure looked like a giant venomous worm wrapped in grey tin-foil, and Bond would not have been surprised to see the rest of it trailing slimily along the carpet behind.

from *Doctor No* by IAN FLEMING

And now the reader must deduce that Doctor No is, emotionally and physically, inhuman. In all, a terrible enemy to confront.

For our final description of a person we look at a young girl from the book *Shirley* by Charlotte Brontë. Here is the description of this young girl, together with the reader's deductions.

SHIRLEY

To her had not been denied the gift of beauty; it was not absolutely necessary to know her in order to like her; she was fair enough to please, even at the first view.... her face was expressive and gentle; her eyes were handsome, and gifted at times with a winning beam that stole into the heart, with a language that spoke softly to the affections. Her mouth was very pretty; she had a delicate skin, and a fine flow of brown hair, which she knew how to arrange with taste; curls became her, and she possessed them in picturesque profusion. Her style of dress announced taste in the wearer; very unobtrusive in fashion, far from costly in material, but suitable in colour to the fair complexion with which it contrasted, and in make to the slight form which it draped. Her present winter garb was of merino, the same soft shade of brown as her hair: the little collar round her neck lay over a pink ribbon, and was fastened with a pink knot; she wore no other decoration.

from *Shirley*
by CHARLOTTE BRONTË

DEDUCTIONS

The reader deduces that the girl's appearance is a real guide to her character — with this girl, a first impression is a true impression.

Her outward beauty parallels a beauty of character. More definitely, she is intelligent, gentle and affectionate.

In all, it is just as though she were posing for a painting.

Nothing in the way she dresses causes the reader to change his or her overall deduction that the writer is portraying the girl as an angel, both in appearance and in character.

Your Turn to Write

Imagine you are one of the people in the panel below. Describe your life and relate some of your experiences.

Poetry 13

Rhyme

A word that has the same end-sound as another is said to rhyme with it. Look at these example of rhyming words:

rang	cook	might	moon	wait	mare
sang	look	bite	tune	hate	fair

You'll quickly realize that the rhyming parts of words are not always spelt the same way. Read the following limerick. The words in heavy type rhyme with each other, as do the words in italics. Keep in mind that rhyme depends on sound, not on spelling.

A Teacher Called Green

There once was a teacher called **Green**,
Who invented a caning **machine**;
On the 99th *stroke*
The rotten thing *broke*,
And hit poor old Green on the **bean**.

Rhyming fun

Here's a chance to have fun with rhyming words. Use the clues and insert rhyming words of your own. The number of letters required is shown in each case. The first one has been done to give you the idea.

CLUES	RHYMING WORDS
(1) A happy parrot	a <u>j o l l y</u> polly
(2) A cat who tells funny stories	a witty _ _ _ _ _
(3) A fat husband	a chubby _ _ _ _ _ _
(4) A bigger volcano	a _ _ _ _ _ _ _ _ crater
(5) A short Indian leader	a brief _ _ _ _ _ _
(6) A cattle rustler	a _ _ _ _ _ thief
(7) A cook who can't hear	a deaf _ _ _ _ _
(8) A clothes-maker in the navy	a sailor _ _ _ _ _ _ _
(9) A stupid seabird	a dull _ _ _ _ _
(10) An inexpensive woolly animal	a _ _ _ _ _ _ sheep

(11) An adolescent female monarch   a _ _ _ _ _ queen

(12) A shaking stomach   a jelly _ _ _ _ _ _

(13) A stupid Sherlock Holmes   a defective _ _ _ _ _ _ _ _ _ _

(14) A delicate mollusc   a _ _ _ _ _ _ snail

(15) A cranky employer   a _ _ _ _ _ _ boss

(16) A crazy fashion   a _ _ _ _ fad

(17) A dishonest fowl   a _ _ _ _ _ _ chook

(18) A less generous meal   a _ _ _ _ _ _ _ _ dinner

Limericks

Read through the following limericks and notice the rhyming pattern common to them all.
Then write down the two limericks you like best and underline the rhyming words.

A Young Lady of Guam

A daring young lady of Guam,
Observed, 'The Pacific's so calm.
   I'll swim out for a lark'
   She met a large shark ...
Let us now sing the ninetieth psalm.

A Silly Young Fellow

A silly young fellow named Hyde
In a funeral procession was spied;
   When asked, 'Who is dead?'
   He giggled and said,
'I don't know; I just came for the ride.'

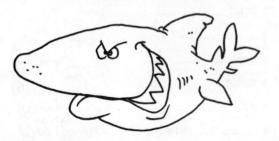

A Lovely Young Maiden

A lovely young maiden named Carol,
At Niagara donned swimming apparel.
  We heard from the shore:
  'Oh, swimming's a bore!'
So she went down the falls in a barrel!

CHARLES BARSOTTI

Trapeze Artist

A man on the flying trapeze
Emitted a terrible sneeze.
The consequent force
Shot him right off his course,
And they found him next day in some trees.

A Dentist

'Open wide,' said a dentist called Bert
To a man-eating shark whose teeth hurt.
'When I've finished the drilling
I'll give you a filling.'
He did — and the filling was Bert.

Old Man in a Trunk

There was an old man in a trunk,
Who inquired of his wife, 'Am I drunk?'
She replied with regret,
'I'm afraid so, my pet.'
And he answered, 'It's just as I thunk.'

OGDEN NASH

An Old Man of Nantucket

There was an old man of Nantucket
Who kept all his cash in a bucket;
But his daughter, named Nan,
Ran away with a man —
And, as for the bucket, Nantucket.

Fly and Flea

A fly and a flea in a flue
Were imprisoned, so what could they do?
Said the fly, 'Let us flee!'
'Let us fly!' said the flea,
So they flew through a flaw in the flue.

Twickenham

There was a young lady of Twickenham,
Whose boots were too tight to walk quickenham.
    She bore them awhile,
    But at last, at a stile,
She pulled them both off and was sickenham.

Bump!

Things that go 'bump' in the night,
Should not really give you a fright.
    It's the hole in each ear
    That lets in the fear,
That, and the absence of light!

SPIKE MILLIGAN

Spelling 13

PROBLEM PAIRS

recent	formally	vocation	profit	coarse
resent	formerly	vacation	prophet	course
incite	eligible	principle	cereal	ascent
insight	illegible	principal	serial	assent

Picking from the Pairs

Select the correct words from the brackets to complete the following sentences.

(1) The lifesaver .... read the riot act to Nino, who had .... lived in Italy. **[formerly/formally]**

(2) When he began to .... the lifesaver, Nino did not have much .... into the Australian temperament. **[insight/incite]**

(3) Nino tended to .... the interruption of his swimming. **[recent/resent]**

(4) The lifesaver had a definite .... of action. **[course/coarse]**

(5) At that time, Nino was the .... offender in the surf. **[principal/principle]**

(6) Nino was taking a short .... **[vocation/vacation]**

(7) The faded sign was practically .... **[eligible/illegible]**

(8) After the riot act had been read, Nino nodded his .... **[assent/ascent]**

(9) Nino was able to .... from his surfing experience. **[prophet/profit]**

(10) The boy ate .... while he watched the television .... **[serial/cereal]**

Words and Meanings

Given the meanings, supply the correct words from the spelling box.

(1) In the past: ....

(2) Of poor quality, rough: ....

(3) Gain: ....

(4) A divinely inspired religious leader: ....

(5) The career to which one is called: ....

(6) Fit to be chosen, qualified: ....

TEAM SELECTION

(7) Any grain used for food: ....

(8) A period of rest from work or study: ....

(9) An upward slope: ....

(10) To urge to action, arouse: ....

(11) A fundamental truth, a rule of conduct: ....

(12) According to fixed customs or rules: ....

Fun with Clues

Using the following clues, write down the appropriate words from the spelling box.

(1) These two words end with a small coin.

(2) These two words end with the past participle of 'send'.

(3) This word ends in a very healthy manner.

(4) This word is sick at the beginning.

(5) This word ends with a friend.

(6) These two words have a feline in their middle.

(7) These two words rhyme with 'horse'.

(8) These two word rhyme with 'light'.

Try Thinking 13

Jumbled Products

Here are ten jumbled words, each preceded by a clue. The first letter of each word has been underlined, and the clue gives the *source* of the jumbled product. Noting the example, find the items.

(1) A dairy produces L̲MKI.   ......MILK......

(2) An orchard produces I̲RFTU.   ....

(3) A brewery produces E̲BRE.   ....

(4) A bakery produces D̲AREB.   ....

(5) A colliery produces A̲LCO.   ....

(6) A mint produces Y̲NOME.   ....

(7) A studio produces IMF̲SL. ....

(8) A kiln produces ETROP̲TY. ....

(9) A fire produces AH̲TE. ....

(10) A dynamo produces CRITTIYC̲EEL. ....

Cracking the Colour Code

Use the code key below (i.e. the square and the circle) to decode the names of six colours 'spelt out' in code underneath.

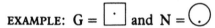

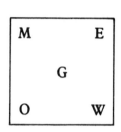 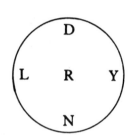

Missing Persons

If you fit six of the seven names across each grid in the correct order, the seventh name in the list will appear, reading from top to bottom in the indicated squares. (Answers on p. 259.)

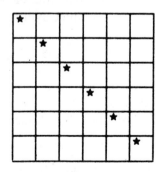

No. 1:
AGATHA
ELAINE
ESTHER
MAXINE
OLIVIA
SABINA
SOPHIE

No. 2:
BERTIE
CARLOS
LESTER
SIDNEY
STEVEN
WARREN
WESLEY

Unit Fourteen

Comprehension 14

Gerald Durrell, the famous naturalist, once had a very lively time with an archer-fish — a creature that uses a kind of machine-gunning to bring down its prey.

THE SPITTING FISH

This is a rather handsome creature found in the streams of Asia. It has evolved a most ingenious method of obtaining its prey, which consists of flies, butterflies, moths, and other insects. Swimming slowly along under the surface it waits until it sees an insect alight on a twig or leaf overhanging the water. Then the fish slows down and approaches cautiously. When it is within range it stops, takes aim, and then suddenly and startlingly spits a stream of tiny water droplets at its prey. These travel with deadly accuracy, and the startled insect is knocked off its perch and into the water below, and the next minute the fish swims up beneath it, there is a swirl of water and a gulp, and the insect has vanished for ever.

I once worked in a pet-shop in London, and one day, with a consignment of other creatures, we received an archer-fish. I was delighted with it, and with the permission of the manager I wrote out a notice describing the fish's curious habits, arranged the aquarium carefully, put the fish inside and placed it in the window as the main display. It proved very popular, except that people wanted to see the archer-fish actually taking his prey, and this was not easy to manage. Eventually I had a brainwave. A few doors down from us was a fish shop, and I saw no reason why we should not benefit from some of their surplus bluebottles.* So I suspended a bit of very smelly meat over the archer-fish's aquarium and left the door of the shop open. I did this without the knowledge of the manager. I wanted it to be a surprise for him.

It was certainly a surprise.

By the time he arrived, there must have been several thousand bluebottles in the shop. The archer-fish was having the time of his life, watched by myself inside the shop and fifty or sixty people on the pavement outside. The manager arrived neck and neck with a very unzoological policeman, who wanted to know the meaning of the obstruction outside. To my surprise the manager, instead of being delighted with my ingenious window display, tended to side with the policeman. The climax came when the manager, leaning over the aquarium to unfasten the bit of meat that hung above it, was hit

_____

* *Bluebottles:* blowflies.

accurately in the face by a stream of water which the fish had just released in the hope of hitting a particularly succulent blue-bottle. The manager never referred to the incident again, but the next day the archer-fish disappeared, and it was the last time I was allowed to dress the window.

from *Encounters with Animals*
by GERALD DURRELL

How Well Did You Understand?

(1) What does the archer-fish feed on?

(2) How does the archer-fish act when it sees its prey?

(3) What three things does the fish do when it comes within range of its prey?

(4) What happens after the startled insect is knocked off its perch?

(5) Where did Gerald Durrell once work?

(6) What did he do with the archer-fish that had come into his possession?

(7) Why did Durrell want some of the bluebottles (blowflies) from the fish shop?

(8) How did he attract them to the archer-fish's aquarium?

(9) What surprise did the manager find awaiting him when he arrived at the shop?

(10) Why was a policeman also attracted to the shop?

(11) How did the manager become involved, unpleasantly, with the archer-fish?

(12) What were the consequences of the manager's unfortunate experience?

Dictionary Words

Give the meaning of each of the following words. You might like to use the back-of-the-book dictionary.

(a) evolved   (b) ingenious   (c) consignment   (d) climax   (e) succulent.

Language 14

Prefixes

Prefixes are very important in the formation of our words. Many of them come from Latin and Greek. A prefix is a word-part added at the beginning of a word to alter the meaning or make a new word.

prefix **ex**hale **dis**appear **re**claim **post**pone **pre**view	

Working with prefixes

Select one prefix from the box to add to the words or word-parts in each of the eight groups that follow — one prefix per group. The meaning of each prefix is given with it in the box.

bene (well)	**per** (through)	**circum** (around)	**inter** (between)
trans (across)	**con** (together)	**super** (above)	**tele** (far)

(1) (a) .... navigate
    (b) .... stances
    (c) .... ference
    (d) .... scribe

(2) (a) .... phone
    (b) .... graph
    (c) .... vision
    (d) .... scope
    (e) .... type

(3) (a) .... spirator
    (b) .... vene
    (c) .... current
    (d) .... gregation
    (e) .... form
    (f) .... clude

(4) (a) .... port
    (b) .... fer
    (c) .... fusion
    (d) .... late
    (e) .... mit
    (f) .... plant

(5) (a) .... visor
    (b) .... intendent
    (c) .... stition
    (d) .... sonic

(6) (a) .... factor
    (b) .... fit
    (c) .... volent
    (d) .... diction
    (e) .... ficial

(7) (a) .... colator
    (b) .... spective
    (c) .... spire
    (d) .... forate
    (e) .... manent
    (f) .... plex

(8) (a) .... val
    (b) .... cept
    (c) .... loper
    (d) .... mediate
    (e) .... rupt
    (f) .... jector

GO TO
FRONT
OF WORD

PREFIXES

Suffixes

There are many suffixes in the English language. A suffix is a word-part added at the end of a word to alter its meaning or form. Most suffixes consist of one syllable.

> sense**less**   accept**able**   colon**ial**   doubt**ful**   botan**ist**   surviv**or**

Using suffixes to form diminutives

By adding the suffix **let** to the word 'book' we get the word **booklet**. This means 'a small book', and is therefore a *diminutive* of the word 'book'. Form diminutives by adding the correct suffixes from the box to the words in italics. Sometimes you'll need to alter the original word slightly before adding the suffix.

> **et   ette   let   ling   ock**

(1) a small *statue*

(2) a little *hill*

(3) a young *duck*

(4) a small *kitchen*

(5) a young *goose*

(6) a minute *drop*

(7) a young *bull*

(8) a small *stream*

(9) a small *wagon*

(10) a small *cod*

(11) a small *island*

(12) a very small *river*

(13) a young *pig*

(14) a small *brook*

(15) a young *owl*

(16) a small *flat*

Word Origins

1 **Auto** is a Greek prefix meaning 'self'. For each of the clues below, write down a word beginning with 'auto'.

   (a) A person's signature   auto...............

   (b) A word for a motorcar   auto...............

   (c) Working by itself   auto...............

   (d) A ruler who has total control   auto...............

   (e) A book about one's own life   auto...............

2 **Scope** comes from the Greek verb *skopein*, meaning 'to look at, examine'. Here are five words that contain 'scope': microscope, periscope, telescope, horoscope, stethoscope. Insert them correctly into the following sentences.

   (a) His .... predicts that he will be famous one day.

(b) With her ...., the doctor listened to the patient's heartbeat.

(c) 'Up ....!' shouted the submarine captain.

(d) The astronomer viewed the stars through his ....

(e) The biologist examined the bacilli through her ....

3 **Dictum** is the past participle of the Latin verb *dicere* ('to say, tell'). A dictator is an all-powerful ruler who tells people what to do. Here are some other words with the same root: verdict, abdicate, indicator, dictionary, contradict, dedicate, dictate, diction. Insert them correctly in the spaces below.

(a) It is sometimes unwise to .... your teacher.

(b) A king who gives up his throne is said to ....

(c) The jury could not reach a ....

(d) The manager had to .... the letter to her secretary.

(e) Her .... is always clear.

(f) The car's .... was not working.

(g) The nurse wanted to .... her life to the care of the sick.

(h) He used a .... to find the word's meaning.

4 **Ped** is a prefix and suffix that comes from the Latin word *pes* ('foot'). See whether you can explain how each of the following words is connected with feet:
(a) pedestrian (b) centipede (c) pedal (d) biped (e) quadruped (f) expedition
(g) pedestal.

Creating words

Using the Latin roots in the brackets, write the missing words into the following sentences.

(1) Electric lights have been installed to .... the caves. [*lumen*, 'light']

(2) The builder began to re........... the house. [*novus*, 'new']

(3) The .... listened to the concert in the .... [*audio*, 'I hear']

(4) The troops were able to re........... the attack. [*pello*, 'I drive, push']

(5) A hermit leads a .... life. [*solus*, 'alone']

(6) The accident victim's life was saved by a blood .... [*fundo*, 'I pour']

(7) The athlete had .... his leg. [*frango*, 'I break']

(8) We had no trouble finding the .... [*locus*, 'place']

(9) Many countries have .... currency. [*decem*, 'ten']

(10) Animals that eat other animals are .... [*caro*, 'flesh']

Punctuation 14

Quotation Marks

The *actual* words that a speaker uses are enclosed in quotation marks (also known as inverted commas).

EXAMPLE: Bob Hope once said, 'People who throw kisses are hopelessly lazy.'

Note: (a) a comma is used before the first quotation mark;
     (b) the first word inside the quotation marks begins with a capital letter;
     (c) the full stop is placed *inside* the closing quotation mark.

Sometimes, the actual words spoken come first.

EXAMPLE: 'The first thing that struck me on my visit to the supermarket was a loaded trolley,' said the shopper.

Note: (a) the first word begins with a capital letter;
     (b) the comma is placed at the end of the spoken words and *inside* the closing quotation mark.

Exercise

Enclose within quotation marks the actual words the speaker uses in each of the following. Pay particular attention to commas, capital letters and full stops.

(1) Jim said you are at the Admiral Benbow Inn, Black Hill cove, my good man
Take me straight in to the captain, or I'll break your arm whispered Pew quietly

(2) There were footprints said Dr Mortimer
I suppose they belonged to a man or woman mused Holmes
Dr mortimer looked strangely at us for an instant, and then his voice sank almost to a whisper as he said No, Mr Holmes, they were the footprints of a gigantic hound

(3) Bacchus, the god of wine, said to Midas choose anything you like for a gift, and it shall be given to you
Midas said what I should like is that everything I touch should be turned to gold

Creative Writing 14

The following piece of descriptive writing is from *Storm Boy* by Colin Thiele. Hide-Away, Fingerbone and Storm Boy live by a flat, shallow waterway called the Coorong, which they cherish as a bird sanctuary. With the coming of the morning, the birds awaken.

BIRD SANCTUARY

Some distance from the place where Hide-Away and Fingerbone had built their humpies, the whole stretch of the Coorong and the land around it had been turned into a sanctuary. No one was allowed to hurt the birds there. No shooters were allowed, no hunters with decoys or nets or wire traps, not even a dog.

And so the water and the shores rippled and flapped with wings. In the early morning the tall birds stood up and clapped and cheered the rising sun. Everywhere there was the sound of bathing — a happy splashing and sousing and swishing. It sounded as if the water had been turned into a bathroom five miles long, with thousands of busy fellows gargling and gurgling and blowing bubbles together. Some were above the water, some were on it, and some were under it; a few were half on it and half under. Some were just diving into it and some just climbing out of it. Some who wanted to fly were starting to take off, running across the water with big flat feet, flapping their wings furiously and pedalling with all their might. Some were coming in to land, with their wings braking hard and their big webbed feet splayed out ready to ski over the water as soon as they landed.

Everywhere there were criss-crossing wakes of ripples and waves and splashes. Storm Boy felt the excitement and wonder of it; he often sat on the shore all day with his knees up and his chin cupped in his hands. Sometimes he wished he'd been born an ibis or a pelican.

from *Storm Boy*
by COLIN THIELE

Examining the Writer's Technique

(1) 'Everywhere there was the sound of bathing — a happy splashing and sousing and swishing. It sounded as if the water had been turned into a bathroom five miles long, with thousands of busy fellows gargling and gurgling and blowing bubbles together.'

Here, the writer uses sound-words — words that echo the sounds they describe — to capture the senses and imagination of the reader as he or she pictures the watery wonderland of the Coorong. One such sound-word is 'splashing', used here for the sound of the water being slapped by birds' wings.

Supply the sound-words, from the two sentences just quoted, for the following:
(a) .... is the sound of water moving rapidly past feathered bodies.
(b) .... is the sound of water being sucked into little whirlpools.
(c) .... is the sound of water being rolled and blown around in the throat.

(2) Another way in which a writer can focus a reader's attention is by linking words that begin with the same letter. For example, listen to the 's' sound in 'splashing and sousing and swishing'. See if you can give at least four other examples, from the *whole* passage, of words linked by the same letter.

(3) What impression does Thiele give the reader by the repeated use of 'some' in the second paragraph?

(4) Why is 'pedalling' a good word to use for big birds trying to take off, in '. . . running across the water with big flat feet, flapping their wings furiously and pedalling with all their might'?

(5) The words 'ripples and waves and splashes' give the reader a lively impression of water being stirred up as birds take off or land.

Suppose you were thinking of describing (a) clouds moving across the sky (b) grass being rippled by the wind. Think up three words to describe each movement and leave a reader with a lively impression.

(6) Storm Boy sometimes 'wished he'd been born an ibis or a pelican'. Why?

Storm Boy Goes Walking

Now, for sheer enjoyment, let's follow Storm Boy walking along the sand; and let's focus, with him, on some of the birds that live in the sanctuary. As you read, notice the wonderful comparisons that are made, and also the use of sound-words.

When Storm Boy went walking along the beach, or over the sandhills, or in the sanctuary, the birds were not afraid. They knew he was a friend. The pelicans sat in a row, like a lot of important old men with their heavy paunches sagging, and rattled their beaks drily in greeting; the moor-hens fussed and chattered; the ibises cut the air into strips as they jerked their curved beaks up and down; and the blue crane stood in silent dignity like a tall thin statue as Storm Boy went past.

Your Turn to Write

Try your hand at writing about *one* of the following:

(1) Describe as vividly as you can a place that should be preserved for future generations.

(2) 'My Solution to Pollution.'

(3) The Ideal Zoo.

(4) What is your favourite bird? Describe it, and, in a paragraph or two, give reasons for your choice.

Poetry 14

The narrator in this poem is a man of great courage — except, of course, when there is a spider in his bath.

THE SPIDER

I have fought a grizzly bear,
Tracked a cobra to its lair,
Killed a crocodile who dared to cross my path;
But the thing I really dread
When I've just got out of bed
Is to find that there's a spider in the bath.

I've no fear of wasps or bees,
Mosquitos only tease,
I rather like a cricket on the hearth;
But my blood runs cold to meet
In pyjamas and bare feet
With a great big hairy spider in the bath.

I have faced a charging bull in Barcelona,
I have dragged a mountain lioness from her cub,
I've restored a mad gorilla to its owner
But I don't dare to face that Tub...

What a frightful-looking beast —
Half an inch across at least —
It would frighten even Superman or Garth.
There's contempt it can't disguise
In the little beady eyes
Of the spider sitting glowering in the bath.

It ignores my every lunge
With the back-brush and the sponge;
I have bombed it with 'A Present from Penarth';
But it doesn't mind at all —
It just rolls into a ball
And simply goes on squatting in the bath...

For hours we have been locked in endless struggle;
I have lured it to the deep end, by the drain;
At last I think I've washed it down the plug-'ole
But here it comes a-crawling up the chain!

Now it's time for me to shave
Though my nerves will not behave,
And there's bound to be a fearful aftermath;
So before I cut my throat
I shall leave this final note:
DRIVEN TO IT — BY THE SPIDER IN THE BATH!

MICHAEL FLANDERS and DONALD SWANN

Thinking about Attitudes and Feelings

(1) 'I have fought a grizzly bear, / Tracked a cobra to its lair ....' What is the narrator trying to prove to the reader?

(2) What are the narrator's feelings towards a cricket on the hearth?

(3) What are the narrator's feelings towards 'a great big hairy spider in the bath'?

(4) Why is it a particularly brave act to have 'dragged a mountain lioness from her cub'?

(5) What attempts has the narrator made to remove the spider from the bath?

(6) How has the spider reacted to these attempts?

(7) 'There's contempt it can't disguise / In the little beady eyes ....' Why do you think the spider is contemptuous of the narrator?

(8) What is the 'fearful aftermath' likely to be?

(9) Which act of bravery on the part of the narrator did you find the most impressive. Give a reason for you choice.

(10) Did you enjoy reading 'The Spider'? Why or why not?

Spelling 14

THE ARCHER-FISH

permission	consignment	opportunity	eventually	entertainment
popularity	generosity	obstruction	irritate	energetically
attitude	referred	enthusiasm	exhibition	industrious
accuracy	succulent	aquarium	cautiously	exaggerate

Missing Words

Read through *Archie* and copy into your workbook the words that correctly fit the blank spaces. Select your words from the spelling box. Note the helpful letters.

Archie

There is one fish in the .... in our pet-shop which must be approached .... because it spits e.......... and with great a.......... at any s.......... morsel it happens to see. This fish is called the archer-fish but our particular specimen is .... to by us as 'Archie'.

Archie has achieved great p.......... because onlookers find such e.......... value in his activities. You see, Archie has a very i.......... a.......... towards hunting, and he spits rather like a machine-gun. Archie seizes any o..........to shoot down blowflies, and does so with much e.......... . I do not e.......... when I say that Archie's performance has become the number-one attraction at our pet-shop.

Word Forms

Change each of the words in heavy type into its correct form.

(1) The archer-fish is **popularity** with pet-owners.

(2) A **generosity** supply of blowflies is needed to feed the archer-fish.

(3) Do you need a **permission** to keep an archer-fish?

(4) Visitors to the aquarium are asked not to **obstruction** the shop doorway.

(5) The archer-fish is an **energetically** hunter.

(6) The manager showed **irritate** when the fish spat in his face.

(7) A **cautiously** approach is needed when dealing with any wild creature.

(8) It is no **exaggerate** to say that the archer-fish is a fantastic hunter.

Working with List-words

Persons

Give the person that comes from each of the following words:
(1) industrious   (2) entertainment   (3) enthusiasm.

Similar words

Find list-words that are similar in meaning to the following:

(1) juicy   (2) busy   (3) chance   (4) annoy   (5) blockage.

Opposite words

Find list-words that are opposite in meaning to the following:

(1) soothe   (2) rashly   (3) meanness   (4) lazily   (5) understate.

Try Thinking 14

Occupations

Sort the people in the box into their job fields in the table at the bottom. There are five people to each job field. Note the example.

PEOPLE				
banker	dentist	magician	physiotherapist	contestant
doctor	judge	reserve	pilot	police officer
actor	mechanic	lawyer	accountant	umpire
driver	musician	coach	juror	passenger
referee	nurse	auditor	cashier	playwright
creditor	solicitor	ballerina	pharmacist	bus conductor

Health	Business	Entertainment	Sport	Law	Transport
doctor					

Match-ups

Each word in the left-hand column has a word in the right-hand column which has a similar meaning. See if you can match them up.

swamp	canyon
digit	bravery
trail	sign
odour	dwelling
remedy	marsh
gorge	edge
mariner	track
warrior	inside
moisture	smell
mischief	weakness
margin	finger
residence	sailor
valour	cure
conversation	soldier
feebleness	talk
omen	dampness
interior	trouble
malady	illness

Odd One Out

In each of the rows A and B there is one outsider. Which, and why? (Answer on p. 260.)

Unit Fifteen

Comprehension 15

When a raging, uncontrollable wildfire sweeps across dry grassland and dense eucalyptus forest, Pete, Bill, Jan, Steve and Fizzer find themselves fighting together for their very survival.

FIRESTORM

Fire was exploding in the forest. Such high flame flashes and explosions meant that a rapid distillation of eucalyptus gases was taking place. It meant a high-intensity fire. Each of them felt he was sitting on a time-bomb. So far as Bill was concerned the only good point was that Steven must now see for himself how necessary he was in this battle for survival. Surely he wouldn't bolt now.

The whole roof was rattling and banging and lifting at the edges, threatening to take off. If they lost the roof they would never survive; beneath the iron there was only a flimsy lining-board ceiling which would burn like kindling if a spark landed on it. So they battled with the roof while smoke poured into their lungs and the iron grew hotter and hotter. At every edge the wind raised Bill hammered in another nail while the other two held the sheet down with their bodies. Not until they were absolutely sure that no more nails would be needed did they come down. Their hands and faces were burnt by sparks and glowing sticks, flying ahead of the main body of fire.

In the meantime, Jan and Fizzer had become the bucket gang, trying to obey Bill's shouted commands from the roof, to aim high. With Bluey at the tap. A bleary-eyed, shaking Bluey, yet sufficiently conscious of what was happening not to let the buckets overflow or to waste a drop of water. He felt the responsibility of age for youth; he was determined that these youngsters should be saved. That was what kept him on his feet.

Then the door of the hen-house which housed Gran's twelve fowls blew open and

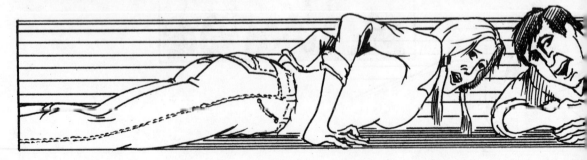

the hens ran out squawking, wings flapping, and the wind lifted them and carried them out of sight to their fate. It blew down the hen-house, flattened Gran's small vegetable garden and deposited another sheet of iron at the kitchen door. This time the iron proved a godsend instead of a desperate problem. The bucket-carrier — either Bill or Pete — going the long haul to wet down the rear of the house was able to hold the iron in front of him to protect his body from radiated heat. For the rest of them, the shield for their faces against the heat was a spade or shovel.

Masses of burning debris were flying overhead. Great slivers of candlebark, burning from end to end, some six feet long, rode on the wind like long burning cigars.

For hours they had not been able to distinguish between night and day; the cottage was dark except for the eerie, flickering movement of glow and shadow. They didn't relight the lamp. It was not only Steven who could not bear to light another flame.

Now another noise assailed the walls, tried to penetrate the roof and blocked their eardrums, so that they had to scream to make themselves heard. The noise of the flames, added to the noise of wind.

Flames that rose up, twenty-footers, like waves, but with red crests instead of white. Mad, rushing flame that gyrated, leaped, thrust and screamed.

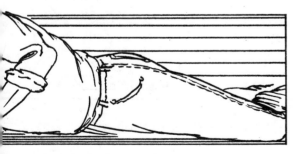

'It's on us — a fire-storm,' Bill said, quietly. 'Fire gone mad. God knows what it will do next.'

Strangely, they all heard him, despite the noise; as though it was something they had to hear, had to know. That the danger was — extreme.

They looked out of the smeared window and saw the great sheets of flame hurl themselves across the clearing. They licked at the walls of the cottage and the heat inside became so great that it seemed the house itself must explode.

'Lie on the floor!' Bill shouted. 'Get down, Bluey!' There was more oxygen at ground-level.

The old teamster was so obsessed now with the thought that he must save these young ones that Bill had to take the bucket forcibly from his hands, and insist that he stretch out on the floor. As they lay there, the cat leapt down from the mantelpiece and crouched in a corner, green eyes glowering.

Now they dared not open the door to cast another bucketful on the wooden walls. If they did, the fire would sweep in. They could only pray that the flames would be satisfied to lick the water from the wood and pass on.

The boom of the flames as they flung across the clearing was like the passing of a hundred jet planes. But afterwards, the sound only partially passed away; the crackle of the fire remained to shrivel and destroy everything it touched.

But the dreadful intensity of burning lasted only a few minutes. When the first wall of flame had swept over, Bill sprang to his feet. 'Main body's passed! Now I'll have to get more water on the walls. We're over the worst.'

from *Wildfire*
by MAVIS THORPE CLARK

How Well Did You Understand?

(1) In what way did Bill feel that the fire could be a help to Steven?

(2) Why would those in the house have no hope of survival if the roof took off?

(3) What did they do to try to keep the roof on?

(4) What suffering did they have to endure?

(5) What evidence can you find to show that the wind was very strong?

(6) In what way did the sheet-iron prove to be a godsend?

(7) What evidence can you find to suggest that Bluey was older than the others?

(8) Why was it better to lie on the floor than to stand up?

(9) What evidence can you find that the noise of the fire was extremely loud?

(10) What clues in the story indicate that Bill was the leader of the group?

(11) There is a number of onomatopoeic words (sound-words) in the passage — e.g. 'rattling', 'banging'. What other onomatopoeic words can you find?

(12) What did you learn about the character of (a) Bluey (b) Bill (c) Steven?

Dictionary Words

Write down the meaning of each of the following words from the passage. You may like to use the back-of-the-book dictionary to help you.

(a) flimsy (b) distillation (c) debris (d) assail (e) gyrate (f) glowering.

Language 15

Word Families

In the process of learning about nouns, verbs, adjectives and adverbs, you may have noticed that many words belong to families. Some words have large families, while other words have small families. The word 'argue', for instance, belongs to a large family — *argue* (verb), *argument* (noun), *argumentative* (adjective), *arguably* (adverb). See whether you can complete the following word families. The first one has been done for you.

Noun	Verb	Adjective	Adverb
selection	select	selective	selectively
attraction			
	compete		
		prosperous	
			hastily
mystery			
	educate		
		memorable	
			widely
product			
	terrify		
		admirable	
			inclusively

Family selections

Select the appropriate words from the word families in the boxes and place them in the gaps. Each word is to be used once only.

> extend   extending   extent   extension   extensively   extensive

(1) The .... to the house was completed within two months.

(2) .... damage was done to the car.

(3) We will be .... our holidays.

(4) A vast .... of the forest was damaged by the fire.

(5) The farmer decided to .... his orchard.

(6) The tourists had travelled .... through America.

> managed   managerial   management   manageable   manager

(1) The supervisor displayed excellent .... skills.

(2) The .... of the cinema raised the admission charges.

(3) The farmer said that the wild bull was ....

(4) The hockey player .... to control his temper.

(5) The new .... had dramatically increased the shop's sales.

> operating   operator   operation   operational   co-operate

(1) The lift .... was absent from work.

(2) The union decided to .... with the government.

(3) The whole .... took only a few minutes.

(4) The patient lay on the .... table.

(5) The machinery was fully ....

> strong   strongest   strength   strengthened   strengthening   strongly

(1) His .... slowly returned after his illness.

(2) He is the .... of the three weightlifters.

(3) Concrete is often .... by steel cables.

(4) She has a very .... will.

(5) The swimmer swam ....

(6) The old bridge needs ....

Nouns

Match up the nouns on the left with their meanings on the right.

(1) gazette   a list of things to be done or dealt with

(2) diary   the life story of a person written by that person

(3) anthology   a book providing information

(4) legend   a book giving names and addresses, or other listings

(5) agenda   a collection of poems or literary extracts

(6) summary   an official or government publication

(7) directory   a book in which one records one's daily experiences

(8) autobiography   a recounting of events

(9) manual   a popular tale handed down by tradition

(10) narrative   a short statement of the main points

Verbs

Write out *The Bushfire* and insert the appropriate verbs from the box into the blank spaces.

burst	fled	grew	ignite	was flying	had seen
paused	was	heard	saw	was travelling	had caught

The Bushfire

I w........... in lofty timber, and, as I p..........., I h........... the mighty crackling of fire coming through the wood. At the same instant, the blinding smoke b........... into a million tongues of flickering flame, and I .... the fire — not where I .... it before, not creeping along among the scrub, but up above, a hundred and fifty feet overhead. It .... the dry tops of the higher boughs and w........... f........... along from tree-top to tree-top like lightning. Below, the wind was comparatively moderate; but up there, it .... twenty miles an hour. I saw one tree .... like gun-cotton, and then my heart .... small, and I turned and ....

from *The Recollections of Geoffrey Hamlyn*
by HENRY KINGSLEY

Adjectives

Form an adjective from each of these words by adding the suffix **ous, ant, ible, able, ive** or **al**. Sometimes you'll need to make a slight change to the end of the word before you add the suffix — e.g. exclude/exclusive.

(1) possess	(7) describe	(13) contempt	(19) deceive	(25) justify
(2) nature	(8) irritate	(14) spire	(20) nerve	(26) influence
(3) intellect	(9) treachery	(15) explode	(21) terror	(27) excite
(4) tolerate	(10) attract	(16) signify	(22) observe	(28) origin
(5) digest	(11) envy	(17) reverse	(23) instruct	(29) notice
(6) persuade	(12) experiment	(18) defy	(24) avoid	(30) occasion

Adverbs

Replace the words in italics in each sentence with an adverb from the box.

steadily	accidentally	annually	immediately	inaudibly
daily	humbly	repeatedly	perpetually	successfully

(1) The proud man did not speak *in a modest manner*.

(2) The pensioner *over and over again* requested help.

(3) He answered the letter *without any delay*.

(4) The taxi crashed into our car *without meaning to*.

(5) The school prize-giving ceremony is held *once every year*.

(6) The surf pounds against the rocks *without ever ceasing*.

(7) We have the paper delivered *every day*.

(8) The student's work was improving *in a firm, regular way*.

(9) The television star spoke *in such a way as to be unheard*.

(10) The ship was launched *with a favourable result*.

Punctuation 15

The Apostrophe — To show contraction

One use of the apostrophe is to show that one or more letters have been dropped from a word.

EXAMPLES: **I've** found it   (I have found it)
He's ready   (He is ready)

Opening up

Give the full form of each of the following.

(1) You'll go.

(2) It doesn't matter.

(3) They'd done it.

(4) We're willing.

(5) It needn't be long.

(6) He can't stand it.

(7) They're prepared.

(8) It wasn't planned.

(9) That'll be satisfactory.

(10) I'm sure.

Closing up

Use an apostrophe to contract each of the following.

(1) They are off.

(2) I will wait.

(3) We need not hurry.

(4) You cannot be late.

(5) I am packed.

(6) Let us go.

(7) We must not complain.

(8) I have checked.

(9) That is a good plan.

(10) She did not wish to apply.

Creative Writing 15

Descriptions of Places

In a piece of creative writing that describes a place, there will often be a *dominant feeling* that is present and recognizable. Read carefully the three descriptions of places which follow. Each is accompanied by questions on the writer's technique, and these will help you to see just how the place and its dominant feeling are related.

In the first description, the place is the Malaysian jungle. The dominant feeling that emerges as you read is that of the suffocating profusion of the plant-life....

Here the tall trees with their barks of a dozen hues, ranging from marble white to scaly greens and reds, thrust their way up to a hundred feet or even double that height, straight as symmetrical cathedral pillars, until they find the sun and burst into a green carpet far, far above; trees covered with tortuous vines and creepers, some hanging like the crazy rigging of a wrecked schooner, some born in the fork of a tree, branching out in great tufts of fat green leaves or flowers; others twisting and curling round the massive trunks, throwing out arms like clothes-lines from tree to tree. In places the jungle stretches for miles at sea level — and then it often degenerates into marsh, into thick mangrove swamp that can suck a man out of sight in a matter of minutes....

The War of the Running Dogs by NOEL BARBER

Questions

(1) How does the writer present to the reader the idea of a great range of colour amongst the trees?

(2) Why is the comparison of forest trees to cathedral pillars an appropriate one here?

(3) What is the word used by the writer to indicate the 'explosion' of vegetation that occurs when the trees find the sun?

(4) When the writer comes to describe how the vines and creepers cover the trees, words and sounds are repeated — e.g. 'some hanging ... some born', 'twisting ... curling ... throwing', 'tree to tree'. Can you say what impact such repetition is likely to have on the reader?

(5) What comparison describes how the vines and creepers are hanging in the trees?

(6) The last sentence contrasts sharply with what has gone before. In what ways is it sharply in contrast?

In the next passage the description is of the sea as it pounds a remote coastline. The dominant feeling that emerges as you read is one of uncontrolled wildness and savagery.

They call it the Ninety Mile Beach. From thousands of miles round the cold, wet underbelly of the world the waves come sweeping in towards the shore and pitch down in a terrible ruin of white water and spray. All day and all night they tumble and thunder. And when the wind rises it whips the sand up the beach and the white spray darts and writhes in the air like snakes of salt.

from *Storm Boy* by COLIN THIELE

Questions

(1) What words does the writer use to impress upon the reader the power that the waves have built up before they hit the beach?

(2) 'The waves come sweeping in towards the shore ...'
If you say these words aloud, you hear long sounds in a flowing rhythm. What do they suggest to you?

(3) 'And pitch down in a terrible ruin of white water and spray.'
Now the sounds chop and change, and are short and confused. Why the sudden change?

(4) Why did the author write 'All day and all night' instead of simply 'All day and night'?

(5) When you say the last sentence aloud, you seem to hear a hissing sound. Which words help to create this effect?

The final description is of a clear, frosty night in the forest. The dominant feeling that emerges as you read is one of stillness and moonlit brilliance, all magically captured and bound together by the intense cold.

> A clear frosty night. Unusual brilliance and coherence of everything. Earth, sky, moon and stars, all seem riveted together by the frost.
>
> Shadows of trees lie across the paths, so clear-cut that they seem carved in relief. You keep thinking you see dark figures endlessly crossing the paths, now here, now there. Big stars hang on the branches like blue lanterns. Small ones are all over the sky like daisies in a summer field.

from *Doctor Zhivago* by BORIS PASTERNAK

Questions

(1) 'Coherence' suggests that everything is somehow connected and united. How does the writer continue this idea even more forcefully?

(2) What is it that seems to be common to everything?

(3) How does the writer introduce a feeling of mystery into the wintry night's scene?

(4) Why do you think the writer makes use of the word 'you' in his description of the tree shadows and the paths?

(5) 'Big stars hang on the branches like blue lanterns.' Can you explain how stars can be linked with tree branches, when the stars are so distant and the branches so close?

(6) 'Small ones are all over the sky like daisies in a summer field.' This is an appealing comparison, but can you say *why* stars and flowers are compared in this way?

Your Turn to Write

Employ your powers of description as you write on *one* of these:

(1) You have won a competition that will allow you to go as a tourist, all expenses paid, to any country in the world. Which country would you choose? Why?

(2) The Ideal Holiday Resort.

(3) The View from Above.

(4) Write a composition ending, 'I will never go *there* again.'

Poetry 15

Fun with Poetry

The next three pages present a selection of humorous poems. Have fun as you read them through; then choose the one you like best and explain why you chose it.

TOOTHPASTE

Who's been at the toothpaste?
I know some of you do it right
and you squeeze the tube from the bottom
and you roll up the tube as it gets used up, don't you?

But somebody
somebody here —
you know who you are
you dig your thumb in
anywhere, anyhow
and you've turned that tube of toothpaste
into a squashed sock.
You've made it so hard to use
it's like trying to get toothpaste
out of a packet of nuts.

You know who you are.
I won't ask you to come out here now
but you know who you are.

And then you went and left the top off didn't you?
So the toothpaste turned to cement.

People who do things like that should . . .
you should be ashamed of yourself.

I am.

MICHAEL ROSEN

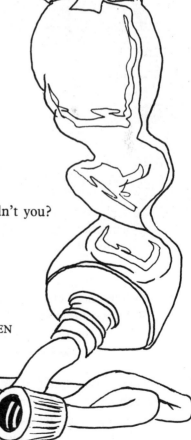

LOVELY MOSQUITO

Lovely mosquito, attacking my arm
As quiet and still as a statue,
Stay right where you are! I'll do you no harm —
I simply desire to pat you.

Just puncture my veins and swallow your fill
For, nobody's going to swot you.
Now, lovely mosquito, stay perfectly still —
A SWIPE! and a SPLAT! and I GOT YOU!

DOUG MACLEOD

ORDER IN THE COURT

Order in the court,
The judge is eating beans.
His wife is in the bathtub
Counting submarines.

THE BOY STOOD IN THE SUPPER-ROOM

The boy stood in the supper-room
　　Whence all but he had fled;
He'd eaten seven pots of jam
　　And he was gorged with bread.

'Oh, one more crust before I bust!'
　　He cried in accents wild;
He licked the plates, he sucked the spoons —
　　He was a vulgar child.

There came a burst of thunder-sound —
　　The boy — oh! where was he?
Ask of the maid who mopped him up,
　　The bread crumbs and the tea!

ODE TO AN EXTINCT DINOSAUR

Iguanodon, I loved you,
With all your spiky scales,
Your massive jaws,
Impressive claws
And teeth like horseshoe nails.

Iguanodon, I loved you.
It moved me close to tears
When first I read
That you've been dead
For ninety million years.

DOUG MACLEOD

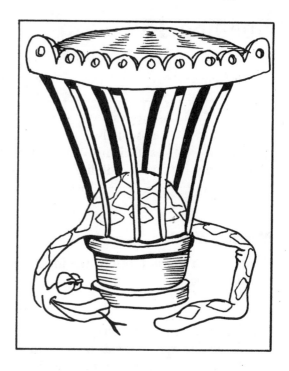

VICTOR R.I.P.

Remember the fate of Victor McGage
Who ventured too close to the reptile cage.
A hungry old snake took a liking to Victor
So, now he's a lump in a boa-constrictor.

DOUG MACLEOD

AUNT LOUISA

When Aunt Louisa lit the gas
    She had the queerest feeling.
Instead of leaving by the door
    She vanished through the ceiling.

MAX FATCHEN

Spelling 15

WILDFIRE

fierce	survival	deposit	penetrate	unfortunately
surround	absolutely	inflammable	increase	wearily
intensity	sufficiently	distinguish	conscious	scheme
completely	responsibility	partially	regrettable	exceptionally

Missing Words

Read through *Rescued*, below, writing down the words from the spelling box which will fit the blank spaces.

Rescued

The f.......... fire had s.......... them c.......... . The teacher and his students were amazed, then terrified by the i.......... of the heat. Soon, they were c.......... of the fact that their very s.......... was at stake. The teacher realized that it was his .... to p.......... the ring of flames somehow and get his students to safety. However, he couldn't think of any s.......... that was s.......... safe. Just when they had given up hope, a figure p.......... hooded in a wet hessian bag appeared. They were able to d.......... a fire-extinguisher in one hand. Their rescuer applied a d.......... of chemical foam to the i.......... material from which the flames were springing. He then led them to a stream, where they w.......... refreshed themselves. They were e.......... fortunate to be alive.

Miscellaneous

Go to spelling-box words for an answer to each of the following.

(1) Another word for a plan is: ....

(2) What kind of person can you form from 'survival'? ....

(3) The opposite of diminish is: ....

(4) To be awake and aware is to be: ....

(5) The opposite of 'luckily' is: ....

(6) By adding the prefix **un**, **ir** or **in**, change these words into their opposites: (a) responsibility (b) complete (c) conscious (d) sufficiently.

(7) A word meaning 'in a tired way': ....

Word Forms

Select the correct form of the word in brackets to fit each of the blank spaces in the following sentences.

(1) As she regained .... [**conscious**] she opened her eyes.

(2) The dropping of a lighted cigarette was .... [**responsibility**] for the bushfire.

(3) After the fire, the house was a .... [**completely**] ruin.

(4) There is an .... [**increase**] danger of bushfires in the area.

(5) The flames from the burning oil produced .... [**intensity**] heat.

(6) The .... [**fierce**] of the blaze kept onlookers at a distance.

(7) They were lucky to have .... [**survival**] the bushfire.

(8) Damage by both fire and water has left the house in a state of .... [**partially**] collapse.

Try Thinking 15

City and Country

Given the city on the left, link it with its country in the centre and a famous feature of that country on the right.

City	Country	Famous Feature
London	France	Amazon River
Athens	USSR	Eiffel Tower
Rio de Janeiro	Australia	Loch Ness monster
Paris	Egypt	Buckingham Palace
Rome	Scotland	Red Square
Sydney	Japan	Acropolis
Moscow	England	Pyramids
Edinburgh	Italy	Mount Fuji
Tokyo	Brazil	Harbour Bridge
Cairo	Greece	Colosseum

You Dig?

Transfer the data gleaned from the clues into the grid, using a tick to indicate a positive assumption and a cross for a negative one. You will then be able to cross-refer data inside this grid with the aid of logical deduction. (Answer on p. 260.)

Professor Rubble, the renowned archaeologist, and five keen young volunteer diggers are working on a prehistoric-cum-Roman site. On the first five days, each volunteer unearthed a particularly interesting find. Can you work out when, where and what it was?

1. The boy digging in the foundations of a building found a flint-head axe; that wasn't Roger, whose find was in an ancient well.
2. Maria found the bronze brooch, but not on Monday.
3. Josie made her find on Wednesday in the storage pit.
4. The knife-blade was found in the grave, but not by Hank.
5. Andy's find was on Friday; and Josie's was unearthed before the pottery fragment.

	Axe-head	Brooch	Knife-blade	Needle	Pottery	Foundations	Grave	Hearth	Storage pit	Well	Monday	Tuesday	Wednesday	Thursday	Friday
Andy															
Hank															
Josie															
Maria															
Roger															
Monday															
Tuesday															
Wednesday															
Thursday															
Friday															
Foundations															
Grave															
Hearth															
Storage pit															
Well															

Unit Sixteen

Comprehension 16

Noel Monkman, in this passage from his book *Escape to Adventure*, graphically recounts his narrow escape from death under the reef.

THE REEF TUNNEL

This life we have chosen has only one serious disadvantage: a submerged but ever-present anxiety that accident or sickness may overtake one or both of us when we are in the depths of the jungle, or on some isolated, uninhabited island far from medical aid. Risks are inseparable from the type of work we do, and although we try to avoid unnecessary dangers they cannot always be foreseen. The desire to photograph some particular scene or subject is so apt temporarily to put the sense of judgment into abeyance, and then only chance or good luck can save the day.

As Kitty says, usually after the event: 'You and your one-track mind! How do you think I would feel being left all alone? If you die under the sea I might not see even your body again, and if we are in the jungle, am I to dig a grave and bury you there, then try to find my way out alone?' Listening in submissive silence, I know she is right to scold me: but awkward situations seem silently to creep up on one, and to become evident only as *faits accomplis*.

Wearing the aqualung, I was swimming along the inner edge of a coral reef with my winged undersea camera. A big shoal of rainbow-hued parrot-fish sped out from a deep canyon in the coral reef. They made a glorious picture as, brightly lit, they swam in the open sea with the sombre gloom of the canyon as a background. Tilting the wings of the camera, I swam downwards towards them. As I approached they turned back towards the reef and disappeared into a deep narrow channel. They were swimming leisurely, so I knew they had not been frightened by my approach, and I swam into the channel after them in the hope that they would again swim out into the open where I could get a good picture. As I swam forward, the channel grew narrower overhead, and I realized it was becoming a tunnel under the coral. There was a turn just a short distance ahead, and I decided to swim round the corner, and, if the parrot-fish had disappeared, return again to the inner edge of the reef.

I turned the corner, and it was like looking along a tube. At the far end was the lovely translucent blue of the open sea with the parrot-fish moving slowly past. It looked too good to miss, so I swam on down the tunnel. When I reached the opening the shoal had moved some distance away, so again I followed them out into the open, intent on securing my picture. They still showed no sign of fear, but most tantalizingly stayed just out of range for a good undersea picture. One of the great difficulties in underwater photography is to get close enough to the subject to overcome the mistiness caused by the sediment and microscopic life in the sea.

Concentration on the job prevented my noticing a dull, rhythmic, thudding sound, and it was only when the shoal moved steadily away into the distance that I realized the sound had been going on for some time. It is very difficult to identify sounds under the sea, so I swam upwards towards the surface. As I ascended, the sea became very bright, but so full of air bubbles it was impossible to see where I was going. Then my head broke the surface, and I struck out desperately to escape being dashed by the waves on to the reef. I was on the outer edge of the reef where the breakers from the open sea were pounding down on to the coral, and the tide had turned and was sweeping in over the exposed reef. That submarine tunnel I had come through ran from the smooth water in the lee of the reef to the open water of the Coral Sea. Kitty and the dinghy were on the other side of the reef in the sheltered water, and there was no way for her to reach me even if the dinghy could have remained afloat in those angry seas. If I tried to swim with the incoming tide across the shallow reef I would be torn to pieces on the coral; the only hope was to find that many-times accursed tunnel, and return the way I had come. I had come out of the tunnel and followed the fish to the right of the opening.

Down I went into the quiet waters beneath the churning seas, and swam in again towards the cliff-like face of the reef. As I swam, I realized I should have known where I was as soon as I came out of the tunnel, for now I was near the reef I could see the cliff face going sheer down until it faded away in the awesome blue of the depths. There was nothing between me and the floor of the sea but several thousand feet of deep blue ocean. The continental shelf ends abruptly beyond the northern Outer Reef, but the sea inside the Great Barrier Reef is comparatively shallow: reef-building corals cannot grow at a depth of more than one hundred and fifty feet. Sheer carelessness — I should have known better than to allow my interest in obtaining one not very important shot to put me in this predicament.

Steadily I swam along, keeping the face of the submarine cliff on my left. The tunnel opening must now be near. I saw an opening and struck out more strongly. It looked like the tunnel. I paused and peered into the opening. No, that's not it; it is evidently only a deep cave; the coral walls disappear into darkness, and there is no sign of light shining through from the other end in the lee of the reef. I swam on. Another opening — well, that was lucky, it didn't take long to find. But this was not it, only a coral grotto extending back twenty or thirty feet into the cliff face. I began to swim faster. How many false openings would I have to explore before finding the right one? I began to breathe heavily. Steady up — the faster you swim, the more air you'll use up. This is a time to keep cool — I feel cold. Calm — that was the word — keep calm — things are bad enough without starting to panic. I wonder how much compressed air remains in these steel bottles? Forget it — you can't put any more in now. Where is that tunnel? I must have passed it — I've come a good deal farther along this way than when I followed that shoal of fish. You fool! Of course, you have — that wasn't a cave you passed the first time, that was the tunnel! Don't you remember the turn near the other end? Of course, the light doesn't show through — how do you think the light can turn corners? Round I swung and started back. The entrance! It looks familiar, but I could be wrong. Well, if I am wrong — I could be dead. In I go.

The light grew dimmer as I swam inwards until I could barely see the walls of jagged coral, which seemed to be slipping past me at an ever-increasing speed. Fear gives wings to one's feet, so I have heard. I seemed to be doing quite well with ordinary rubber flippers on my feet. Very dark now. Then I realized why I was moving so fast. I was in the tunnel all right, but the incoming tide was racing through it like a mill race! If I touched the sides of the tunnel I would have only a short period to appreciate what 'death by a thousand cuts' meant. The air was coming feebly from my bottles, and I pulled the emergency wire which releases a last five minutes of air. Then I saw a wall of coral rapidly growing nearer and brighter — the turn in the tunnel! I swam hard towards the right-hand side so that I could turn sharp around the corner. It was bright and clear now. I reached the turn and swam strongly forward towards the exit, but the racing waters carried me towards the wall on the left. Frantically I lashed out with my flippers. Almost round. An agonizing pain bit into my leg. I had kicked savagely against a mass of branching coral. Forget it — keep kicking! I was round the turn and speeding towards the calm water inside the reef. Leg was a bit sore — but not too bad — my emergency air supply was still functioning smoothly — I surfaced and swam towards Kitty and the dinghy.

from *Escape to Adventure*
by NOEL MONKMAN

How Well Did You Understand?

(1) How do you know that the author, Noel Monkman, leads a life full of adventure?

(2) How does his wife Kitty feel about this kind of life?

(3) When he is working as a photographer, what can cause Monkman temporarily to lose his sense of judgement?

(4) How did Monkman know that his approach had not frightened the rainbow-hued parrot-fish?

(5) What is one of the great difficulties of underwater photography?

(6) What was the 'dull, rhythmic, thudding sound'? Why hadn't Monkman noticed it earlier?

(7) Why could Kitty not have used the dinghy to rescue her husband?

(8) When he couldn't find the tunnel, Monkman began to swim faster. But why was he concerned about his swimming speed?

(9) What made Monkman realize that he had mistaken the tunnel for a cave?

(10) 'Then I realized why I was moving so fast.' What caused him to be swimming so fast along the tunnel?

(11) What does 'death by a thousand cuts' mean?

(12) What did you learn about the character of the author, Noel Monkman?

Dictionary Words

Write down the meaning of each of the following words. You might like to consult the back-of-the-book dictionary.

(a) abeyance   (b) submissive   (c) tantalizingly   (d) sombre   (e) translucent
(f) grotto.

Language 16

Revision

Nouns

Form nouns from these words. The first one has been done to help you.

(1) dark ......*darkness*......	(9) hinder	(17) satisfying ....
(2) interfere	(10) humiliate	(18) begin ....
(3) intend	(11) inferior	(19) heroic ....
(4) prepare	(12) grieve	(20) complain ....
(5) insure	(13) equal	(21) simple ....
(6) recover	(14) shrink	(22) complete ....
(7) qualify	(15) various	(23) postpone ....
(8) warm	(16) protect	(24) assist ....

Verbs

The poem that follows depicts various creatures in action. But the verbs, in italics, have been jumbled. Write out the poem with the verbs unscrambled.

Frogs *mpju*
Caterpillars *pmhu*

Worms *gligwe*
Bugs *glegij*

Rabbits *pho*
Horses *pocl*

Snakes *idsel*
Seagulls *eidlg*

Mice *ercpe*
Deer *plea*

Puppies *uncobe*
Kittens *uncope*

Lions *ktlas* —
But —
I *lwka!*

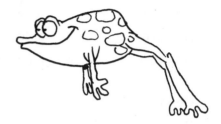

Shades of meaning

From the box, select the most appropriate adjective to complete each of the fifteen groups that follow. The first one has been done to help you.

delicious	diminutive	freezing	foul	exhausted
opulent	prehistoric	invulnerable	expert	saturated
forlorn	idiotic	chivalrous	evil	devoted

(1) palatable	tasty	appetizing	......*delicious*......
(2) sad	unhappy	despondent	....
(3) old	antiquated	ancient	....
(4) small	little	tiny	....
(5) silly	foolish	stupid	....
(6) cool	cold	chilly	....
(7) bad	harmful	sinister	....
(8) tired	weary	fatigued	....
(9) capable	skilful	accomplished	....

(10) unclean	dirty	filthy	....
(11) safe	secure	protected	....
(12) fond	affectionate	loving	....
(13) damp	moist	wet	....
(14) rich	affluent	wealthy	....
(15) civil	polite	courteous	....

Opposites

By adding the prefix **un**, **in**, **im**, **ir**, **il**, or **dis**, give each of these adjectives an opposite meaning.

(1) convenient	(7) loyal	(13) visible	(19) honourable
(2) logical	(8) truthful	(14) mortal	(20) healthy
(3) popular	(9) mobile	(15) adequate	(21) experienced
(4) considerate	(10) relevant	(16) controllable	(22) polite
(5) advantageous	(11) frequent	(17) accurate	(23) digestible
(6) movable	(12) worthy	(18) responsible	(24) clement

Using the better word

In your writing, always strive to use the very best words you can. In the following sentences, replace each *lot* with a more expressive word from the box.

cluster	pack	choir	flotilla	volley	orchard
swarm	troupe	bouquet	cairn	mob	team

(1) A *lot* of ships proceeded out of the harbour.

(2) A *lot* of cattle suddenly blocked our way.

(3) A *lot* of acrobats arrived in the town.

(4) The florist sent three *lots* of flowers.

(5) A *lot* of bees attacked the picnickers.

(6) A *lot* of footballers went onto the field.

(7) A *lot* of wolves attacked the settlers.

(8) The farmer planted a *lot* of fruit-trees.

(9) The explorers erected a *lot* of stones.

(10) The countess had a *lot* of diamonds on her finger.

(11) The infantry fired a *lot* of shots.

(12) A *lot* of singers stood at the front of the auditorium.

Misused words

There are words in our language which people often confuse. When words are misused communication is hindered. Write out the following sentences, selecting the correct word from the brackets.

(1) The politician was trying to [**canvass/canvas**] votes.

(2) The [**moral/morale**] of the troops is excellent.

(3) He was a [**veracious/voracious**] eater.

(4) The millionaire lives in a [**luxuriant/luxurious**] home.

(5) Her invention was [**ingenuous/ingenious**].

(6) The horse has hurt [**its/it's**] leg.

(7) Because he is so [**human/humane**], he will never hurt anyone intentionally.

(8) The [**populous/populace**] rejoiced when peace was declared.

(9) The first [**peel/peal**] of the bell was the signal for the [**peasants/pheasants**] to attack the castle.

(10) The judge [**wandered/wondered**] why some of the key witnesses had not been [**persecuted/prosecuted**].

(11) This belt is [**lose/loose**].

(12) [**Their/There**] books have been left over [**their/there**].

Punctuation 16

Revision

Correctly punctuate each of the following sentences.

(1) ladislo biro invented the ball-point pen now known as the biro

(2) one of mr pedricks inventions was a network of giant peashooters to shoot snowballs from the polar regions and thus irrigate the arid areas of the world

(3) whose rat is it asked Tony

(4) who cares about stupid old careers louie groaned

(5) get that rat out of here screamed the terrified teacher standing on a chair

(6) the deputy-head said boys i want you to be quiet and attentive during the important talk that is to follow on careers

(7) with a wonderful spring forward mary rodgers began her sprint to the tape

(8) possibly anne frank would have become a great writer if she had survived the war

(9) in the middle of the cavern the monstrous animal awaited its next victim

(10) luke jabba the hutt is expecting us said leia

(11) dingoes are fond of eating the following grubs frogs rats mice lizards and any other small bush creature

(12) here is a list of the things to look for in dingo country paw marks on the sand a scrap of fur caught on a bush a musky smell bones scraps of food

(13) alan marshalls greatest wish was to swim out into the lake alone

(14) johns thoughts soared like a balloon

(15) the german soldiers guns were pointed at the dutch family gathered round their kitchen table

(16) the childrens fears were confirmed when they heard the feet pounding up the stairs

(17) look out theres a shark warned the diver urgently

(18) where is it asked his companion fearfully

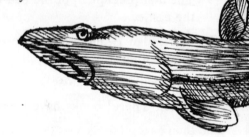

Creative Writing 16

Here is a piece of writing about a powerful inhabitant of the sea. This creature is driven through the depths by a single, overwhelming urge. . . .

THE EEL

He was eight feet long. At the centre of his back he was two feet in circumference. Slipping sinuously along the bottom of the sea at a gigantic pace, his black, mysterious body glistened and swirled like a wisp in a foaming cataract. His little eyes, stationed wide apart in his flat-boned, broad skull, searched the ocean for food. He coursed ravenously for miles along the base of the range of clifs. He searched fruitlessly, except for three baby pollocks which he swallowed in one mouthful without arresting his progress. He was very hungry.

Then he turned by a sharp promontory and entered a cliff-bound harbour where the sea was dark and silent, shaded by the concave cliffs. Savagely he looked ahead into the dark waters. Then instantaneously he flicked his tail, rippling his body like a twisted screw, and shot forward. His long, thin, single whisker, hanging from his lower snout like a label tag, jerked back under his belly. His glassy eyes rested ferociously on minute white spots that scurried about in the sea a long distance ahead. The conger eel had sighted his prey. There was a school of mackerel a mile away. . . .

He roamed about for half an hour, a demented giant of the deep, travelling restlessly at an incredible speed. Then at last his little eyes again sighted his prey.

Little white spots again hung like faded drops of brine in the sea ahead of him. He rushed thither. He opened his jaws as the spots assumed shape, and they loomed up close to his eyes. But just as he attempted to gobble the nearest one, he felt a savage impact. Then something hard and yet intangible pressed against his head and then down along his back. He leaped and turned somersault. The hard gripping material completely enveloped him. He was in a net.

from *The Conger Eel*
by LIAM O'FLAHERTY

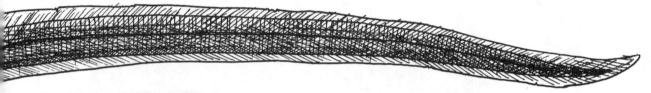

Studying the Description

This description of an eel is arranged in three paragraphs, each of which gives us a different view of the eel. The opening sentence of the first paragraph has only five words, yet it presents us with a startling fact that makes us sit up and take notice. We want to read on and find out more about this large creature. Having been told its size, we look at its body, and then pass on to its eyes and head. And all the while, the eel is searching ravenously for food.

Notice the way the words 'Slipping sinuously', used together, seem to follow the twists of a long, powerful body. Read the words aloud and you 'see' the picture of the twisting eel even more clearly. Finally, the short sentence 'He was very hungry' ends the paragraph neatly. Furthermore, it points the way to the main idea contained in the next paragraph.

If you had to think up a heading for the second paragraph, you might choose 'He Searches for, and Sights, his Prey'. This paragraph takes a longer look at the eel's movements. See if you can find several words that describe movements and other features of the eel. Notice, at the end of this paragraph, the use of the dots . . . hinting that something is going to happen.

In the third and last paragraph, the eel reaches its prey. Words such as 'demented' (maddened), 'rushed' and 'gobble' portray the savagery of the eel as a hunter. But what, in turn, envelops the eel? (What title would you give to *this* paragraph?) Finally, notice the short sentence that ends this description: 'He was in a net.' Simple? But satisfying, isn't it? Try, in your own writing, to experiment with simple yet satisfying beginnings and endings of this kind.

Your Turn to Write

Let your imagination go as you write about *one* of the following:

(1) 'If I Won a Million Dollars.'

(2) 'My Crazy Ideas for Making Money.'

(3) 'If I Were a Television Celebrity.'

(4) 'If I Were Prime Minister.'

(5) 'The Hold-up.' (Imagine you are a customer in a bank during a hold-up. Describe the experience.)

Poetry 16

Fun with Animals

Ogden Nash is at his humorous best as he introduces us to a man's best friend.

AN INTRODUCTION TO DOGS

The dog is man's best friend.
He has a tail on one end.
Up in front he has teeth.
And four legs underneath.

Dogs like to bark,
They like it best after dark.
They not only frighten prowlers away
But also hold the sandman at bay.

A dog that is indoors
To be let out implores.
You let him out and what then?
He wants back in again.

Dogs display reluctance and wrath
If you try to give them a bath.
They bury bones in hideaways
And half the time they trot sideaways.

They cheer up people who are frowning,
And rescue people who are drowning,
They truck mud on beds,
And chew people's clothes to shreds.

Dogs in the country have fun.
They run and run and run.
But in the city this species
Is dragged around on leashes.

Dogs are upright as a steeple
And much more loyal than people.

OGDEN NASH

Thinking about Dogs

(1) 'The dog is man's best friend.' What proof does the poet offer for this statement?

(2) What comment would you make about the poet's physical description of a dog in the first stanza?

(3) What is the meaning of 'hold the sandman at bay'?

(4) What is the meaning of 'To be let out implores'?

(5) How does a dog react if its owner tries to give it a bath?

(6) What are some of the good things dogs do?

(7) What are some of the bad things dogs do?

(8) What is the difference between the life of a country dog and that of a city dog?

(9) What does the poet mean by 'Dogs are upright as a steeple'?

(10) Write down the stanza you liked best and explain why you chose it.

Ogdeniana

Here are a few more of Ogden Nash's wonderful poems. Select the two that you like best and, in a few sentences, explain why you chose them.

THE KANGAROO

O Kangaroo, O Kangaroo,
Be grateful that you're in a zoo,
And not transmuted by a boomerang
To zestful tangy Kangaroo meringue.

THE OSTRICH

The ostrich roams the great Sahara.
Its mouth is wide, its neck is narra.
It has such long and lofty legs,
I'm glad it sits to lay its eggs.

THE PORPOISE

I kind of like the playful porpoise,
A healthy mind in a healthy corpus.
He and his cousin, the playful dolphin,
Why they like swimmin like I like golphin.

THE CAMEL

The camel has a single hump;
The dromedary, two;
Or else the other way around.
I'm never sure. Are you?

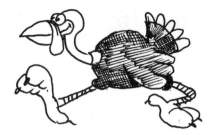

THE TURKEY

There is nothing more perky
Than a masculine turkey.
When he struts he struts
With no ifs or buts.
When his face is apoplectic
His harem grows hectic,
And when he gobbles
Their universe wobbles.

THE LION

Oh, weep for Mr and Mrs Bryan!
He was eaten by a lion;
Following which, the lion's lioness
Up and swallowed Bryan's Bryaness.

THE CANARY

The song of canaries
Never varies,
And when they're molting
They're pretty revolting.

THE RHINOCEROS

The rhino is a homely beast,
For human eyes he's not a feast.
Farewell, farewell, you old rhinoceros,
I'll stare at something less prepoceros.

Spelling 16

REEF PERIL

perilous	glorious	panic	agonizing	functioning
submerged	channel	difficult	exploration	identify
tunnel	photographer	rhythmic	escape	dinghy
familiar	leisurely	frantically	attempting	temporarily

Missing Words

Insert the most appropriate word from the spelling box into each of the spaces. Sometimes a letter is given to help you.

An Encounter with Death

In his book *Escape to Adventure*, Noel Monkman, underwater ...., describes his narrow .... from death while he was a.......... to photograph a big shoal of rainbow-hued parrot-fish. Because the parrot-fish made such a g.......... picture as they were swimming in a l.......... manner towards the reef, Monkman decided to follow them — even when they began to disappear into a deep, narrow c.......... . As he swam forward he realized he was swimming through a t.......... under the coral.

   T.......... forgetting everything except the fish, Monkman suddenly became aware of a dull, r.........., thudding sound. Because it was d.......... to .... sounds under the sea, he swam to the surface, where he learnt that he was in a p.......... situation. He was now on the outer edge of the reef, and unable to return except by the way he had come. Monkman quickly s.......... and passed a.......... minutes as he f.......... searched for the tunnel. Fortunately, this hurried underwater e.......... ended happily when, with only a few minutes left in his air-bottles, he surfaced and swam towards his wife Kitty and the d.......... .

Substituting List-words

Substitute a list-word for each of the words or phrases in italics.

(1) The gash Noel Monkman received from the coral was *extremely painful*.

(2) When he turned on his emergency air-supply, his situation was *very dangerous*.

(3) The rainbow-hued parrot-fish were swimming in an *unhurried* manner.

(4) It was very *hard* for Monkman to *get free* from the tunnel in the coral.

(5) The sight of the fish was *splendid*.

(6) Noel Monkman was *endeavouring* to save his life.

Forming New Words

Create new words by inserting letters into the blank spaces.

(1) indentif __ c __ t __ __ __

(2) familiar __ t __

(3) rhythm __ c __ __ __ y

(4) photograph __ c

(5) difficult __ __ s

(6) __ __ peril

(7) glor __ f __

(8) escap __ e

(9) function __ l

(10) pani __ __ ed

(11) explor __ t __ __ y

(12) ding __ __ __ s

Try Thinking 16

Ship Endings

Find the word that ends with 'ship' for each of the following. The first one has been done for you.

(1) Knowing and liking someone: F r i e n d ship

(2) Suffering difficulty and poverty: H __ __ __ ship

(3) Being in charge: L __ __ __ __ __ ship

(4) Learning a trade: A __ __ __ __ __ __ __ __ ship

(5) Addressing an aristocratic male: Your L __ __ __ ship

(6) A collection of houses and streets: T __ __ __ ship

(7) People go to church in order to W __ __ ship

(8) An aristocratic female is Her L __ __ __ ship

(9) This usually occurs before marriage: C __ __ __ __ ship

(10) A ship used in warfare: B __ __ __ __ __ ship

(11) When you join a club you become part of its M __ __ __ __ __ ship

(12) A top competition in sport is often called this: C __ __ __ __ __ __ ship

Sea Search

Search for fishy things and creatures in the sea of letters. Search across, down and diagonally for the words grouped at right.

SEA OF LETTERS

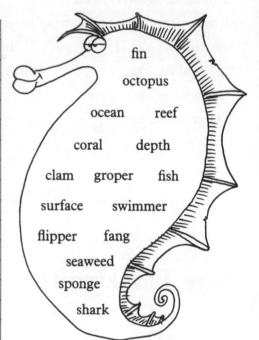

S	U	R	F	A	C	E	P	E	F	I	S	H	E	E	G
W	O	V	T	N	L	S	U	A	X	B	Y	D	Y	C	R
I	P	S	R	G	F	H	S	S	H	A	R	K	T	R	O
M	L	S	P	E	L	T	Y	C	L	U	T	G	U	V	P
M	T	P	G	R	I	F	S	E	A	W	E	E	D	X	E
E	P	O	I	N	P	S	R	E	R	R	L	A	A	M	R
R	P	N	T	H	P	H	K	W	K	A	E	N	P	C	R
M	P	G	R	H	E	G	R	E	C	O	C	E	A	N	S
C	E	E	C	P	R	E	R	E	D	S	H	S	P	J	P
F	O	T	E	V	T	S	U	A	E	L	M	F	F	H	O
F	Y	R	Z	S	O	P	F	E	L	F	Q	T	A	D	T
L	T	O	A	T	S	D	C	T	C	N	P	X	C	N	L
B	C	L	E	L	H	E	C	L	T	O	P	L	C	R	G
F	C	T	R	U	V	P	V	S	R	O	S	C	L	O	R
I	P	B	L	O	C	T	O	P	U	S	O	Q	A	P	G
N	A	C	O	L	M	H	S	H	S	R	S	T	M	C	L

fin

octopus

ocean   reef

coral   depth

clam   groper   fish

surface   swimmer

flipper   fang

seaweed

sponge

shark

Match the Catch!

Which positive corresponds to the negative? (Answer on p. 260.)

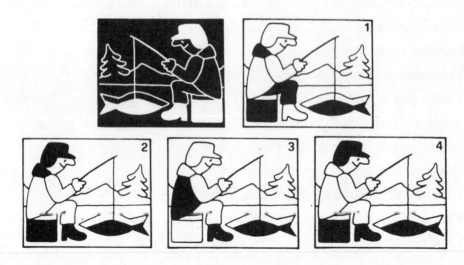

Answers

Page 31. (1) Connie (2) Mary (3) Jean (4) Mabel (5) Clara.

Page 47.
- *Rungs of a ladder.* No rungs will be covered with water. Boat and ladder will rise with the tide.
- *Family tally.* Three girls and four boys.
- *A weather forecast.* In 72 hours' time it will again be midnight, and unless I am near the North or South Pole it is safe to predict that the sun will not be shining.

Page 61. (1) DOG/DOT/ROT/RAT (2) SAW/SAY/SLY/FLY (3) SAND/LAND/LANE/LAKE (4) SINK/SANK/BANK/ BARK/DARK (5) BULL/DULL/DOLL/DOLE/DOZE (6) WET/SET/SAT/SAY/DAY/DRY.

Page 62. Here is the path through the maze, from A to Z.

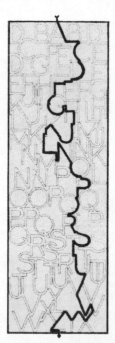

Page 78. 1–D, 2–C, 3–A, 4–B.

Page 93. (1) For disabled persons (2) Danger! (3) 'Let your fingers do the walking' — Yellow Pages (4) The dollar sign (5) First Aid or hospital (6) Pedestrian crossing (7) Food or dining-room facilities (8) Volkswagen (9) Scorpio — sign of the zodiac (10) No fishing! (11) Slippery when wet (12) The Nazi swastika (13) Capricorn — sign of the zodiac (14) Children crossing (15) Leo — sign of the zodiac (16) Peace (17) No smoking! (18) Love (19) Mercedes-Benz (20) No way (21) Gemini — sign of the zodiac (22) McDonald's (23) A doctor. This symbol shows a serpent entwined about a staff (*caduceus*); the staff is the symbol of Hermes, messenger of the gods. (24) A shower is available (25) Flammable material! Beware! (26) Female (27) Male.

Page 108. One way of imposing common sense on the highway is shown below. This is a seven-move solution.

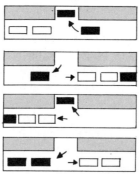

Page 124. The Maydays with 1 child (Clue 1), don't go gardening (Clue 2), to the cinema (Clue 3), the bush (Mundays, Clue 3) or the beach (Clue 4); so they stay at home and watch television.

The Heydays with 5 children (Clue 4), don't watch television (above), go to the beach (Clue 4), or the cinema or the bush (Clue 3); so they are the gardeners.

The beach family isn't the Maydays or Heydays (above), the Mundays (Clue 3) or the Freedays (Clue 4); so it is the Fundays, who thus (Clue 4) have 4 children.

Since the Mundays go for a bush walk (Clue 3), the Freedays must (by elimination) go to the cinema; thus (Clue 3) they have two children. So the Mundays have 3 children.

The cottage-dwellers are not the Maydays (Clue 1), the Heydays (gardeners/semi, Clue 2), the Freedays (cinema, Clue 3) or the Mundays (Clue 3); so they are the Fundays.

Since the Fundays (above) have 4 children, the flat-dwellers must (Clue 2) have 1 child, so they are the Maydays.

The Freedays don't live in a semi, cottage or flat (above), or a terrace (Clue 3), so they have a townhouse. Therefore, by elimination the Mundays live in a terrace.

Summary:
Freedays: Cinema, townhouse, 2 children.
Fundays: Beach, cottage, 4 children.
Heydays: Gardening, semi, 5 children.
Maydays: Television, flat, 1 child.
Mundays: Bush walk, terrace, 3 children.

Page 157. Second vase from the left on shelf C.

Page 175. (1) Look before you leap (2) Long overdue (3) Missing person (4) Broken promise (5) X-ray (6) Sideshow (7) Divide and conquer (8) Lost in the woods (9) Wind in the willows (10) It's out of this world.

Page 209.

```
E S T H E R    W A R R E N
O L I V I A    B E R T I E
A G A T H A    L E S T E R
S A B I N A    C A R L O S
M A X I N E    S T E V E N
S O P H I E    S I D N E Y
```
Missing Persons: Elaine and Wesley.

Page 223. (A) The hen in the lower right-hand corner is the only one scratching with her left claw. (B) The man third from the left has his hair combed back — all the rest have theirs combed forward.

Page 240. Josie's find in the storage pit on Wednesday (Clue 3) wasn't the flint axe-head (Clue 1), bronze brooch (2), knife-blade (4) or pottery fragment (5); so it was the bone needle.

Roger (digging in the well) didn't find the axe-head (Clue 1), brooch (2), needle (above) or knife-blade (4); so he found the pottery fragment; and after Josie (Clue 5), therefore on Thursday, since Andy's find was on Friday.

Maria's bronze brooch (Clue 2) wasn't in the foundations (Clue 1), the well (Clue 1), the storage pit (3) or the grave (4); so it was in the hearth. She didn't find it on Monday (2), Wednesday (3), Thursday (above) or Friday (5); so on Tuesday.

Hank didn't find the needle, pottery or brooch (above), or knife-blade (4); so he found the axe-head in the foundations (Clue 1). He didn't find it on Tuesday, Wednesday or Thursday (above), or Friday (Clue 5), therefore on Monday.

Therefore Andy found the knife-blade in the grave on Friday.

Summary:
Andy: Knife-blade, grave, Friday.
Hank: Axe-head, foundations, Monday.
Josie: Needle, storage pit, Wednesday.
Maria: Bronze brooch, hearth, Tuesday.
Roger: Pottery, well, Thursday.

Page 256. No. 4.

Acknowledgements

The authors and publishers are grateful to the following for permission to reproduce copyright material.

Prose: Prentice-Hall Inc. for two extracts from *Why Didn't I Think of That?* by Webb Garrison © 1977; Routledge & Kegan Paul PLC for two extracts from *The Book of Heroic Failures* by Stephen Pile; Don Congdon Associates Inc. for the extract from *Shane* by Jack Schaefer © 1963; John Murray (Publishers) Ltd for the extract from *A Pattern of Islands* by Arthur Grimble; Associated Book Publishers Ltd for the extract from *Let the Balloon Go* by Ivan Southall; Longman Cheshire Pty Limited for extracts from *I Can Jump Puddles* by Alan Marshall; Curtis Brown Group Limited on behalf of Doris Lessing for the extract from *The Habit of Loving* by Doris Lessing © 1957; Ann Elmo Agency Inc. for the extract from *Leiningen versus the Ants* by Carl Stephenson; William Heinemann Ltd for the extract from *Goodbye to the Rat* by Prudence Andrew; Angus & Robertson Publishers for the extract from *This School Is Driving Me Crazy!* by Nat Hentoff and the extract from *Escape to Adventure* by Noel Monkman; Hodder and Stoughton Ltd and the Evelyn Singer Agency for the extract from *The Hiding Place* by Corrie ten Boom; Vallentine, Mitchell & Co. Ltd for the extract from *The Diary of Anne Frank* by Anne Frank; Michael Dugan for the extract from his book *Dingo Boy*; Rex Collings Ltd for the extract from *Shardik* by Richard Adams; Penguin Books Ltd for the extract from *This Sporting Life* by David Storey © 1960; Lucasfilm Ltd and Ballantine Books (a division of Random House, Inc.) for the extracts from *Return of the Jedi* by James Kahn; David Higham Associates Ltd for the extract from *Vets Might Fly* by James Herriot, published by Michael Joseph Ltd; Burke Publishing Co. Ltd for the extract from *The Day of the Bomb* by Karl Bruckner; Jonathan Cape Ltd for the extract from *Doctor No* by Ian Fleming and the extract from *The Conger Eel* by Liam O'Flaherty; Hodder and Stoughton (Aust.) Pty Ltd for the extract from *Wildfire* by Mavis Thorpe Clark; Rigby Publishers Ltd for extracts from *Storm Boy* by Colin Thiele; Granada Publishing Limited for the extract from *Encounters with Animals* by Gerald Durrell; Victor Gollancz Ltd for the extract from *Z for Zachariah* by Robert C. O'Brien.

Poems: Curtis Brown Ltd for 'The Microscope' by Maxine Kumin; Pam Ayres for her poems 'Goodbye Worn-out Morris 1000' and 'Ever Since I Had Me Op'; Australian Consolidated Press Limited for 'Missionary Bill' by Eric C. Rolls; Angus & Robertson Publishers for 'Sports Field' from *Collected Poems 1942–1970* by Judith Wright and 'Lifesaver' by Elizabeth Riddell; Longman Cheshire Pty Limited for 'Outside the General Hospital' by Bruce Dawe from *An Eye for a Tooth*; David Higham Associates Ltd for 'Timothy Winters' from *Collected Poems* by Charles Causley, published by Macmillan Limited, and for 'Cat!' from *Silver Sand and Snow* by Eleanor Farjeon, published by Michael Joseph Ltd; *The New Yorker* for 'Catalogue' by Rosalie Moore; Dr Sy M. Kahn for her poem 'Boy with Frogs'; The Hogarth Press for 'Frogs' from *Selected Poems* by Norman MacCaig; Ann Elmo Agency Inc. for 'Song of the Storm Trooper' by Bertolt Brecht, as translated by H. R. Hays; Faber & Faber Publishers for 'The Refugees' by Herbert Read; Maurice Carpenter for his poem 'Solar Travel'; Norma Farnes for 'Bump!' by Spike Milligan from *Silly Verse for Kids*; Curtis Brown Group Ltd for 'Old Man in a Trunk', 'An Introduction to Dogs', 'The Kangaroo', 'The Ostrich', 'The Porpoise', 'The Turkey', 'The Camel', 'The Canary', 'The Lion' and 'The Rhinoceros' by Ogden Nash from *Custard and Company*.

Photos, puzzles, comic strips: Alan Foley Pty Ltd p. 27; Mirror Books, London, pp. 31, 223, 256; Land Commission of NSW p. 41; Associated Book Publishers Ltd p. 47; Field Enterprises Inc. pp. 51, 204; Ms Densey Clyne of Mantis Wildlife Films p. 56; Frederick Muller Ltd p. 62; John Fairfax

& Sons Ltd pp. 72, 250; Doubleday and Co. Inc. p. 78; Austral-International Press Agency and Photographic Library (Sydney) pp. 86, 184; News Ltd pp. 102, 169, 234; Dunlop Footwear p. 118; Lucasfilm and Twentieth Century–Fox (Australia) pp. 126, 132, 134; United Feature Syndicate Inc. pp. 129, 152, 154; Permanent Building Societies Association Ltd p. 150; Barry McKinnon of the Sydney *Daily Telegraph* p. 218.

Drawings by Randy Glusac

Cover by Jan Schmoeger

While every care has been taken to trace and acknowledge copyright, the publishers tender their apologies for any accidental infringement where copyright has proved untraceable. They would be pleased to come to a suitable arrangement with the rightful owner in each case.

Dictionary

The following abbreviations are used in this dictionary:

adj adjective	*adv* adverb	*n* noun	*n pl* noun plural
pp past participle	*pr p* present participle	*v* verb	*sing* singular

abeyance *n* temporary disuse or inactivity

academic *adj* of higher learning, scholarly; relating to skills of the mind

acclaimed *pp* applauded, saluted with enthusiasm

adhesive *adj* sticky, clinging (e.g. adhesive tape)

annihilate *v* to destroy fully, utterly

assail *v* to attack vigorously

asymmetrical *adj* not evenly proportioned; not regular or balanced in form

butt *n* the thicker, larger or blunt end (e.g. of a weapon or tool)

churn *v* to move in an agitated way (as by violent stirring)

clamour *n* loud outcry or noise

climax *n* event or point of highest intensity or interest

conception *n* notion, idea; thing conceived

consignment *n* goods delivered for a specific purpose (e.g. to be sold)

contravene *v* to go against (e.g. a regulation); to violate, infringe

contribution *n* a giving in common with others

cornea *n* the transparent front part of the external coat of the eye, covering the iris and the pupil

courtiers *n pl* attendants or hangers-on (e.g. at the court of a sovereign)

cranny *n* a small, narrow opening; crevice, chink

debris *n* scattered fragments, remains or wreckage; rubbish

disarmingly *adv* in such a way as to remove hostility or suspicion; winningly

discern *v* to perceive, make out; to distinguish

distillation *n* the purification or concentration of a substance, or its separation from another, by evaporation and condensation of a liquid that contains it

ecstatically *adv* with utter joy, rapture, overpowering delight

emaciated *adj* thin and feeble, wasted away

epilepsy *n* a nervous disorder usually characterized by a brief loss of consciousness, with or without convulsions

evolved *pp* developed gradually or by natural process

excreting *pr p* separating and expelling (e.g. waste from a body)

expanse *n* a wide area or extent

expedient *n* a means to an end; a suitable resource

flimsy *adj* very weak or inadequate, frail

forlorn *adj* downcast, unhappy, miserable

futile *adj* useless, coming to nothing

glowering *pr p* staring angrily or with sullen dislike

grotesque *adj* odd, fantastic or unnatural in shape or form; distorted, strange

grotto *n* a cave or cavern

gyrate *v* to move in a circle or spiral; to whirl

haemorrhage *n* discharge of blood; profuse bleeding

idolatrous *adj* blindly worshipping; adoring

incarnate *adj* embodied in flesh; endowed (e.g. a quality or an idea) with a bodily form; typified, personified

infinitely *adv* boundlessly, immeasurably

ingenious *adj* inventive, clever

insomnia *n* inability to sleep (especially if habitual)

inspiration *n* the arousing of feelings, ideas or impulses, especially of those leading to creative activity; an influence that awakens such feelings

intercostal *adj* between the ribs

irrationally *adv* without reason, illogically, absurdly

irremediable *adj* unable to be remedied or cured

irritable *adj* quick to anger, easily irritated, touchy

lecture *n* a talk or discourse delivered in front of a class or audience for the purpose of instruction

limpid *adj* clear, transparent (as water)

lure *n* something to entice or decoy; a bait

manacle *n* a handcuff; a device used to shackle the hand

munitions *n pl* military weapons, ammunition, and other materials of war

mutt *n* a stupid or blundering person

nuzzle *v* to rub up or press with the nose (*into* or *against*); to snuggle or cuddle up

permissible *adj* allowable

pharynx *n* the tube or cavity behind the nose and mouth, connecting them with the oesophagus (gullet)

phenomena *n pl* observed events or occurrences (particularly those that impress as extraordinary or remarkable); *sing* phenomenon

pneumonia *n* inflammation of the lung or lungs

precariously *adv* insecurely or perilously; without stability

psychiatrist *n* a medical specialist in the treatment of mental diseases

reconnaissance *n* examination or survey, especially of enemy territory

relentless *adj* not lessening in severity or determination; not softening

residential *adj* suitable for or occupied by private dwellings

reverberating *pr p* echoing, resounding

self-deprecating *adj* understating one's worth; modest

sensation *n* a feeling; perception through the senses

serrated *adj* having a notched or toothed edge

silhouetted *pp* outlined in black against a lighter background

slavering *adj* dripping with saliva; slobbering

sombre *adj* dark, gloomy, shadowy

spasm *n* sudden involuntary convulsive movement; uncontrollable wrench or jerk

squint *n* a look with the eyes partly closed

submissive *adj* yielding, humbly obedient

succulent *adj* juicy; tasty

surpassing *pr p* going beyond, overtaking, exceeding

sustained *adj* kept up or kept going, constant; continuous

tantalizingly *adv* temptingly but just out of reach; teasingly

tenacity *n* persistence; a holding firm

tentatively *adv* hesitantly, not definitely, cautiously

toxic *adj* poisonous

trachea *n* the windpipe — the main air-passage of the body, from larynx to bronchial tubes

translucent *adj* allowing light through but not transparent

undignified *adj* lacking dignity; not noble or elegant in manner or conduct

upheaval *n* a violent disturbance or change

writhe *v* to squirm, twist

Other titles in

Home Building Work
Bill Goodson

With this book at hand you should
have no difficulty in making a satisfactory job
of any building additions and improvements to
the house and garden. Basic information is
given on the main building crafts, including
bricklaying, carpentry and joinery, and
everything is explained in clear and simple
terms. The construction of brick, timber and
pre-cast buildings is fully described and the
projects covered in detail include sheds, home
workshops, garages, and a small conservatory
as well as many simple indoor improvements
such as built-in cupboards and wardrobes. The
basic requirements of the Planning
Regulations and Building Regulations
are explained.

Contents:
Introduction · Foundations, solid floors and pavings ·
Brickwork and blockwork · Fireplaces, flues and
chimneys · Small brick buildings · Carpentry–floors and
joists · Roofing and roof construction · Joinery–tools,
materials, joints. Windows, doors and staircases.
Garage doors, fences and gates. Small timber
buildings · Plastering and rendering · Index.
112 pages   0 408 00276 X

Home Repair and Maintenance
Tony Wilkins

How to keep your home in first-class condition,
both indoors and outdoors. Protecting
paintwork, metal, brick and woodwork from rot
and general deterioration will avoid major
repair costs later on.

Contents:
Introduction · The tools you will need · Materials for
repairs · Timberwork · Metalwork · Walls and
ceilings · Damp · Repairs at roof level · Outside jobs.
Twenty common problems · Seventy repair tips · Index.
112 pages   0 408 00242 5

Home Improvement
Tony Wilkins

Guidance on nearly 400 problems commonly
encountered in home maintenance and
improvement, categorised for easy reference
and set out in question-and-answer form.

Contents:
Painting and decorating · Woodwork and
woodfinishing · House defects · Floors · Plumbing ·
Electrical work · Central heating · Insulation · Tools ·
Adhesives · Garden · Unclassified problems · Index.
112 pages   0 408 00403 7

Home Plumbing
Ernest Hall

A complete guide to the maintenance
and repair of home plumbing systems, this
book is intended for DIY enthusiasts and
householders who want to know how their
domestic plumbing system works, how
to protect it from frost and corrosion, how to
identify faults and how to carry out
emergency repairs.

Contents:
Introduction · Cold water services and the cold water
storage cistern · Domestic hot water supply – cylinder
storage systems · Water heating by electricity and
gas · Taps, stop-cocks and ball-valves · The
lavatory · Baths and showers · Sinks, basins and
bidets · The drains · Hard water problems · Coping with
frost · Plumbing techniques for the householder ·
Some rural plumbing problems · Index.
112 pages   0 408 00246 8

Home Decorating
Tony Wilkins

Practical information and useful hints
on both interior and exterior decorating. In this
book the reader will find answers to his
decorating problems concerning preparation,
choice of materials and application.
In addition to painting and wallpapering, there
are chapters with instructions for the best
methods of laying carpets and floor tiles and
also woodfinishing.

Contents:
Introduction · Colour and pattern · Tools ·
Materials · Preparation · Paintwork · Interior walls ·
Exterior walls · Ceilings · Floors · Wood finishing ·
Wrinkles and tips · Index.
112 pages   0 408 00243 3

Home Electrics
Geoffrey Burdett

This book includes information on
the home electrical installation and electrical
appliances which the household requires to
know in order to carry out any repairs or
replacements in safety. The book explains in
simple language what to do in an electrical
emergency whether great or small.

Contents:
Introduction · Your electrical installation · Rewiring · The
lighting system · Lamps · Power circuits · Circuit for
electric cookers · Electric water heaters · Night storage
heaters · Outdoor electrical extensions · Electrical
hardware · Electrical repairs about the home · Tools · A
guide to lighting fittings · Control of lighting and
heating · Hints on safety · Index.
128 pages   0 408 00245 X